PIERS MACKESY

THE COWARD OF MINDEN

THE AFFAIR OF
LORD GEORGE SACKVILLE

ST. MARTIN'S PRESS
NEW YORK

ISBN 0-312-17060-2

Library of Congress Cataloging in Publication Data

Mackesy, Piers.
    The coward of Minden.

    includes index.
    1. Sackville, George Sackville Germain, 1st Viscount,
1716-1785. 2. Great Britain – History, Military – 18th
century. 3. Great Britain – Politics and government –
1760-1789. 4. Generals – Great Britain – Biography.
5. Statesmen – Great Britain – Biography. 1. Title.
DA67.1.S2M32 1979   94107'2'0924 [B]   78-26204
ISBN 0-312-17060-2

FOR
ANTHONY MACKESY

CONTENTS

LIST OF PLATES

The author and publishers are grateful to the following for permission to reproduce photographs: The National Army Museum for nos 1, 9, 13; The National Portrait Gallery for nos. 2, 4; The Trustees of the British Museum for nos 3, 10, 14; The Hon. Giles St Aubyn and The Bomann Museum, Mündhausen Bettensen Collection for no. 15. Nos 5, 6, 7, 8, 11 and 12 are reproduced by gracious permission of Her Majesty the Queen.

LIST OF MAPS

ACKNOWLEDGEMENTS

I have to acknowledge the gracious permission of Her Majesty the Queen to make use of the Duke of Cumberland's papers in the Royal Archives. Two branches of Lord George's family have helped me generously: Lord Sackville and the Hon. Hugh Sackville West at Knole, and Mr L. G. Stopford Sackville at Drayton. Among many kindnesses for which I am grateful I must mention particularly that of Mr Ewan Fraser, for giving me notes or copies from three letters in the Bute papers at Mount Stuart, and for other information; Mr Damon Wells, Mr E. G. W. Bill, Librarian of Lambeth Palace, Mrs Nancy Parker of the Fondren Library at Rice University, and Sir Robin Mackworth-Young, Librarian of Windsor Castle, for helping me to pursue Captain John Smith; Mr C. W. Stewart for the loan of two family letters at Glenharvie, and Major T. L. Ingram for depositing at York City Library two letters from the Hickleton papers; Lieut.–Col. R. M. Pratt, D.S.O., D.L., for an excerpt from the diary of Captain Bell of the 5th Fusiliers; Dr Michael Ingham, once again, for astronomical information about the early hours of 1 August 1759; Mr C. Batt, of the Brighton Area Library, for an excerpt from the *Sussex Weekly Advertiser*; Mr N. Higson, archivist of Hull University Library, for his special helpfulness with the Hotham papers; Elizabeth Mavor, who called my attention to Mrs Thrale's journal; the Hon. Giles St Aubyn for information about the portrait of Prince Ferdinand, which is reproduced by his kind permission; and Sally Mackesy for valuable suggestions.

INTRODUCTION

Historians have not judged Lord George Sackville with charity. I
first encountered him, when I was a boy, in the pages of Sir John
Fortescue's *History of the British Army*, which tells the story of how
'this deplorable man' ignored repeated orders to bring up his
cavalry at the battle of Minden. 'It is possible', wrote Fortescue,
'that on the day of Minden Sackville's courage failed him.'
Dismissed from the army, Sackville vanished from the battlefields.
'But we shall meet with him again', Fortescue warned the reader,
'and the meeting will not be a pleasant one.'

   Fifteen years passed before I made the promised encounter:
exactly the same interval as had passed between Sackville's fall and
his reincarnation as Lord George Germain, Secretary of State for
the American colonies and minister in charge of subduing the
American Revolution. Starting the research for a book about the
War of Independence, I found that almost everything that had been
written painted Germain as a disastrous minister. The attempt to
subdue the Americans was regarded as a moral iniquity and a
humiliating defeat, and he was the perfect scapegoat. His earlier
misfortune at Minden became entangled with his role as war
minister. Some contemporary historians, including Smollett, had
exonerated his conduct at Minden; but after his death his whole
career was reflected in the mirror of American independence, and
the tradition of his disgrace at Minden slowly hardened. The
Victorian Sir George Otto Trevelyan ascribed his conduct to 'a fit
of the sulks'; but by Edwardian times the naval historian Sir Julian
Corbett could refer simply and unhesitatingly to 'his cowardice –
for it can be called nothing else'; and in his study of the Seven Years

Introduction

War the index, that great betrayer of an author's prejudices, refers the reader to Sackville's 'evil influence'. The assumption persists. In 1966 Sir Reginald Savory's history of the German campaigns damned Sackville without qualification: 'Seldom, if ever, has there been in battle such disgraceful disobedience.' Occasionally the quiet voice of scepticism breaks through, usually in an article by some Staff College graduate who has noted the deplorable confusion of the staff work in the battle.

When I met Sackville again, many things had happened in the intervening years to open my mind to the possibility that he might not have been simply the cowardly soldier and foolish statesman of historical tradition. One of the first documents I read about the War of Independence was a private letter from Lord George to a friend commenting on the heavy losses sustained by the British infantry in the opening operation at Concord. His guess about the cause of their failure was shrewd, knowledgeable and open-minded. There was no trace of the prejudice against the irregular tactics of America that one might have expected of an officer trained in the German school. Lord George saw at once that the British troops had lost their grasp of the light-infantry training which they had evolved in America in the Seven Years War. He relied on General Howe to revive it.

Was the writer of this letter the man to whose ignorant blunders tradition imputed the disasters of the War of Independence? Gradually, as the evidence accumulated, it became apparent that tradition was wrong. With straitened resources and against great physical difficulties Germain had waged the war beyond the Atlantic with courage, imagination and perhaps even a trace of wisdom. He had evolved operational plans for dealing with the new problem of a people in arms. Yet he had not allowed the struggle in America to hypnotize him: in a world war against the great maritime nations of Europe he had maintained a balanced sense of priorities.

The truth seemed to be that Sackville was a man of splendid capacity, marred by faults of temperament which prevented him from rising to the highest positions. He commanded an expeditionary force but was never commander-in-chief of an army, and

Introduction

was Secretary of State but never Prime Minister, though Lord
Shelburne, who hated him, judged that he had the ability to be
both. He was a capable leader, but did not inspire devotion; an
effective politician, but not the head of a party; loyal to his assistants
in politics and the army, but easily moved to rancour against his
colleagues and superiors; courteous and pleasant in private life, but
in public life apt to bear grudges, and unable to resist the
temptation to deploy a wounding irony.

We shall never know for sure what made him so. American
historians have tended to explain what they see as his arrogance by
the fact that he was the son of a duke, forgetting that his second-in-
command and successor, the accessible and convivial Lord Granby,
was not only a duke's son but the heir to a dukedom; and that it was
Sackville's equals rather than his inferiors who disliked him. The
flaw in his character seemed to be insecurity rather than arrogance.
As I closed my story of the War of Independence on his declining
years in retirement and his final struggle to subdue his ancient
resentment against the authors of his Minden troubles, I wondered
what forces had blighted this man's life and left him, in the exercise
of great power, still vulnerable to the barbs of his enemies for events
long buried in his past. This book is a search for the answer.

P. M.
Pembroke College, Oxford

ONE

A MEETING OF ALLIES

THE COMING OF FERDINAND

The moment of assuming supreme command must be a lonely one; and few generals can have felt sharper pangs of solitude than Prince Ferdinand of Brunswick as he drove into Hamburg from the east one day in the late November of 1757 to command His Britannic Majesty's army in Germany. Behind him he had left his service in the Prussian army, the iron machine forged by the Hohenzollerns and driven by the harsh will of Frederick the Great. Ahead lay what? A gathering of disparate strangers: a defeated force.

Two months earlier the Duke of Cumberland, commanding the British-paid army in Hanover, had capitulated to the French at Kloster Zeven, removing his army from the war. The Hanoverian troops were to be neutralized, and their Hessian and Brunswick auxiliaries dispersed. Cumberland had had little choice. Outnumbered and defeated near Hameln in July by Marshal d'Estrées in the hard-fought battle of Hastenbeck, he had retreated across the Electorate to the estuary of the Elbe, abandoning the capital. Pinned against the river at Stade without supplies, he capitulated on the authority of his father George II to save his army from destruction and the Electorate from ruin.

But the news of his capitulation hit the British government with a chilling shock. For George II was King of England as well as Elector of Hanover, and England was engaged in a world-wide struggle with France. The German army in Hanover was financed with British subsidies, and the cabinet had higher priorities than saving the old king's German Electorate from a French occupation.

A Meeting of Allies

The success of Britain's colonial campaigns in India, Canada and the West Indies depended on keeping the war alive in Europe, and her only major ally, Frederick the Great of Prussia, was being hammered by the combined assaults of France, Austria, Russia and Sweden: in October Berlin itself was occupied for a week by Austrian raiders. In this desperate situation the capitulation of the Hanoverian army tore open Frederick's western flank, and exposed him to attack by yet another French army. If Prussia collapsed under this pressure, the nightmare of isolation which haunted British statesmen would be realized. France could forget about Europe and concentrate on maritime warfare and invasion.

To save Frederick there was only one choice: to repudiate Cumberland's capitulation and bring the Hanoverian army back into the war. Even the king, who hated the Hohenzollerns and had authorized the surrender, felt a 'Prussian qualm' when Frederick protested, and Cumberland returned to England to find that his father had disowned and disgraced him. 'I think like a *German*,' the old man told his Prime Minister, the Duke of Newcastle. A kind of excuse for repudiating the convention was provided by the French, who tried to disarm the Hessian troops in alleged breach of its terms. The allied army was reactivated, and the king decided to look for a German prince to replace the fallen Cumberland. In the opening days of November the Hanoverian Major-General von der Schulenburg arrived at Frederick's head-quarters to ask for the loan of Prince Ferdinand of Brunswick to lead the army in Hanover.

It was a command fit for a prince: a conglomerate of little sovereign forces which only the charisma of royal blood could hold together. England had collected the army, and England paid for it, though as yet there were no British troops. But besides the Hanoverian redcoats there were blue-coated Brunswickers and Hessians, with a British colonel to count the men and disburse the cash; some regiments of Prussian dragoons and hussars lent by Frederick; and serving in the Hanoverian force under separate treaties with the Elector, a brigade of Bückeburg artillery and a regiment of foot from Saxe-Gotha. Since Cumberland's departure this amalgam had been held together by the ancient Hanoverian

General Zastrow, now nearly eighty years old. A new commander was needed to restore the morale of his defeated and bewildered army.

Once in her history England had produced a commoner with the stature for the task; but half a century had passed since the victories of the great Marlborough, and a royal commander was needed to unite the conglomerate force. The British royal house was a martial dynasty, but it was fifteen years since George II had commanded at Dettingen, and fifty since he had fought under Marlborough at Oudenarde. In his middle seventies he was too old for soldiering. His younger son the Duke of Cumberland, a veteran of Fontenoy and Culloden, had been the obvious choice for the command when war broke out, just as in the next generation the Duke of York would be the inevitable commander for a combined army of British and Russians. But Cumberland was now disgraced, and Prince Ferdinand was the British government's choice to pick up the pieces and make a fresh start. He looked like a winner. Aged about thirty-eight, he had learned his trade and made his reputation under Frederick, the greatest general of the age. And he had the right blood. His brother was the reigning Duke of Brunswick, Frederick the Great was his brother-in-law, the King of England a relation. If anyone was qualified by birth and training to succeed a British royal duke as commander-in-chief of King George's German army, it was His Serene Highness Duke Ferdinand of Brunswick-Lüneburg. On 5 November he distinguished himself in Frederick's great victory at Rossbach, and a few days later he departed to command the army in Hanover.

The only friends he took with him were two young aides-de-camp and his private secretary Westphalen, and he arrived at his new headquarters to find that even his brother's Brunswick troops were there under duress. Four nights before his arrival they had marched stealthily out of the allied lines towards the French to execute the terms of Kloster Zeven. General Zastrow had learned the secret and acted firmly. With a force of Hanoverians he blocked a canal bridge on their line of march, while behind them Hessians moved up to channel them back to their quarters; the Brunswick generals were deprived of their swords and arrested. Of such troops and commanders was Ferdinand's army composed. It was their confidence that he had to win as he led them back into the war. His impact was immediate and lasting. Hardy and contemptuous of self-indulgence, he rode about in the freezing December weather without a greatcoat, enduring the pangs of rheumatism so that the troops could recognize their new commander by his decorations. He had to restore not only the army's morale, but its administrative machine and means of movement. Pay was raised and rations were improved; and confidence flowed back into the grounded army. Horses and wagons were collected to convert a static neutralized body of troops into a force fit for the field.

But there was no time for deliberate preparation. The French were concentrating from their winter quarters to fight him, and the race was on to seize the crossings of the river Aller before the enemy. Within three days of joining the army Ferdinand was moving it south towards the enemy, mobilizing it with improvised transport as he went, and hardening the men for war as they marched through the snow.

But his soft troops in their worn-out boots moved slowly, and his improvised supply train bogged down on the slushy roads. The French reached the Aller crossings before him, and he fell back to Lüneburg to complete his training and preparations. In the middle of February he was ready. His operations were as dazzling in their hardihood and boldness as Washington's crossing of the Delaware nineteen years later. Struggling forward across the heaths in deep slush and mud, his army surprised the right wing of the French army. At Verden a bridge submerged in the flooding waters of the Aller was seized intact, and an advanced guard commanded by the Hereditary Prince of Brunswick raced forward to the Weser. The night was dark and stormy when it reached the banks of the river, and the local boatmen were reluctant to launch their boats through the ice floes in the swirling floods. But gold coin persuaded them. A detachment was put across the river and surprised the French bridge-guard at Hoya from the rear. The line of the Weser was won, and the French scarcely stood again as they fled back to the Rhine with devastating losses of men and material. Ferdinand's brilliant opening offensive had liberated Hanover, cleared the French from Westphalia, and ended the threat to the western flank of Prussia. Frederick the Great never had to fight a Frenchman again.

A pause followed the lightning advance; but on 1 June Ferdinand resumed the offensive, and the army began to cross the Rhine near the Dutch border on a pontoon bridge for which boats had been secretly collected in Holland. His plan was to sweep down the Rhineland from the north into the rear of the French holding the river line, pin them against the Rhine and destroy them.

This time boldness was less successful. The army was too small for its extended front, and far off at Frankfurt Marshal Soubise launched a French force into Hesse to threaten Hanover from the south in Ferdinand's absence. On the Rhine General Chevert pushed down the right bank to threaten the allies' bridges; and though Ferdinand won a victory at Krefeld, superior French forces on the left bank threatened to trap him. Ferdinand slipped back across the river, breaking his bridge behind him.

The operations across the Rhine had been indecisive, but Ferdinand returned a hero, and it is now that we have our first sight of him through British eyes. A new commissary, Colonel Durand, had joined the army on the eve of the Rhineland operations and met the commander-in-chief for the first time. Ferdinand took care to make a friend of this solitary representative of the British army. Durand was allowed to join the handful of officers who accompanied the prince on reconnaissances, and became his devoted admirer. On one occasion he was present in the dark of an early morning when Ferdinand briefed his generals for an attack in a tent specially pitched out of line. Ferdinand's briefings were famous, and Durand was struck by 'his politic, cool and clear manner of explaining himself'. Durand also noted Ferdinand's secrecy – 'he wisely never declares his intention to any body here'. Ferdinand kept his own counsel. He travelled with a single aide-de-camp and no escort, and on reconnaissance took only a few essential staff officers, among whom Durand was flattered to be included. When the army was marching he kept his plans secret till the last possible moment, and even generals commanding detached forces operated under sealed orders to be opened on specific dates. Ferdinand's only confidant was his secretary Westphalen, the friend among strangers, who encouraged his secretiveness. Though Durand admired the prince's reticence, it could offend the commanders of the national contingents in his army, who felt entitled to his confidence.

Behind Ferdinand's mask of courteous serenity there lurked a flaw which even those who were close to him did not discover. Perhaps only his secretary Westphalen knew that Ferdinand was a prey to doubt. It was a weakness which seems to have afflicted the house of Brunswick, fostered perhaps by their dependent relationship with the kings of Prussia and the Prussian army, and especially by the dominating character of Frederick the Great, who could undermine the self-confidence of the best of his subordinates. Ferdinand's nephew, the brilliant young hereditary prince who had seized the Weser crossing, was afflicted by similar self-doubt. A generation later as Duke of Brunswick during the French Revolution, when he commanded the Prussian invasion of France in 1792, he roused France to a fury of resistance by publishing the disastrous 'Brunswick manifesto', against his own convictions and in deference to the King of Prussia. The same deference to the Prussian king was to push him forward to defeat and death at the hands of Napoleon at Jena in 1806. Prince Ferdinand shared this lack of self-confidence, and had shown it when he failed to seize the Aller crossings during the winter. In his disappointment he had drafted a letter to Frederick asking to be recalled to the Prussian army, though he had only commanded the Hanoverians for a few weeks. He was saved by Westphalen, who dissuaded him from sending the letter. Others who worked close to Ferdinand lavished praise on his cool perception and judgement, his unselfishness, military skill and a dozen attributes which a supreme commander needs: none of them hint at his self-doubt. Westphalen wrestled with the doubts, and never betrayed them.

The men Ferdinand commanded were experienced, disciplined Germans who had never lost their courage and cohesion even during Cumberland's retreat to Stade. Colonel Durand saw them in action during the Krefeld campaign, marching into an attack full of spirit and resolution yet silent and attentive to their officers. The Hanoverian artillery particularly impressed him, and at Krefeld he 'never saw artillery better served nor do more execution'.

The largest contingent were the thirty-four squadrons and twenty-three battalions of Hanoverians. 'Better, more loyal, more willing troops do not exist in the whole world,' Colonel Mauvillon of Ferdinand's staff declared in his memoirs. They regarded themselves as the army's soul, and the other contingents as existing only through them and for them. The Brunswickers, at first only seven battalions, were totally devoted to their own Prince Ferdinand, and his problem with them was not to make his affection too obvious to the other troops. The Hessians were more tricky to handle. These ten squadrons and ten battalions were certainly splendid troops. Always hired out by their Elector as mercenaries, they were accustomed to serving in combined armies and in this sense were the easiest of all to control. 'War is their element,' wrote Mauvillon; but they were quarrelsome, and if trouble broke out with other troops the whole Hessian corps took part, and their hot tempers made the dispute very hard to damp down. To their ruler's profit they were the worst-paid troops in the army, yet squandered their money like mercenaries for whom lasting peace would never dawn and who never knew what tomorrow might bring. There was a strong reciprocal dislike between the Hessian officers and the better-paid and thriftier Hanoverians, and an outbreak of serious quarrels would have had appalling consequences.

The other components of the army gave little trouble. The fifteen squadrons of Prussian hussars and dragoons were strictly disciplined, and among the little force of Bückeburgers disorders were unknown. But there were problems enough for Ferdinand's diplomacy. All his tact and skill were needed to damp down quarrels and settle disputes impartially. In distributing duties he took care to give the different troops the task for which they were best suited, without showing that he knew their weaknesses. Individuals were praised for their success, and their errors were concealed to protect their honour. So at least says Mauvillon; but we shall see.

Ferdinand knew how to cope with his German troops. But a new problem was about to test his art of management to the limit: the British.

THE BRITISH ALLY

One result of Ferdinand's swift advance from the Weser had been to threaten the French hold on the port of Emden at the mouth of the Ems; and Marshal Clermont was already urging its evacuation when Commodore Holmes brought two British warships up the unbuoyed channel by a brilliant feat of navigation and cut off the garrison's supplies. The French hastily abandoned the town, opening a short sea route from England to the theatre of war. As soon as the news reached London a battalion was embarked to garrison the port, and soon Brudenell's regiment, the 51st Foot, was holding open the door to Germany.

The British Government had been hesitating between amphibious raids on the coast of France and continental warfare in Germany. Ferdinand had let it be known that he needed another 10,000 men to hold his own, and the news of his victory at Krefeld tilted the cabinet in favour of the continent. Six regiments of British cavalry and six battalions of foot sailed for Germany, adding about 7,000 British troops to the allied army.

Their pleasant summer voyage of twelve days was a time of anticipation for young British officers who had never been on active service. It was glamorous to tell one's family to address their letters to 'His Britannic Majesty's Army in Germany', and stirring to see the low coastline of Europe for the first time as the transports groped their way into the shallow estuary of the Ems. Four miles below Emden the ships berthed one at a time at the end of a new 200-ft jetty bridging the mud-flats, and the troops tramped resoundingly across the planks on to German soil.

The British were now in the field. They knew all that could be taught on barrack squares and camps of exercise but had still to learn about life on active service. As they marched south to join Prince Ferdinand, they could not guess that a whole year would pass before they faced the test of a general action: a year to shake down in the field and accustom themselves to the country.

The British Ally

Every morning at two or three o'clock the camp was roused by the drums beating the *générale* in the darkness. Half an hour later the battalions fell in, and in another half hour marched off. The weather was a miserable introduction to war. Torrents of rain flooded the Ems valley, and at times the infantry were up to their waists in mud and water as they plodded towards their rendezvous with the army in Westphalia. On 19 August their commander, the third Duke of Marlborough, met Prince Ferdinand; on the 21st his troops marched into the allied camp near Bocholt; and on the following day the prince reviewed them and sent an approving letter to the British Secretary of State. 'I do not know how to express my pleasure, my Lord,' he wrote in his excellent French, 'at the satisfaction I felt at the good state of these fine troops.' The British for their part saw a German general about five feet six inches tall, with a fair complexion rather pitted with the smallpox. 'Of a pleasant countenance,' a farrier of the Greys recorded in his journal, 'seems always smiling in presence of his troops.'

Behind his smiles, what did Ferdinand think of his reinforcements with their bright new uniforms and equipment? Colonel Mauvillon's assessment when the war was over gives us a clue: 'Braver troops there cannot indeed be found in the world when on the battlefield and under arms before the enemy; but here their military virtue ends.' So indiscriminately was the infantry recruited, compared with the conscripted German peasants of Hessen, that it was difficult to maintain a shadow of discipline; and the officers with their purchased commissions gave little thought to their duties. From the subaltern to the general they were ignorant and comfort-loving, and expected to sleep every night in undisturbed ease. The cavalry troopers were better material than the infantry; but, said Mauvillon the staff officer, 'a foolish love of their horses makes them astonishingly greedy about forage'. They would eat a district bare far sooner than the Germans, who could be kept to a fixed ration.

Such was the British force as seen through German eyes. It was the harshest of judgements, and on the battlefield the troops were as good as Mauvillon conceded: steady, brave, and well drilled. The infantry's fire drill was deadly, and they knew the importance of the ramrod. To get the best out of the musket, whose smooth bore was appreciably enlarged by half a dozen shots, the ball had to be rammed down hard with wadding, so that it compressed the powder and did not roll forward out of the barrel before it was fired. The British excelled in loading drill, and the thrust of the iron ramrod in Brown Bess's gullet made the shot fly hard and straight. The artillery officers were an exception to Mauvillon's criticism. They were professionals, separately administered by the Board of Ordnance and trained in their own military academy. 'No other country', an American declared at Quebec in the following year, 'can boast of greater proficients in the art of gunnery than those produced by that excellent academy at Woolwich.' At Minden the British artillery matched the Hanoverians with their bold movements and deadly fire.

Off the battlefield, however, the faults of the British troops were already visible. The march from Emden through a Catholic countryside brought complaints of troops breaking down wayside crucifixes, and after they joined the army marauding became a serious problem. Houses were pillaged and outrages were committed against civilians. Some of the trouble was due to inexperience or to troops 'trying it on' before they had shaken down on active service. Men marking quarters were rubbing out the names of generals on the doors and appropriating the houses for their own units. Hygiene was another problem for an inexperienced army, and men with dysentery were being sent back to hospital in the empty bread wagons. This was forbidden in orders; but if it was unavoidable, thick layers of straw were to be put down and cleared out and burned before the fresh bread was loaded at the bakery.

As marauding appeared, German discipline began to bite. The pickets and cavalry patrols had orders to shoot at offenders instead of seizing them, and the Grand Provost was instructed to go his rounds daily and hang without mercy every marauder he caught. Fraternizing with the enemy's advanced posts was forbidden on pain of cashiering for the officers and death for the non-commissioned officers and men. But Ferdinand applied discipline with common sense. It was the reality which mattered, not the forms; and officers on duty were forbidden to salute him by removing their hats. He had also to take care that German discipline did not make the new allies resentful. Not for them the full summary justice of a German army, any more than he could string up a fraudulent contractor as Frederick the Great would have done. The British were proud and touchy; and with what Mauvillon called their quiet natural arrogance and contempt for foreigners, they treated their allies as hired inferiors, an attitude which the Hanoverians defending their homeland found particularly offensive. At the same time the British army was not quite sure of itself. It was not loved or respected at home, and had not proved itself in this war like the German troops. 'I think it very important', a British general was to write not long before the battle of Minden, 'that the army should get up a little from the odium under which it has lain for want of being known.'

Arrogant and touchy, the British needed all Ferdinand's tact to handle them. He had to avoid using them in roles in which they were unreliable, without revealing that he thought them unsuitable or giving his German troops the impression that the British were being spared the hard work because they were the paymasters. He could not afford to alienate the British by harsh discipline, but must not appear to favour them by punishing other troops more severely; so the British presence imposed some slackening of discipline in the whole army. The selfishness with which the British troops spread their quarters and foraging areas at the expense of neighbouring formations caused resentment and some dangerous collisions. Ferdinand damped down these outbreaks impartially. Within a few days of the British joining the army a Hanoverian trooper who drew his sword on the British baggage guard was ordered to be confined and punished with his N.C.O., and Ferdinand issued a general order that swords must not be drawn in disputes between the national contingents, but complaint made to the nearest officer.

The new arrivals were as curious about their allies as the German troops must have been about them. The Hanoverian chasseurs impressed them as accurate shots and smart-looking troops, but the Prussian death's-head hussars were a surprise.

A Meeting of Allies

A nasty looking set of rascals [wrote a British officer about these hard-living outpost troops], the picture you have in the shops in London is very like them though it does not represent their rags and dirt – they make no use of tents; at night or when they rest they run their heads into some straw or any stubble and the rest of their persons lies soaking in the rain. It's said that some private hussars have this campaign got about 2,000 German crowns, nay some advance it to pounds. They drink more brandy than water and eat I believe more tobacco than bread.

A FIRST VIEW OF LORD GEORGE

No one could seriously dislike the British commander, the third Duke of Marlborough, nor was he likely to impress a professionally minded German general. Among the memoir-writers of the day Lord Hervey stressed his good sense, modesty and generosity, and Horace Walpole his ignorance, carelessness and profuseness, and both views are probably true. In the last war he had resigned in protest at the conduct of the Hanoverians, which does not suggest that he was the most suitable commander for a contingent in a German army, and as soon as he arrived he headed straight for another collision with the Hanoverians. Discovering that Lieutenant-General Spörcken, who had served under him in England, had been promoted general over his head by an antedated commission, the duke protested. He would not have his army made into 'cleavers of wood and drawers of water for the Hanoverians'; and he threatened to resign if he were not made senior to Spörcken. He was promptly given a general's commission antedating Spörcken's, underlining the special British position in the alliance.

If Marlborough was likely to raise problems for the German supremo, another of the British generals was still more likely to make trouble. It was at the Bocholt meeting that Ferdinand first made acquaintance with Marlborough's second-in-command Lord George Sackville, the third son of the Duke of Dorset and soon to become one of the most notorious Englishmen of the century. Ferdinand saw a tall, rather heavy man of about forty-two, some four years older than himself, with a clear blue eye, strong features with an ugly snout of a nose and protruding lower lip, and a quick expression with a touch of melancholy and reserve.

Lord George was an able man with a good military record. Born in 1716 at the Sackville's family seat at Knole, he had been educated at Westminster School and then at Trinity College, Dublin, 'half beer garden and half brothel' but even so a more serious place of education than eighteenth-century Oxford or Cambridge. He was in Dublin because the Duke of Dorset was Lord Lieutenant of Ireland, and he received his first taste of political affairs as his father's private secretary and Clerk of the Council. After a brief intermission in Paris and a return to Dublin to serve the new Lord Lieutenant, Lord George was called away from politics to war, and began the other half of his double career, as a soldier.

During his first stay in Dublin he had been commissioned in a cavalry regiment on the Irish establishment, and in 1740 became lieutenant-colonel of General Bragge's regiment of foot, the 28th. Three years later he went to war with his regiment in Germany. At Dettingen in 1743 he fought in his first battle, and his good conduct caused King George II, who commanded the army, to appoint him one of his aides-de-camp. In 1745 he was wounded and captured in the heavy-fire fight at Fontenoy, where his battalion suffered 139 casualties. Soon afterwards he was ordered home to fight the Jacobite rebellion, and at the end of the campaign his commander-in-chief the Duke of Cumberland wrote to his father that 'he has shown not only his courage, but a disposition to his trade which I do not always find in those of higher rank'. At the end of the continental war Cumberland sent him to negotiate an armistice with the words, 'I need prescribe no rule of conduct to an officer who has already shewn so much gallantry and conduct.' As colonel of James Wolfe's regiment Sackville discovered his merits and pushed him on, and may later have suggested him for the command of the attack on Quebec. Wolfe evidently trusted and respected him. 'I know he is very sincere,' he wrote; and when Sackville gave up the colonelcy of his regiment Wolfe lamented that with one exception 'no possible successor can in any measure make amends for his loss'.

A Meeting of Allies

In 1755 came promotion to major-general. Sackville was now recognized as a serious soldier and a power in the army. 'I find it highly essential to my interests', wrote a Guards officer, 'to procure as much of Lord George Sackville's friendship as I possibly can . . . he is become, by means of his parts rather than his extraction, one of the most powerful officers in the army.'

The source of Sackville's influence was only partly his ability as a soldier, for he was climbing fast in politics. Since 1741 he had been Member of Parliament for Dover, a borough in his father's gift as Lord Warden of the Cinq Ports. During his father's second spell as Lord Lieutenant of Ireland from 1751 he served him as Chief Secretary, the position in which the Duke of Wellington and Sir Robert Peel were to serve their political apprenticeships. Sackville's tenure of the secretaryship did not prove that he had political judgement, for his energy stirred up a hornet's nest of Irish antagonism which forced his father to quit the lord lieutenancy. But his political career scarcely faltered. Returning to England in 1754 he soon became a central figure in the Prince of Wales's opposition group at Leicester House, led by the future Prime Minister Lord Bute. He was on the Cabinet-list for the ministry which Bute intended to form when the prince succeeded to the throne, and high political office seemed sure to come. In 1757 Henry Fox wanted to offer him a secretaryship of state; and when the Pitt–Newcastle coalition was formed Pitt and Bute pressed Sackville's claims to the secretaryship at war. This the king refused, complaining that Lord George had 'most ungratefully abandoned him' by attaching himself to the rival court at Leicester House. At the end of 1757, however, office came at last when Lord Ligonier succeeded the disgraced Cumberland as commander-in-chief, and Sackville took Ligonier's place as Lieutenant-General of the Ordnance. The reason for the appointment was political. He was brought in by Pitt to add a skilful speaker to the ministry and give Leicester House a stake in the government.

In spite of this promotion, Sackville's political position was insecure. In the first place his relations with Leicester House were beginning to cool. The group had identified itself with the 'blue water' strategy of coastal raiding expeditions in opposition to the

'Hanoverian' strategy of commitment to Germany. Sackville served in the St Malo expedition of 1758 as second-in-command to Marlborough, but shared the army's dislike of the raids, which were risky, indecisive and likely to discredit the generals. If the army commander did not preserve his communications with the fleet, he risked being cut off and forced to capitulate; if he stayed near the coast and his shipping, he exposed himself to charges of timidity and worse from the ever ungenerous navy, not to mention the armchair strategists of Westminster and even his own more hot-headed juniors. General Jack Mostyn, who could not be accused of being a thinking soldier, complained of 'cruising like a marine with the fleet', and Sackville echoed a common feeling when he told his friends that he was 'sick of coasting' and 'tired of buccaneering' and asked Pitt to send him to Germany. The offer appealed to Pitt. As second-in-command of the force for Emden, Sackville would make Leicester House appear to share responsibility for the German strategy; and though Bute was annoyed by Sackville's criticisms of the coastal raids he could not easily disown him for an opinion with which most soldiers agreed.*

Nevertheless Sackville's association with the German war made his political position precarious. It alienated his friends at Leicester House, for they regarded his posting to Germany as a betrayal of their 'blue water' principles and disliked his association with Pitt, whom they were coming to hate as a turncoat who had sold himself for the sake of office. Pitt, however, was no sure anchor for Sackville. He was an individualist totally devoted to his own career: a good friend in prosperity, he would throw Sackville overboard as soon as it became popular to do so. As dangerous as Pitt's friendship was the enmity of George II. For two days he had resisted Sackville's appointment to Germany, and finally gave way, grumbling that there was nothing left for him to do but sign papers. He had a long-standing dislike of Marlborough, and having these two generals imposed on him left him, as the Prime Minister Newcastle wrote, 'a little out of humour'.

It was said that Sackville left for Germany without the

*On this point I am indebted to Mr Ewan Fraser's unpublished thesis.

conventional formality of coming to court and kissing hands, a discourtesy which enraged the little drawing-room tyrant of St James's. Whatever the truth of that, his posting to Germany had weakened his friendship with Bute and Leicester House without gaining that of the most passionate advocate of German war, the king himself. George II was more German than the Germans. Prince Ferdinand wrote to the King of Prussia in French, but to the King of England in German; and it was in German that George corresponded with the commander of his Hanoverian troops. We glimpse him at court through Horace Walpole's eyes, standing 'in one spot, with his eyes fixed royally on the ground, and dropping bits of German news'. The king's addiction to Hanover was dangerous for Sackville because it was both single-minded and unpredictable. Cumberland's misfortune in the previous year stood as a warning. After the defeat at Hastenbeck he had wanted to retreat eastwards out of Hanover towards the Prussian army, knowing that he could not be supplied on the lower Elbe. But the king his father, thinking obsessively of the political interest of Hanover, had forced him to retreat into the trap at Stade, promising supplies from England and begging his son to make terms and save his troops. The king then felt his 'Prussian qualm' and Cumberland was disgraced for doing what the king had wanted.

This shabby story showed that the British generals in Germany could rely on the king's support only so far as their actions supported Hanoverian interests, and not even then if the king changed course. One condition of retaining the king's approval would be loyal cooperation with the German commander-in-chief. Ferdinand had insisted on direct access to George II when he accepted the command, and corresponded with him regularly. In any collision between the British generals and their German supremo, the king would back the German.

Such was Lord George's record, but what of the man? What lay behind the mask of melancholy, reserve and ambition, and is it possible to put together a coherent portrait rather than a bundle of conflicting attributes collected from the memoir-writers? There is certainly a conflict of testimony. Horace Walpole, the most quarried source for Lord George's character, said many and various things about him in the vast output of writing which extended over a couple of generations, his attitude changing as his personal vanity was flattered or affronted and as the interests of his closest friends were affected by Sackville's actions. A superficially more consistent source is Lord Shelburne, one of the most original statesmen of the century, yet a distrusted failure known to his enemies as the Jesuit of Berkeley Square. Shelburne's portrait of Sackville is consistent in its savage malice. Sackville emerges as an incompetent soldier and a coward; an intriguer who exploited his connections and imposed on the world; an implacable and vindictive enemy who surrounded himself with low adventurers of doubtful morals and integrity; sanguine at the outset of an enterprise but easily dashed by difficulties, and liable to sink from overbearing optimism into unreasonable despondency. But even Shelburne granted him ability of a kind. His military disgrace at Minden, he wrote, saved the rest of the Empire from following America into independence, 'for I do not conceive that anything but the checks which stopped his military career could have prevented his being Prime Minister'.

What can one make of the dark and secret portrait which Shelburne left at the end of his life for posterity? It tells one as much about Shelburne as about Sackville, and is paralleled though scarcely equalled by Shelburne's abuse of Pitt and Ligonier. But Sackville had friends who left memoirs, as well as enemies. They were not of his own social standing, and most of them made their mark in literature rather than public affairs. One was the editor and literary critic Percival Stockdale, who served under his command. He remembered Sackville as polite and well informed, with an elegance and dignity of deportment; well read and conversant with human nature; a good conversationalist; even – in contrast to Shelburne's opinion – magnanimous.

> But [Stockdale added] there was likewise a reserve and haughtiness in his manner, which depressed and darkened all that was agreeable and engaging in him; it . . . naturally and very fairly hurt the reasonable self-love of his acquaintance and friends. His integrity commanded esteem, his abilities praise; but to attract the heart was not one of those abilities.

Though very different from Shelburne's portrait, Stockdale's still shows that dark shadow of haughtiness and reserve. Another portrait with lights and shadows is Richard Cumberland's, but the emphasis shifts. Cumberland was a playwright and minor politician who served in Sackville's department in the American War of Independence. In a tribute written soon after Sackville's death he admitted that he had an exterior reserve, a grave and thoughtful bearing. His manners, said Cumberland, lacked the easy freedom fashionable in the seventeen-eighties. Like others, Cumberland had received an initial impression of cold reserve; but Sackville's kindness when he first visited his country house at Stoneland melted this unfavourable impression. 'The fact is,' he wrote, 'sincerity was his nature; reserve, contracted by long exile from society, was the result of his misfortune.'

Men who had known Sackville in earlier life might have challenged the explanation, for the reserve had been with him before his disgrace at Minden. Yet clearly there was a more likeable person beneath the haughty surface. Cumberland found him an agreeable talker and companion, and a good listener who was patient of interruptions. In the office he soon came to respect Sackville's ability. 'In punctuality, precision, dispatch and integrity he was not to be surpassed; he was fitted both by habit and temper for business . . . a spirit incapable of despondency.' The politician and memoirist Nathaniel Wraxall described him in later life as having 'a quickness of perception which seemed at times to partake of prescience and intuition'. Like Cumberland he called him a stranger to circumlocution.

One dimension of Sackville's reputation does not appear in these memoirs. Though he was married in 1754 to Elizabeth Sambrooke, and the first of his five children was born in 1756, he was widely believed to be an active homosexual, and sodomy was not merely a private matter affecting his social relations: it was a capital crime, a sin and an outrage. The gossip caused by his relationships in later life will be examined in due course, but it was already in the air during his command in Germany. It is difficult to know what weight to put on a scurrilous pamphlet published after his disgrace, which alleged that a relationship he had formed in Ireland had led to the promotion of a 'beautiful warrior'; but some of his military enemies later associated his behaviour at Minden with his sexual character. Burgoyne, they told each other after Saratoga, 'ought not to be sacrificed to a Minden b—g hero'; to which was added on the letter in another hand, 'I'll tell you what, Monsieur le capitaine de dragons, you may kiss my arse.' Fruitshop Betty, the gossiping flower-woman of St James's, earned their applause and no doubt their custom outside the clubs when the Board of Trade was separated from Lord George's department in 1779 and given to Lord Carlisle. 'It is dirty in Lord Carlisle', she said, 'to take half of such a b—r's bed.'

One forms an impression of a man who was socially isolated among his equals. This may merely mean that he was not a convivial man, but it is remarkable that his staff in Germany contained so few officers of high social rank. Ferdinand had Fitzroy, Ligonier and the young Duke of Richmond: these had few equals on Sackville's staff. Apart from the adjutant-general, Colonel Hotham, the landed and political families of England were not represented there, though Welsh and Scots names of obscurer pedigree appear. The Scots were an unpopular crew in eighteenth-century England. At worse they were regarded as go-getting intriguers, at best as nobodies. The attitude was to persist. 'The Scots were chiefly engaged,' a lady wrote after the battle of Quatre Bras in 1815, 'so there are no officers wounded that one knows.' The scarcity of established names on Sackville's staff does not necessarily endorse Shelburne's in-sinuation that he collected adventurers, but may mean that he was more at ease with his social inferiors, and preferred to help and befriend them: he may not have found it easy to show the affable side of his nature to his equals.

The touch of melancholy described by Shelburne reflected a depressive vein in the Sackvilles of that day which affected both his brothers. The elder, Charles, who succeeded to the dukedom, was talented, solitary and eccentric; the younger, John, spent the latter part of his life under supervision as a madman in Switzerland. Though friends who knew him in later life described Lord George's temperament as equable amid the strains of the American war, he was by then mellowed by age, and occasional outbursts in

Parliament when under personal attack show that all was not calm beneath the serene and dignified surface. Even at that later period of his life he had an irritable, impatient streak, and an official who worked for him remarked that he could never bear delay or disappointment in the small arrangements of his life. 'I once imagined that I could not have lived without constant business,' Sackville himself observed in 1775 when he thought that age had brought him serenity.

Here then was the man with whom Ferdinand had to work: powerful in politics and the army, but vulnerable to political change and the prejudice of the king. A man whose drive and energy were not tempered by tact or the power to win the love of those who worked with him. Undoubtedly able; yet his Irish career suggests a defective sense of the expedient. Visibly ambitious, clever, confident and sharp-tongued; yet within the walls of his personality unsure of himself in a crisis, sensitive to slights, and at times perhaps vulnerable to the see-saw of depression. An isolated man, who could not depend on prudent advice from wise friends in trouble. Sackville did not admit people to his interior, and inside the mansion there were locked rooms to which even he may not have possessed the keys.

As second-in-command of the British force Sackville would clearly be a problem for Ferdinand, for he was said to dominate his chief, the Duke of Marlborough. But he was to be more important in the army's life than Ferdinand could have guessed in those early days in Westphalia. For in October Marlborough suddenly died, and Ferdinand confronted in Sackville the 'commander in chief of the British forces with the allied army in Germany'.

IN WINTER QUARTERS

The campaign ended quietly, and as the British settled down in the army they discovered that under Ferdinand's command their business was to obey and not to understand. 'Everything is conducted with so much secrecy that we never know what is to be done before the order arrives,' an officer of the Scots Greys told his family, 'and as for news it is only to be met with in the English papers.' Rumour substituted for information. 'We have always a lie of the day, and one day contradicts the next,' wrote another cavalry officer.

The army went into winter quarters. The British infantry were at Münster, and half of the British cavalry was quartered along the Ems under General Elliot, with the rest under General Mostyn detached to form part of a linking force in the bishopric of Paderborn. The allies were unpopular in Westphalia, and the local deputies protested that they were unable to provide its rations. Determined not to draw on the magazines which would be needed when the army took the field again, Ferdinand threatened to seize all the forage that could be found in town or country, which frightened the deputies into supplying the army above the level of absolute want. The shortage, however, caused some friction between the British and Germans. General Whitefoord collected what forage he could find in his area into the town of Rheine, to prevent 'the Jews and Hanoverians, both damned pilferers', from carrying it off in the night. A Hanoverian unit which occupied a village in his area was invited to depart with the threat of sending their commander as a prisoner to Münster. 'I wish our Hanoverian chiefs would keep their people in better discipline,' he complained. Evidently German complaints of the British tendency to spread their quarters were reciprocated.

Ferdinand and Sackville had their headquarters in the city of Münster, with a garrison of four British battalions and two of Hanoverian Guards. Discipline in the town was strict. Each British gate guard had a Hanoverian corporal attached to it as interpreter, and to safeguard the supplies to the town market the soldiers were forbidden to go out and buy provisions in the neighbouring villages or to stop the country carts coming into the city. The soldiers' quarters were not to be kept too warm, to keep the men hardy, and at first no stoves were allowed at all. Any soldier caught robbing an inhabitant on the streets at night was to be punished without mercy or excuse as the law directed; this, as regiment orders pleasantly reminded the troops, meant breaking on the wheel.

The inhabitants, on the other hand, who were unfriendly, were forbidden to go on the streets after eight o'clock at night without a lantern, and refractory behaviour towards the occupation was punished by 'military execution': a party of troops was quartered on the offender and confined him to his house, and every twenty-four hours the 'execution party' levied a fixed payment for their trouble. A different sort of execution took place in the New Year, when a French emissary was hanged in the cathedral square. The town gates were shut, the streets patrolled, and at nine in the morning grenadiers fetched the condemned man from the prison. Two sentries guarded the gallows till the order was given to cut him down.

For the cavalry quartered on the Ems life was freer, though the Scots predictably complained about religion. 'Very bad quarters, they all being Roman Catholics,' grumbled the farrier of the Greys. Westphalia was a country of scattered dwellings rather than villages, and the troops of horse were dispersed away from their officers' eyes. Lodgings were primitive. The peasants shared their rooms with their cows, hogs and horses; and Captain Davenport of Mordaunt's dragoons slept with three of his horses on the other side of a lath-and-plaster partition, of which they occasionally kicked a hatful into his bedroom in the night. The girls were not encumbered with breeches under their skirts like the Dutch girls, but alas, were well chaperoned; and the maid fancied by Davenport was constantly watched by the mistress of the house, who took care to send another girl in to light his fire. But there were compensations. If the beef and beer were bad, there were plenty of wild fowl, partridges, hares and poultry; and pike, tench and perch from the slow north-German streams. If one wanted to sample country hospitality winter was the season for weddings, and an invitation guaranteed a living scene from Breughel: a hundred drunken people gathered in a barn, all singing different tunes, with four fiddles playing, twenty couples dancing, the drum beating, ten couples fighting; some sleeping, some eating and others throwing up their food to make room for more. In these conditions, with dysentery encouraged by small beer and *Brandwein*, sickness and desertion flourished; and though not a man of the British force had been killed or wounded, its losses were proportionately the highest in the army.

Society at headquarters in Münster was more elevated, and the staff amused themselves with customary refinement. 'My love to all the scrubs,' wrote an officer on leave in London. Colonel Hotham, also in England, received the usual messages from his friends. 'All the beauties and *your love in particular* are quite enchanted with the fine things I have said in your name,' wrote Major Keith, a future ambassador in Vienna, 'and Reden [Hotham's opposite number on Ferdinand's staff] kissed me for half an hour together, with open mouth, out of sheer friendship to you.'

Sackville himself was not endeared to the German allies. A dispute with General Schulenberg about quarters led Schulenberg to challenge him, but Ferdinand intervened and settled in the German's favour. A Hanoverian officer told the Prince of Wales that Sackville was so imperious and satirical that none of the foreign troops could bear him; and later, when he had been disgraced, pamphleteers alleged that there had been disagreements with Ferdinand, which Walpole bears out. But the only substantial hint of personal friction between Lord George and Ferdinand at this time comes from Sir Joseph Yorke, the well-informed minister at The Hague, who reported after Sackville's court martial that Ferdinand was said to have been prejudiced from the outset by Marlborough, who complained that Sackville wished to be thought of as managing him. But Yorke emphasized that this was the only report of the kind which he had heard in the early days, and Sackville's private letters about Ferdinand were admiring, as they generally continued to be right up to the battle of Minden.

The dispositions our General makes of his army upon every occasion [he had written shortly before the death of Marlborough] is [*sic*] so able and in so different a style from everything I ever saw that I think myself extremely happy in having this opportunity of knowing what the duty of a commander in chief is, and I shall endeavour to return to England less ignorant than when I left it. . . .

The Prime Minister was anxious for good relations between the new commander and his German supremo. 'I know,' wrote Newcastle, 'the high regard you have for Prince Ferdinand; and therefore I am sure you will be happy to be under his command.' At

39

the same time, however, he encouraged Sackville to make a stand in a matter which was likely to cause ill feeling: the cost of supplies. It was first raised by Sackville himself, in a letter expressing his uneasiness at the huge sums being spent on forage for the German troops, and hoping some other method of contracting would be found, 'for I am persuaded no country can carry a war at this rate'. This sentiment was music to the First Lord of the Treasury. Sackville was right, he replied, that no country could afford the expense. Newcastle was not the only minister to suspect that England was being skinned by her German allies. Lord Chancellor Hardwicke, his closest political friend, was complaining that the king's Hanoverian ministers regarded the war as a harvest and 'cheat him very much'. Newcastle's letter to Sackville therefore implored him to be economical. He told him that the Treasury was extremely dissatisfied with the extravagant contracts made by the British commissaries, and urged him to get rid of one contract in particular – probably the disadvantageous one with the contractor Prado, for which the ministers blamed the careless Marlborough.

Sackville replied that economy was impossible under the present regulations. The source of the trouble was the king's decision that his Hanoverian territories should pay their war contributions in cash instead of provisions, which they would have had to supply at reasonable rates fixed by the commander-in-chief. Instead the British government was paying three times the proper price for corn. The timid Newcastle was afraid to speak out for fear of making enemies of the Hanoverians and especially of the minister in attendance in London, Baron Münchhausen, and thus alienating the king. Sackville was not prepared to act as Newcastle's fall guy, and the problem of costs was not tackled at the source, but he may have let Ferdinand know that he was aware of the German agents' depredations. Cash payments from Hanover were of small use unless supplies could be bought, and Sackville complained that little hay was being delivered and the army was consequently forced to forage for it. It was a bad system: uncontrollably wasteful of hay and unthrashed corn, and ruinous to the peasants, who would rather have found forage for the army at reasonable prices than be foraged over.

Newcastle lived in terror of personal unpleasantness, and his tireless political skill was largely spent in avoiding scenes, even if it meant sidestepping important questions. It was therefore peculiarly painful for him to break the news in his first letter to the new commander in Germany that Sackville was not to enjoy all the powers of his predecessor. The king had refused to grant him the right to post officers to vacancies in his command. With a man of Sackville's temperament this was sure to cause an explosion, and Newcastle and Lord Ligonier remonstrated with the king. But in vain: Sackville might recommend officers for postings, but he was not to make the appointments himself. Newcastle and Ligonier could now only try to avert the expected explosion, and off went soothing letters of explanation. The king, they said, was upset by some commissions filled by General Bligh, commander of a coastal raiding force, and had resolved to end the practice except in distant colonial theatres. They assured Sackville that the decision was not aimed at him personally, and hoped he would not take it in that spirit. 'Now, my dear Lord,' wrote Ligonier placatingly, 'you will judge wrong if you think this is done to Lord George Sackville, for that is not the case.'

The explosion was not averted. 'It is certainly a very mortifying circumstance to me', Sackville replied, 'to see the powers given to commanders in chief taken from me in the first instance . . . the alteration must be looked upon by the officers in the army as a mark of His Majesty's disapprobation.' He threatened to resign if the change caused difficulties. He did not resign, of course, but he carried the grievance; and treated it as a deliberate mark of the king's disapproval. He could reasonably suspect that things would have been different if the king had liked him.

TWO

PRINCE FERDINAND AT BAY

THE WINTER'S PREPARATIONS

The business of a commander-in-chief when his troops went into winter quarters was to prepare for the next campaigning season, and as soon as the campaign of 1758 was over Sackville was summoned home for 'consultations'. He reached London on 21 December, notified his arrival to Newcastle immediately, and spent the next three months making his military arrangements, trying to obtain reinforcements, and sitting to Reynolds for his portrait. He also attempted to mend his political fences. But he found that his Leicester House ally Lord Bute was remote and inaccessible, and unwilling to see him when he called. Evidently Lord George's criticism of the coastal raids had not been forgiven.

It was soon made clear that the government would spare no more British regiments for Germany. The French were assembling a large force in Flanders which might be used for invasion; and when Sackville spoke to Pitt the minister was adamant that it was politically impossible to send more British troops, though more Brunswickers might be hired. Pitt was as usual looking over his shoulder at his public. It would be dangerous, he explained, 'to stretch the cord too much . . . the public must be humoured'.

Ferdinand, who was made a Prussian field-marshal at the end of the year, showed some bitterness at the British refusal as he surveyed the massive French forces gathering against him. 'The King of England only talks to me of economy,' he complained to Frederick. But on one point he did succeed in obtaining further aid, and here Sackville in his capacity as Lieutenant-General of the

Ordnance was able to help. Ferdinand had been struck by the superiority of the French artillery in numbers and equipment, with their excellent teams of horses and their precision-made cannon with which only British ordnance could compare. He was also being bombarded with advice from Frederick to strengthen his artillery. Frederick had been impressed by the Austrians' huge train of cannon and its skilful use of ground, and realized that though artillery hampered movement he must increase his own, if only to stiffen his infantry as its quality deteriorated with its losses: 'One must conform to the system of numerous artillery, however hampering it may be.' He predicted flippantly that in a few years' time armies would be marching with 2,000 infantry and 6,000 cannon. But – 'one must follow the fashion in spite of oneself'.

Fortified by Frederick's encouragement, Ferdinand applied to England for more artillery. He needed cannon to equip the Hessians, who could find the gunners by converting militia; and he wanted light guns of the Prussian type to re-equip the Hanoverian heavy artillery, whose heavy pieces needed more horses and twice as many men to handle, and could not be moved on the battlefield after reaching their initial battery positions. Since Prussian guns were not available he asked for British six-pounders. He also asked for financial aid to raise two additional companies of Hanoverian artillery and to convert Hessian militiamen and Bückeburg grenadiers. The British obliged with twenty-eight pieces of ordnance – twelve-pounders, six-pounders and howitzers. Ferdinand's persistence in the matter was to reward him. At the battle of Minden he had 181 guns against 162 of the French. Their fire would dominate the field, and the British batteries would play a brilliant part.

Throughout this period of preparation Ferdinand and Sackville corresponded in courtly French about recruits, reinforcements and artillery, with the usual expressions of mutual esteem. Sackville hoped for 'the happiness of meriting your approbation'; and Ferdinand assured Sackville that he was convinced of his friendship since his own for Sackville was as lively as it was sincere. No doubt the question of reinforcements would be difficult; but 'you are capable, my Lord, more than anyone in the world of overcoming those difficulties'.

Sackville returned to Germany towards the end of March, bringing with him some newcomers who were to play a part in his future: General Jack Mostyn, and two young officers who were to join Ferdinand's staff as British aides-de-camp, the Duke of Richmond and Captain Fitzroy. Officers of fashion brought problems with them. Soon after his return Sackville issued an order forbidding soldier-servants to wear private livery instead of uniform.

Jack Mostyn, nicknamed 'Noll Bluff', was a dashing cavalryman who never pretended to be much else. 'I sicken at the sight of pen, ink and paper', he declared; writing and reading were 'two things I never had patience to bear'. When he found himself in temporary command in the following winter, his dislike of desk-work led him into a predictable muddle in overdrawing on his Treasury account. This deficiency was no bar to popularity in the army and at court, where he was a regular member of George II's evening parties. Newcastle, who kept a finger in every pie with his enormous correspondence, hoped that Jack would keep him supplied with hot news from the front. But the labour was too much, though occasional scrawls to Newcastle's nephew Lord Lincoln indicated the main scope of Mostyn's talents. Soon after his arrival in Germany he was hoping for an advance on Frankfurt, to bring him back to Lord Ligonier's quarters of 1743 in near-by Bornheim 'where every woman fucked'. Another scribble was prompted by 'the irresistible temptation of dating one of my letters from my quarters at Ballockshausen; and another from Fuck much'. The other main concern in Mostyn's letters was promotion, and his dashing literary style did not embellish his greed. The colonelcy of a regiment was a lucrative sinecure, and Mostyn's mouth watered at the expected death of General Bland. 'Though Bland calls himself alive I think he is mistaken and that the mistake will soon be found out, and *I* have set my heart on his regiment.' 'The moment the tedious old fool drops, the regiment will be asked for by the *sleek* General Conway'; and Conway would hear of the death sooner than Mostyn in Germany, 'unless Jemmy Brudenell would fuck Mrs. Bland, and by the by why not?' Another plum was the governorship of Chelsea Hospital. 'They say Sir Robert Rich is dying, why should not I *come after* him at Chelsea? I would not hurry the widow out of her lodgings there . . . and it would be a very pretty place for you to dine at in the spring.'

Mostyn was a close friend of Sackville's second-in-command the Marquis of Granby, and in social character he and Lord Granby were at the opposite pole from Sackville. The commander-in-chief was temperate, cold, isolated; his second-in-command was convivial, extravagant, generous and popular. Granby shared Mostyn's dislike of paper-work; his passions were hunting and field sports. Unlike Sackville he had the gift of making himself loved. Bald at the age of thirty-eight, he had the endearing eccentricity of never wearing a wig. He was no administrator, but had a quick eye for a tactical situation; and as a subordinate had attractions for Ferdinand. He was not likely to poke into financial details and make difficulties, or to look out for divergences between British and German interests. Horace Walpole reflected that 'if he wanted any recommendation to Prince Ferdinand besides these ductile qualities, he drank as profusely as any German'; a remark less just to the temperate Ferdinand than to the open-hearted heir to the Duke of Rutland. Walpole added that 'Lord George's haughtiness lost him this young man, as it had lost him the Duke of Marlborough'. The evidence of hostility between Sackville and Granby is of the slenderest kind, but their temperaments were such that they can rarely have met on common ground.

When Sackville returned to Münster the campaigning season was beginning, and field regulations had already been published to prevent marauding. No man was to leave his regiment without his commanding officer's permission, and then only if accompanied by a non-commissioned officer. Two hours before sunset and again at daybreak patrols were to go out three leagues from camp to take up marauders; and foragers' trusses of hay were to be searched for plunder. Bringing in loot meant instant hanging without formal trial at the hands of the Grand Provost; and the same fate awaited all marauders and pillagers, whether soldiers, camp followers or women. Merely to enter a house without an officer or N.C.O. would be severely punished; to take the smallest article meant the gallows.

On 4 April Sackville ordered the lighting of stoves in quarters to cease, to harden the men for the field. Training was under way, and the British infantry were polishing their fire drill and brigade tactics under the eye of Sackville, who ordered them to concentrate on 'alternate firing', the simplified system of delivering rolling volleys which was unofficially beginning to replace the complicated flickering volleys of the platoon-fire system. After the peacetime fragmentation of the army, time was needed to work up its combined training, and Ferdinand was allowing the British troops another couple of months before he would call on them. Sackville, an experienced infantry commander and the friend and patron of Wolfe, would see that they were ready.

Soon the army would be on the road again, with the long columns of guns and baggage wagons and supplies stringing out behind the horse and foot. The grand guard of the day formed the advance guard of the army, followed by the horse, foot and artillery. Then came the baggage, controlled by the regimental baggage-masters under the baggage-master general. In the rear of all the old grand guard formed the rearguard and protected the artillery and train.

Ferdinand's was an army of the *ancien régime*. Not till the French Revolution a generation later would Europe see armies operating without massive supply trains and magazines, and living off the country as they marched. Ferdinand had to spare the population, yet see that his irreplaceable long-service troops were adequately warmed and fed. Without a vast supply system he could not do it. His battalions carried eight days' bread on the march, half of it in the form of a six-pound loaf in the soldier's haversack, the rest in the battalion commissariat wagons. To transport its bread, spare arms and equipment, and the infirmary, each battalion had six military wagons, and on the march was allowed to press another three or four country wagons for its blankets and equipment. The four-horse army-wagon teams, the eight blanket horses, the bat-horses and officers' chargers meant that 113 horses accompanied every battalion of foot in the field.

Behind the battalion transport extended a massive chain of services. The general hospitals and flying hospitals had their own train of six-horse wagons. A dozen miles to the rear of the army's camping ground were the field bakeries, with their six-horse wagons to carry the iron ovens. Still further to the rear, serving the bakeries and magazines, was a provision train of 900 six-horse wagons bringing up the flour and forage from the ports of Emden, Bremen and the Elbe, where the grain was imported from Holland and the Baltic. Navigable rivers running perpendicular to the army's front linked the fighting zone to the ports and gave Ferdinand a wide base for his operations. On the Ems and Weser and their tributaries numerous barges relieved the carriage problem, and without them there would have been an even larger mass of wagon-teams blocking the roads, consuming the forage and wasting the countryside. In 1762, when the army was about a third larger than in 1759, it had more than 9,000 wagons and carriages, made up as follows:

Commissariat (including hospitals, bakeries and regimental transport)	2,554
Private carriages (generals and their staffs, battalion and regimental commanders and staffs)	660
Artillery wagons	1,200
Country wagons allowed to regiments	4,764
Total	9,178

In that year the army had 21,000 cavalry horses, 9,000 for infantry officers, 10,000 for the artillery and 16,000 for the military wagons. This colossal total of 56,000 horses ate up the forage on the allies' front. In addition to these were the horses harnessed to the pressed country wagons, and others impressed for special services such as the 4–5,000 needed for the siege of Münster in 1759.

Ferdinand did what he could to limit the number of vehicles. Tents, blankets and officers' baggage were to be carried on bathorses; only vehicles with tickets issued by the wagon-master general were allowed; and the columns were inspected on the march and unauthorized wagons and carriages were confiscated. Such efforts did no more than set bounds to the clutter of vehicles on the roads. The vast and cumbrous apparatus of supply columns and magazines remorselessly constricted the army's movements.

Problems of supply and movement, however, were merely the medium in which a general plied his art. Like other artists he had to master the techniques of his craft, but the creative act lifted his occupation to a different level. All the art of generalship in Ferdinand would be called forth in the coming operations: the imagination, the political skills to handle men and governments, the daring, the fortitude.

For a massive crisis was building up. He had fewer than 70,000 men to hold the approaches of Hanover against 97,000 French. His western front was threatened by Marshal Contades with 66,000 men at Wesel on the Lower Rhine fronting Westphalia, and at Frankfurt Marshal Broglie faced the southern approaches through Hesse. Against these superior forces Ferdinand had two tasks to fulfil, the defence of Hanover and the protection of the western flank of Frederick the Great; and the roles could conflict. For the French army in the south at Frankfurt had a choice between striking north through Hesse against Hanover, or eastwards through Thuringia against the Prussians in Saxony.

Ferdinand could expect little guidance from his British paymasters, who were torn between their options as George II had been at the time of the convention of Kloster Zeven. Should they give priority to defending the king's German Electorate? Or did the survival of Frederick's Prussia outweigh other considerations? If Frederick went under, the continent was lost. Hanover would sink with Prussia and France could concentrate her resources on maritime warfare against England.

Ferdinand was equally torn between his priorities. He had been engaged by King George to defend Hanover, but his ranging mind took in the whole scope of the war and recognized that Hanover's survival depended on Prussia's. Besides, his old master Frederick was breathing down his neck with domineering advice and pathetic appeals – strengthen your artillery . . . don't be forced to fight in spite of yourself . . . a disobedient subordinate can ruin your plans. Above all Frederick was pleading for help in his own desperate need. He was surrounded by overwhelming numbers of Austrians,

French, Swedes and Russians. The last campaign had seen his costly and unsuccessful manoeuvres against the Austrians to capture Olmütz; the appalling battle of Zorndorf which had stopped the Russians at a cost of nearly forty per cent of the Prussian force; the surprise at Hochkirch in October, when Frederick had lost a hundred guns to the Austrians. He had survived only because his enemies failed to co-ordinate their colossus, and by taking desperate risks. 'You may easily judge my cruel embarrassment,' he wrote to Ferdinand; 'one must hope for the arrival of a deus ex machina to find a happy ending for the play.' Perhaps the King of Spain would die, and a war would flare up in Italy over his inheritance; or the Turks might attack the Austrians' rear. In the meantime Frederick could only sit tight, keep his forces concentrated, and hope that politics or luck would come to his aid. And Ferdinand must help him. Help him by holding Hanover and thus covering Brunswick and Brandenburg. Help him, if the French marched eastwards into Saxony, by joining forces with Prince Henry's defending army.

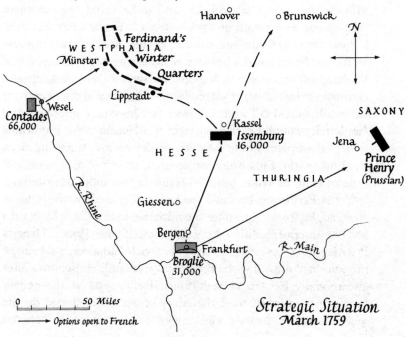

Strategic Situation
March 1759

For Ferdinand, threatened from the west and south, his situation was the classic one of an inferior force defending a central position against two converging enemies; and his classic strategy would be to contain one enemy with an inferior force and strike with mass at the other, using his interior lines for speedy movement. But what seemed simple on a theorist's diagram was more difficult in the uncertainties of real war. The French were reported to be shifting their major concentration from the Lower Rhine to Frankfurt for an advance in Hesse or Saxony. Yet it seemed improbable: their easiest route into Hanover and Prussia was across the north German plain from Wesel. From which direction must he expect the major attack to come?

If the main blow was to come from the south, should he launch a spoiling offensive to deprive Broglie of his options between Hesse and Saxony? It would be risky. Though Ferdinand had the interior position, his two fronts were widely separated, which made mutual support difficult. Could he safely march so far from his western front to attack Broglie? True, he had the fortresses of Lippstadt and Münster to protect Westphalia; and if he could rely on them holding out for a month he could safely march the 120 miles from Lippstadt to Frankfurt and strike at Broglie. But he could not rely on it. The French had a brilliant corps of engineers, the legacy of Vauban; and a fortress which could hold out for three weeks against German engineers might surrender in three days to the French. If Lippstadt should fall while he was away, his communications and magazines would be endangered; if Münster fell, the whole Westphalian plain would be open to the enemy, the route from England by the Ems would be severed, the river navigation and magazines of the Weser lost, and Hanover laid under contribution.

Yet if Ferdinand declined the risk and waited passively to be attacked, he would surrender the initiative to Broglie, who in turn had an interior position between himself and Prince Henry's Prussian force covering Saxony. Frederick had already taken the precaution of obtaining the British government's consent to a joint operation by Ferdinand and Prince Henry, and at the end of February Ferdinand tried the effect of a combined raid on the quarters of the Austrian and Imperial troops who lay between them. But far from easing the pressure in the south, the raid brought a strong French force forward from the Rhine to threaten his right. Nothing had been achieved, no time had been bought. The coming French offensive continued to build up unhindered, and by the middle of March the picture was settling into a pattern which indicated that the blow would come from the south. The enemy intended to envelop Ferdinand's covering force south of Kassel and destroy his magazines in Hesse.

Unless Ferdinand seized the initiative the French would gather at their leisure to destroy him. Faced with this truth he resolved at last to accept the risks of mounting a spoiling offensive. He would advance to Frankfurt, force Broglie to fight or to abandon his big magazine at Friedberg, and thus destroy his preparations for an advance. The risks were considerable; but they would be greater if he gave the enemy time to attack him with united forces. On one favourable factor he did reckon. The enemy were French, and he had already chased them back from the Elbe to the Rhine. They had good engineers, but that was all. Their irresponsible generals and undisciplined troops would not make the most of his difficulties.

This estimate of the enemy left two factors out of the account: their superior numbers, and the position they had been entrenching in front of Frankfurt at Bergen.

Prince Ferdinand slipped quietly out of Münster on 22 March with only two aides-de-camp and no baggage, and no one knew where or why he had gone. Not even the commanders of the three forces concentrating at Kassel had been told his plan; and newly arrived British officers were struck by the confidence of the army in its commander and the absolute ignorance in which he kept it. One of them was Henry Clinton, the future commander in America.

The schemes and designs of our great commander [he wrote] – who by all accounts is the most able general that ever existed – are as impenetrable as his armies have hitherto been, nor is it thought right to dive into them, all that we can say is that 'tis the opinion of every man here that he will meet with all the assistance he can possibly desire from troops who have the greatest opinion, and confidence in him.

General Mostyn's first impression of the prince was as favourable as Clinton's: the best-bred and most agreeable man he had ever seen, but 'as secret in his designs as active in the execution of them, so we never know where we are going'. The most significant comment was that of Sackville, who was kept as much in the dark as his subordinates. Ferdinand, he confessed to the Secretary of State, 'is too wise to trust his secret intentions to anybody further than is absolutely necessary for the carrying them into execution'. To Newcastle he apologized for a letter of 'idle conjectures'. 'If I can give you real and material information I shall do it with greater pleasure.'

Secrecy has its drawbacks. Ferdinand was aware that the more fully a subordinate is informed the better he can execute his tasks, and would have liked to brief the three generals at Kassel for the advance on Frankfurt; his secretary Westphalen dissuaded him. 'I desist from my first wishes,' Ferdinand replied, and kept them in the dark. Even the senior Hanoverian general Spörcken, who was to command the Westphalian front including the British troops in Ferdinand's absence, was not initially trusted with the secret.

Westphalen was also the inspiration behind the plan of operations. He sent Ferdinand a long and detailed memorandum on its execution, beginning with a preliminary push to drive the Austrian and Imperial forces back to the south-east and clear the left flank of the line of advance. Ferdinand accepted the proposals and asked for advice about his own movements. Should he leave tomorrow? Should he join the Hereditary Prince for the preliminary operations against the Austrians, or stay to command the main force which was to thrust at Frankfurt?

The army's winter dispositions had been designed for a rapid concentration to left or right. When the time came to act, Ferdinand's striking force assembled rapidly at Kassel, and on 27 March the advance guard moved forward to clear the French post at Fulda. The Hereditary Prince pushed through to strike the first blow against the Austrians and clear the flank of the advance.

The 'Erbprinz' performed his task with all the dash he had shown a year earlier at the Weser crossing. Moving swiftly eastwards into the Imperial cantonments, he dashed from point to point with his light troops, surprising a couple of battalions here, a regiment there, capturing the magazine at Meiningen, and forcing the enemy to withdraw as far as Bamberg. On 7 April he was back at Fulda to join the advance on Frankfurt, having marched 180 miles in ten days of wintry weather.

In the meantime other troops had been clearing the line of advance, picking up French detachments as they moved. The main army marched on 10 April in difficult weather, and on the 12th was only a dozen miles from Frankfurt. By now Ferdinand knew something of the enemy's reactions. Two strong French columns were on their way from the lower Rhine to reinforce Broglie, who intended to concentrate and stand in front of Frankfurt at Bergen. Ferdinand's plan had depended from the beginning on speed, and knowing that French reinforcements were coming he resolved to attack Broglie without a moment's delay. On the following day he marched straight up to the Bergen position and assaulted it, flinging his troops straight into piecemeal attacks as they arrived on the battlefield. The grenadiers of the advance guard assaulted the village of Bergen itself, the key without which the allies could not break into the French position.

Ferdinand no doubt remembered the French as he had seen them at Rossbach and on the Aller; and though the position was strong, with a short front and secure flanks, he believed that the French had only just occupied it. He therefore disregarded Frederick's advice to be strong in artillery, and launched his first attacks when only four heavy guns had arrived to support them.* But Broglie was well established in the position. He had strengthened it with abattis of felled trees; he had 30,000 men against Ferdinand's 24,000; and forty-five heavy cannon dominated the ground from commanding positions. Ferdinand's grenadiers were stopped by a heavy prepared fire. Other battalions came up to support them, fell back in disorder, and rallied under cover of a Hessian cavalry charge. Though the Germans' fire increased as their cannon arrived and came into action, Ferdinand had brought

---

*A rumour reached Sir Joseph Yorke at The Hague that Ferdinand had been drawn into a premature battle by the precipitate attack of the Hereditary Prince.

only twenty-one of them with the army. The village remained impenetrable, and at nightfall Ferdinand's attacks had all failed. General Issemburg was dead, 2,600 officers and men were killed and wounded, five guns had been lost. And Broglie would be stronger still on the following day when his reinforcements from the Rhine arrived.

The victory on which Ferdinand had gambled had eluded him. His magazines were ninety miles away at Kassel, and the overstretched lines of communication were vulnerable to the Austrians on the east and the French troops from the Rhine on the west. Ferdinand could only retreat, and withdrew with difficulty on flooded roads. Broglie did not leave his entrenchments to pursue, and only light troops harassed the withdrawal, picking up a couple of squadrons of dragoons and some baggage.

The allied army struggled back more or less intact to Kassel; but Ferdinand's opening offensive had been sharply defeated. It was not a shattering failure for the army, but it shook the confidence of its commander.

THE ALLIED RETREAT

The progress of Ferdinand's offensive had been watched anxiously. 'If it pleases God to give us a good issue,' wrote Sir Joseph Yorke from The Hague, 'it may decide the superiority of the allies over the French for the rest of the campaign.' The defeat at Bergen decided otherwise, and the French could now launch their own offensive at leisure.

But when the crisis came, would Ferdinand meet it with the assurance he had hitherto shown against the French? Frederick, who knew his character, guessed that the Bergen defeat had damaged his confidence, and wrote at once to sustain him. 'Treat the affair as trivial and it will indeed become so', he urged him. And again:

> One doesn't make war for long without experiencing some disasters . . . I beg you not to let yourself be intimidated by a lost opportunity, but to be as you were before with the same hopes of success

54

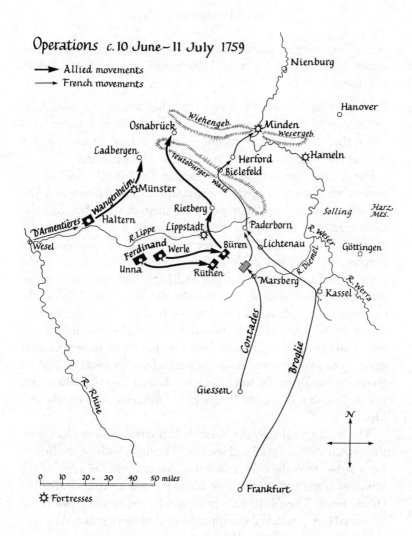

Operations c. 10 June – 11 July 1759

→ Allied movements
→ French movements

Nienburg

Hanover

Wiehengeb.

Osnabrück

Minden
Wesergeb.

Ladbergen

Teutoburger wald

Herford
Bielefeld

Hameln

Wangenheim

Münster

Rietberg

Solling

Harz Mts.

D'Armentières

Haltern

R. Lippe

Lippstadt

Paderborn

R. Weser

Wesel

Ferdinand

Werle

Büren

Lichtenau

R. Diemel

Göttingen

Unna

Rüthen

Marsberg

R. Werra

Kassel

R. Rhine

Contades

Broglie

Giessen

N

0 10 20 30 40 50 miles

Frankfurt

✿ Fortresses

55

and without letting yourself change, for no one is the master of events . . . You must forget what has passed, and think about fresh enterprises.

Ferdinand replied that the king's letter had greatly consoled him, and explained that his cannon had not arrived at Bergen in time. He added that the artillery commander had not done his duty: it was not the last time that he sought to blame a subordinate.

For nearly two months after Bergen Ferdinand watched the French in a state of anxious expectation. The enemy had the initiative, but he could not penetrate their plans. They had the advantage of a rectangular base (to borrow a phrase from the geometrical theorists of war), threatening him from two sides. If he concentrated forward in the salient angle of his front, he could protect the fortresses of Münster and Lippstadt and use them as pivots; but if he did so his own bases on the Weser and Elbe would lie outside the angle of his defences and be open to a wider French thrust round his right. He resolved nevertheless to defend the salient and cover his fortresses. Hesse lay too far off to be defended against the superior forces which were about to assail it, and he therefore withdrew the force covering Kassel into the salient. Its stores were sent down the Weser to the fortresses of Hameln and Minden.

The withdrawal into the Westphalian triangle took place with Ferdinand's usual speed and secrecy. The main body of the British force at last took the field, and joined the army in the angle of the salient at Unna and Werle, from which it could move against either enemy force. The flanks were protected by the two fortresses, and advanced forces watched the approaches at Haltern under Wangenheim and at Büren under Wutginau.

As Ferdinand scanned his intelligence, the enemy at first seemed to be preparing an offensive against his right at Münster, with the main blow coming from the lower Rhine to crack open the way across the northern plain to Hanover. Later it began to look as though the thrust would come from more than one quarter, and there was still the possibility that Broglie, advancing northwards from Frankfurt, would feel his way round Ferdinand's left towards Hanover. This threat Ferdinand intended to meet with light troops

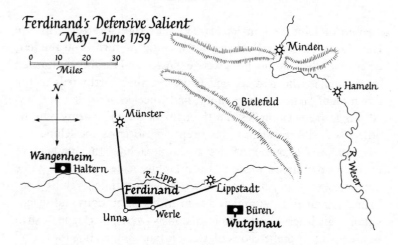

0   10   20   30
Miles

N

Minden

Hameln

Bielefeld

Münster

Wangenheim
Haltern

R. Lippe

Ferdinand

Lippstadt

R. Weser

Unna   Werle

Büren
Wutginau

in the mountains north of Göttingen and a strong garrison in Hameln.

On about 10 June French light troops began to appear on the river Diemel to the south of Ferdinand's salient, and skirmishing started as the French regained contact with the Anglo-German army. It was in fact from this direction that the main thrust was coming. Contades had taken personal command in the south, concentrating 102 battalions in Hesse and leaving only 18 on the lower Rhine under d'Armentières; and it was Contades' main force advancing from Giessen which was beginning to press against Ferdinand's outposts on the Diemel. Further east Broglie's corps was moving forward from Frankfurt towards Kassel.

As the French line of thrust became clearer, Ferdinand moved his army out of its waiting position at Unna to meet it, and concentrated forward of Lippstadt on the heights of Büren. Contades crossed the Diemel at Warburg and occupied the heights on the north bank with an advance guard only six miles from the allies' position, and there was daily skirmishing between the hussars and chasseurs. Here for several days the two armies faced each other. Ferdinand's Büren position was a strong one, with the fortress of Lippstadt in its rear, and its right protected by the Hereditary Prince at Rüthen. But it could be turned on the left, where the allied supply lines were exposed, and Ferdinand learned that Broglie, who had seemed to be pushing northwards in the direction of Hanoverian territory, had wheeled to the left and was closing towards Contades and the flank of the allied army. On the other flank d'Armentières was preparing to cross the Rhine and advance on Münster. 'Affairs are approaching the moment of decision,' the prince wrote to Lord Holdernesse on 17 June. The outcome would depend on his own inner fortitude. 'Whilst I see Prince Ferdinand tranquil and firm in his resolutions and dispositions,' Sir Joseph Yorke wrote anxiously from The Hague, 'I shall bottle up my apprehensions till there is more foundation for them.' 'God grant us success,' he added a week later in expectation of a battle, 'for I shall be a little down in the mouth if Prince Ferdinand is beat.'

On the day of Ferdinand's letter to Holdernesse Broglie's army reached Lichtenau on the road to Paderborn, and the testing time began. On the 18th Contades moved northwards towards Broglie and was evidently feeling his way round the left of the Büren heights. He was now in a position to intercept Ferdinand's supplies from Bielefeld and Minden and could form his army in a plain on the flank of the allies. Their position was not suitable to 'receive' battle from that quarter, and with his supplies threatened Ferdinand had either to attack Contades or withdraw.

But he did not yet feel ready to fight. At ten o'clock on the night of the 18th orders were issued to withdraw from the Büren position, and at two in the morning the army began to retreat, falling back to an intermediate position protected by the guns of Lippstadt. Ferdinand stayed with the rearguard till all the outposts and detachments had come in, but there was no interference from the enemy. At five in the morning the army marched again, tramping through the gates of Lippstadt and across the Lippe, making for a new position a dozen miles to the north at Rietberg. Lippstadt was left to its own resources and could expect a siege. General Hardenberg stayed behind in the fortress with orders to defend it to the last extremity, and a warning that three or four days' delay could be vital. To make doubly sure that the defence would be resolute Ferdinand sent in a British commissary, Colonel Boyd, who had some experiences of sieges, with secret authority to annul any capitulation and a promise that Ferdinand did not regard the fortress as expendable and would do his utmost to relieve it. Flooding of the approaches to the town was begun, but it would take six days to complete unless the Lippe were swollen by heavy rain.

FERDINAND UNDER STRESS

The loss of the Büren position was a heavy blow to Ferdinand. His planned defensive had been swept away. He had intended to support Lippstadt and Münster, the keys to Hanover, by remaining on the Lippe and giving battle on the heights of Büren. But the French strength was overwhelming, and Contades had advanced with caution, keeping his army closed up and giving Ferdinand no opportunity to attack him. The only thing now was to play for time. The French seemed to want a battle: Ferdinand would wear their patience a little longer, wait for their supplies to run short, and hope that somehow their difficulties would increase to the point where Contades would make a mistake.

But the price of delay was high. Ferdinand was dancing to the French initiative, conforming to their movements. With bridge-heads across the Lippe it was in their power to lay siege to Lippstadt, and Münster too if they wanted, for d'Armentières was now across the Rhine. Alternatively Contades could move north-wards to turn Ferdinand's left again, which Ferdinand's secretary Westphalen considered the likelier course. In that case Ferdinand would have to race the French for the defile through the Teutoburger Wald at Bielefeld or risk having his direct com-munications with Minden and the Weser cut. In this crisis he was turning incessantly to Westphalen for advice. 'If Broglie marches to Paderborn, are you of the opinion that I should send a corps to watch him? What do you think? The Hereditary Prince was worried that Broglie's corps could anticipate us at Bielefeld. What do you think?' A note for the English commissary which he showed to

Westphalen produced a telling criticism. Writing notes would never achieve Ferdinand's purpose, the secretary replied – 'this matter cannot be dealt with so well on paper as by a personal word'.

The day after his arrival at Rietberg Ferdinand sent off a batch of letters which were ominous of his state of mind. Addressed to Frederick, George II and Lord Holdernesse, their drift was all the same. If Lippstadt and Münster were besieged he might be unable to relieve them in the presence of Contades' larger army, and the loss of the fortresses might force him to abandon his magazines in Westphalia and retreat across the Weser. The consequences would be so damaging that he was tempted to seek a decision by battle instead. But if he lost the battle that would be still worse. What did Frederick and the British government think he should do? And if he had to cross the Weser into Hanover, should he then retreat towards the sea and lose the hope of help from Frederick, or fall back towards Prussia and lose his communications with England? To Frederick he added that he had only forty-three battalions against Contades' ninety: a spurious exaggeration of the disparity, since French battalions were smaller than British and German ones.

How were the recipients of these letters to reply? How could a minister in St James's or a generalissimo on the Russian front decide whether Ferdinand should fight a battle in Westphalia at some unspecified moment and in circumstances unknown? They could only write as kindly and reassuringly as possible. Frederick had already urged Ferdinand not to wait to be attacked, but to seize the initiative and attack first, making sure this time that he had enough artillery. To this advice he could only add that if Ferdinand crossed the Weser he was lost, and would be pushed back against the sea like Cumberland. 'For the love of God,' he wrote, 'don't be discouraged and don't see things in too dark a colour.' Lord Holdernesse assured Ferdinand that the British government trusted him entirely; and that whatever the outcome, he was certain that Ferdinand's decision would be the best for the protection of Hanover and the preservation of the communications with England and Prussia. George II replied that the relevant circumstances were unknown to him, but that Ferdinand should ensure that Stade was properly provisioned and garrisoned.

Ferdinand was not content with these replies. The British, he complained to Frederick, had simply handed the problem back to him, by telling him to preserve his communications with both England and Prussia, though he could not do both if he were defeated. But Ferdinand's correspondents emerge without discredit from the exchange.

Your Serene Highness [wrote the British minister] is entirely free to follow your own judgment and wishes, and whatever the event His Majesty will always be persuaded that your decision will have been the best and most suitable. Nothing could equal the limitless confidence which His Majesty places in the consummate capacity of which Your Serene Highness has given so many striking proofs.

What words more fortifying could Lord Holdernesse have found?

'No battle fought yet,' wrote Sir Joseph Yorke, 'though we are in a continual stretch of expectation.' Even the British commander was in the dark about Ferdinand's ideas. Sackville saw the situation as critical, and in the absence of a battle could only wait for the enemy to reveal their intentions. 'The Prince seems by his dispositions to intend to gain time and not put the fate of these countries to the decision of a battle without an absolute necessity.'
In this agonizing uncertainty the allies waited in the camp at

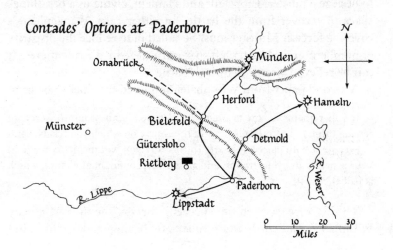

Contades' Options at Paderborn

Rietberg for a week, relieved only by heavy rainfall which speeded the Lippstadt flooding. D'Armentières was moving forward from the Rhine towards Münster, and Contades and Broglie were still in the Paderborn area keeping the allies guessing. At last on the 29th Contades made his move – northwards in the direction of Detmold. It was not to be a siege of Lippstadt, but a thrust into the left flank and rear of the allied field army. Ferdinand fell back the same day towards Gütersloh, retiring parallel to the enemy's line of advance and once again conforming to the French marshal's movement.

Where next? Contades might strike north-eastwards to the fortress of Hameln, to clear the Weser as a supply route and open the way into Hanover. Or he might move due north across the ridge of the Teutoburger Wald to where Minden blocked the gap in the next mountain chain, the dramatic Porta Westfalica where the Weser flowed between the Wiehengebirge and the Wesergebirge into the northern plain. A lucid appreciation by Westphalen etched the enemy's choices, his logic pointing remorselessly to the need to fight. If Contades goes for Hameln, attack him while he is besieging it: if we win this battle we save both Hanover and Westphalia, if we lose it Hameln will merely fall, which it will do anyway if we do not fight for it. If Contades makes for Minden instead, we must still attack him. If we lose, we lose the magazines of Osnabrück and Münster, which we will lose anyway; but the French will still have to besiege Münster, Lippstadt and Hameln, giving us a breathing-space to recover from the battle. In either case, Wangenheim's covering force at Münster must be called in to reduce the disparity of numbers, and Münster left to stand a siege by d'Armentières. It can be relieved after a victorious battle.

A second paper from Westphalen implored his chief to be firm:

> It only remains for me to urge your Serene Highness not to worry; to remain calm; to keep always in sight the course on which you resolve; and to execute it with gaiety of heart. In this way you will inspire courage in your generals and your troops, and all will feel confident of victory, which is half the battle.

This lecture seemed to succeed, for on the following day Westphalen congratulated Ferdinand on having made up his mind to attack the enemy: 'I congratulate you on it with all my heart; the rest will go better than you think.' But the prince's resolution did not last long. Contades wheeled north-west along the southern slopes of the Teutoburger Wald, and cut through the Bielefeld pass towards Minden, still marching with caution, and well closed up. Once again Ferdinand fell back by a parallel march, keeping the hills between him and the enemy. He was evidently preparing mentally for a further retreat. It was certainly difficult to close with Contades, for he could not cross the hills with his artillery and baggage, nor could he find supplies if he marched in the wake of the French. His retreat would have to be away from the enemy towards the magazine at Osnabrück, on which he would depend till he reached the lower Weser. Once there he would be joined by Wangenheim's force from Münster, and would be in reach of his supplies. He would be north of the mountain ranges, and would have to race eastwards to the Weser in order to reach the Minden gap before the enemy.

But there was an alternative. By staying where he was, he could threaten the enemy's supplies and prevent him from advancing further. Contades would then either have to attack him, and give him the battle he needed on ground of his own choosing, or else withdraw. The choice for Ferdinand was clear. He could gain a further respite by retreating to Osnabrück, and then fight for Minden; or stay and offer battle where he was. Ferdinand saw the arguments for both courses, but could decide on neither. He consulted General Imhoff, the Hereditary Prince, Westphalen. But he neither adopted nor absolutely rejected any of their suggestions. Again Westphalen implored him to make up his mind. 'All I ask your Serene Highness to do, is to be very difficult about acceding to any proposal, and only use the ideas of others to form your own plan. On that you must decide for yourself.'

Fresh advice to fight arrived from Frederick. Remember the disproportion at Rossbach, wrote the king: you have seen the French off in the past, and if you concentrate all your forces and use all your cannon you will beat them. There is always risk in a battle; but if you retire you lose your magazines, and spread a panic among the troops which is ten times worse than a lost battle. 'If you only have good courage against the enemy's superiority, all will be well.' Frederick was writing in desperation. His own campaign in the east was in a crisis, between the forces of the Russians and Austrians, and he badly needed a success from Ferdinand. But the prince decided to retreat again; and in the early morning of 8 July he marched for Osnabrück. His withdrawal cleared the threat to Contades' communications. Westphalen deplored the decision. Here we are at Osnäbruck, he wrote to a friend, with the enemy between us and Lippstadt, and in a position to cut us off from Minden. 'The thread is a bit tangled; to unravel the knot we must cut it.'

The price of buying time was still high. Lippstadt had already been summoned to surrender by light troops and was under blockade; and on 7 July d'Armentières summoned Zastrow at Münster. Meanwhile, Contades moved forward to Herford, where he was within a day's march of Minden and little further from Hameln. If Ferdinand was to meet Contades' next move he must anticipate it. The enemy might cross the Weser above Hameln, or enter the Minden basin, or remain in the Bielefeld area to cover a siege of Münster or Lippstadt. Westphalen urged Ferdinand to reflect in an orderly way on the enemy's options and how to frustrate them. If he were mentally prepared for any possible move by Contades he would feel a confidence he could not have at present, and would communicate it to his generals and troops – 'you will soon find in yourself and your army resources which you cannot discover without that'. But if he sought advice without first thinking for himself he would put himself under the influence of his subordinates' local problems.

The more I think over all that has happened in the last month, the more it seems to me that we should not be here, and indeed would not be if your Serene Highness had followed your own views. Your Serene Highness will never achieve the half of what you could do if you act on the ideas of others; and still less if you compromise between opposite opinions.

That day, 9 July, Ferdinand warned the Hanoverian government to be ready to take flight from the capital. What further ideas he may have had for extricating himself we do not know, for once again the enemy took the initiative. On 10 July he learned that they had pushed forward to Minden and attacked it. The fortress was undermanned: if it fell it would give the French cover to besiege Hameln and expose Ferdinand's magazines on the Weser. He had to relieve it.

The enemy force which had attacked Minden could not be more than an advanced detachment which it should be possible to drive off, and the Hereditary Prince was ordered to march immediately to do so. But at the same time Ferdinand resolved to shift the whole army eastwards, and change his base from the magazines of Osnabrück and Münster, supplied from the Ems, to the magazines of the Weser. It was a major strategic movement, and involved the whole cumbrous supply services of the army in what was virtually a flank march across the enemy's front. The fighting troops marched on the following day in the wake of the Hereditary Prince, moving straight for Minden with two days' supply of bread in their packs. For another twenty-four hours the bakery remained at Osnabrück to replenish the regimental bread wagons, which were to follow the fighting troops and join them in two marches as they finished the

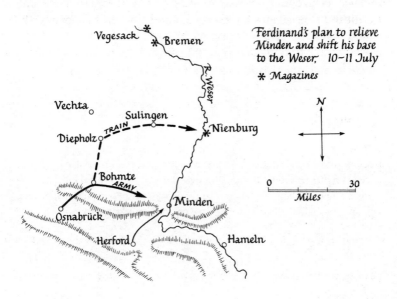

Ferdinand's plan to relieve Minden and shift his base to the Weser, 10–11 July

* Magazines

loaves in their haversacks. All the flour in the Osnabrück magazine which could be loaded in the wagons of the train was moved on a circuitous northerly route through Diepholz behind the cover of the army, to be dumped in the Nienburg magazine which now became the army's forward supply base. Then the heavy iron ovens would trundle round to Nienburg to bake the next supply of bread; but before that reached the army it was likely to go hungry. The forage dump at Osnabrück could not be shifted: it was left with a guard to burn it if the enemy approached.

On the morning of 11 July the army reached Bohmte on its road to Minden, and the Hereditary Prince was pushing forward with the relieving force, still more than twenty miles from the fortress, when he was stopped in his tracks by catastrophic intelligence. Minden had fallen. Though its attackers were indeed only a small advanced force, as Ferdinand had guessed, surprise made up for its lack of numbers. Three hundred volunteers under the partisan leader Fischer crossed the Weser, forced the bridgehead on the right bank, and stormed through the town to open the gates for the rest of the French force. By midday on the 10th the fortress with its stores and cannon was in French hands, and Contades had a fortified bridgehead across the Weser. The northern plain and Ferdinand's magazines lay exposed, and Hanover was open to the enemy.

THREE

THE POINT OF CRISIS

THE LOSS OF WESTPHALIA

Here was the reckoning for Ferdinand's month of retreats. His army found itself in the air between two lines of supply, with his wagon train crawling between Osnabrück and Nienburg. In front of him was the Weser, but the fall of Minden meant that enemy troops were within a day's march of the defenceless Nienburg magazine, from which Ferdinand was separated by the marshland of the Grosses Torfmoor. To reach the Weser and save Nienburg he would have to take the circuitous route of at least two long marches by Diepholz and Rehden, and if the enemy reached the magazine before he did his supply situation would be critical. His alternative was to abandon the Weser magazines to the enemy, sacrificing his contact with Hanover and Prussia; and hold on to Westphalia, supplying his army by the Ems. But if his chance of survival on the Weser was made precarious by the threat to the Nienburg magazine, his survival in Westphalia depended on saving Münster. The fortress had been invested by d'Armentières on the previous day, and the clever French engineers might make quick work of the siege. The fortress was two long marches away, the same distance as Nienburg, and if it surrendered before he could relieve it Westphalia could not give him harbour. He would then have lost both his options.

East to Nienburg, or west to Münster? Indecision assailed him, and ignoring Westphalen's advice to make up his own mind he called for the written opinions of his three contingent commanders. The two Germans took opposite views. Spörcken the Hanoverian was predictably in favour of making eastwards for the Weser and covering Hanover. He argued that the Münster magazines outside the town must already have been taken or destroyed, and that the fortress itself would surrender before Ferdinand could relieve it; but that if Nienburg could be saved, the supply situation and the army's future operations would be assured – at that moment it had only three days' bread. Imhoff the Brunswicker took the contrary view: the enemy would take Nienburg before Ferdinand could reach it, and Ferdinand should march to save Münster instead. And what of the British commander? It seems to have been the first occasion on which Sackville was consulted on a major question: 'the Prince seldom asks opinions', he wrote – a view which might have surprised Westphalen. His answer seemed to balance between the conflicting views of Imhoff and Spörcken, for as he later explained to Bute, 'it is not very easy to form opinions without hearing all that the person knows who puts the question to you'. He declared that in principle he would have favoured saving Münster, because Westphalia would provide good winter quarters and preserve the communications with England and Holland, and it was doubtful whether the French would dare to occupy Hanover with the allied army in their rear. But since Ferdinand was doubtful whether Münster could be saved, Sackville advised him to try to save the Nienburg magazine instead, and accept a battle to do so.

This was not quite the decisive advice for which Ferdinand hoped: Sackville had really stated the options and left the decision to the man who was supposed to take it. Faced with this conflicting advice, Ferdinand summoned the three generals to talk the problem over; and at this point Sackville abandoned his balancing act and came out strongly in favour of saving Münster and the direct communication with England. This meant that two of the generals favoured Münster against one for the Weser. Once again, however, the secretary Westphalen threw his own advice into the scales. Imhoff, he wrote to Ferdinand, had painted the situation on the Weser too black, and had underestimated the danger of marching back to Münster. If there was any chance of saving Nienburg, it must be attempted. With Nienburg secure, the army could march boldly up to attack the enemy, covering its magazines as it advanced, whereas in Westphalia the magazines and supply lines would be exposed to enemy attack if the army moved against either d'Armentières or Contades.

It was now two days since Minden had fallen, and still the prince was dithering. 'It seems to me', wrote Westphalen in his sixth note that day, 'that since your Serene Highness is still unable to reach a firm decision whether to march to Osnabrück or towards Nienburg, you should defer any march till the moment when you can decide.'

At that point Ferdinand made up his mind: he would march for the Weser. That day, 12 July, 600 French cavalry riding hard for Nienburg were met and scattered only five miles from the magazines by a party of German hussars who had come by forced marches from Ferdinand's army with *jäger* riding behind the troopers. The first thrust had been warded off, and now Ferdinand was on the way with the main army. On the 13th he marched to Rehden, and on the 14th arrived at Stolzenau on the Weser and blocked the road to Nienburg against Contades. On the same day General Dreves occupied the free city of Bremen with four battalions to protect the magazines of the lower Weser against a flank thrust by d'Armentières from Westphalia. The magazines of the Weser were secure, the immediate danger had passed, and Ferdinand's operations entered a new phase.

FERDINAND AND SACKVILLE

So apparently did Ferdinand's relations with Sackville. Something had passed between them at the conference which left a lasting resentment in the prince. He never revealed what it was; but probably the truth is contained in a letter which Sackville wrote to Lord Bute after the battle of Minden. 'What I have heard gave most offence', he wrote, 'was my having said I should not be surprised if the British troops were recalled immediately since their country was in danger, as the nearest communication with England was so readily given up.'*

---

*I am indebted to Mr Ewan Fraser for supplying me with this quotation from the Bute MSS.

This was a devastating threat. In 1712, after the dismissal of the great Duke of Marlborough, his successor Ormonde had marched the British troops away from the allied army without notice on the order of Queen Anne's Tory ministers, leaving Prince Eugene at the mercy of a French counter-offensive. More recently, in a situation comparable with the present threat of invasion of the British Isles, British troops had been withdrawn from Flanders to meet the Jacobite rebellion, the Forty-five. It must have seemed perfectly possible to Ferdinand that the British would do it again; and indeed the Duke of Newcastle in 1762 considered ordering a British withdrawal and referred to the Ormonde parallel.

Sackville may have written as he did to Bute in a bid for the sympathy of the anti-German Leicester House party. But if he had really spoken to Ferdinand as he claimed, it was rash and undiplomatic: a disastrous failure to command his irritable temper. The *London Magazine* mentioned this dispute in September, and an account of it evidently reached Sir Joseph Yorke at The Hague, for he referred to it a year later in another context. Lord George, he wrote to Lord Hardwicke, had crossed Ferdinand on every occasion, 'and had gone so far as publickly to accuse him of an intention to abandon the interests of Hanover and England, and to deliver the army up to the King of Prussia'. Sackville seems to have generated· further ill-feeling by criticizing one of Ferdinand's earlier decisions during the retreat.

Perhaps Yorke exaggerated the manner of the offence; but certainly Sackville confided to Bute that he thought Ferdinand's reason for preferring the Weser to Westphalia was to preserve communications with his old master Frederick: 'I only wish we may ever see assistance from that quarter.' Sackville's position as commander of the British contingent was not an easy one. He was under Ferdinand's command and obliged to obey him; yet he was accountable to his government for the advice he gave to Ferdinand, who was not a British subject, had close connections with the King of Prussia, and might not give sufficient weight to England's danger of invasion. Sackville had every right to give his candid advice, but he did not do it with tact and seems to have lost his temper when it was rejected.

It was only to Bute that he confided his objections to the march to the Weser. He did not inform the Secretary of State of them, but merely recorded the choice and the decision – 'the Prince I dare say for the best of reasons preferred the plan of protecting the lower Weser, and by the quickness of his marches, and able dispositions, saved Nienburg and possessed himself of Bremen'. It might indeed have been imprudent to reveal a quarrel with Ferdinand to the Cabinet, knowing as Sackville did how sensitive George II was to the interest of Hanover and his German commander; and he had been sent an official warning that Ferdinand had the ministry's support. 'The King,' wrote the Secretary of State, 'whose confidence in Prince Ferdinand increases every day, has sent him the fullest powers to act as he in his own judgment shall think the best and most conducive to the good of the cause.' Naturally therefore Lord George did not complain of Ferdinand in his official letters. But we shall see that his private letters in the coming weeks before the battle of Minden are also full of praise for Ferdinand's skill and activity, and make no criticisms.

But of this Ferdinand was unaware. What he did learn on 18 July in a letter from Frederick was that the English ministry had been very uneasy about why he had chosen his line of retreat from the Lippe. Frederick pointed out that the English constitution made it necessary to cultivate the confidence of the ministers as well as the king, since they had to explain events to the people; and the people might be quicker than the government to suspect that British interests were being sacrificed to Hanover and Prussia. Ferdinand and Westphalen were upset by Frederick's letter; and they must have suspected, though there is no evidence that it was true, that Sackville had encouraged his government's doubts. The British government's anxiety was the more irritating because they were now talking of seeking another 10,000 German and Danish troops to reinforce Ferdinand. If they had acted on his earlier warnings and provided reinforcements in good time the army need not have been in its present danger. Ferdinand regarded them as negligent and ungrateful allies.

The interruption of communications with England when Westphalia was abandoned was immediate. From Münster d'Armentières' light troops fanned out across the undefended countryside, and on the evening of 16 July an English courier with dispatches from the Secretary of State was intercepted near Vechta, between Osnäbruck and Bremen. The carelessness of the sergeant commanding the French party allowed the courier to destroy his dispatches, and drink and bribery persuaded the sergeant that he was a Dutch merchant and procured his release in the morning. Nevertheless communication with London by the fast route through Holland was severed; and in another ten days French hussars were at the head of the Ems estuary and within three hours' march of the British trooping port at Emden. Preparations were made to shift the British hospital and munitions to Bremen, and the Elbe could also be used if necessary – but for how long, if Ferdinand were driven across the Weser and retired towards the Prussians?

Another source of friction between Ferdinand and his British contingent was supply. The commissary Hunter had been causing him anxiety. 'There is a terrible grievance about magazines,' flapped Newcastle in a letter to Sackville. 'For God's sake, my dear Lord assist me and comfort poor Hunter. It is not now time to have grievances.' The cause of the trouble is obscure. Ferdinand admitted that Hunter lacked neither zeal nor good will, but he was determined to use the system he had learned in the last war in Flanders, and needed time to adapt to Germany. Ferdinand thought that the main cause of the trouble lay in relying on private contractors, combined with a failure by the English commissaries to execute his instructions with speed and precision. He approached George II for help with the problem, and received an assurance that the king would use the information he had sent with the greatest discretion. Is there a hint here that Ferdinand had not received enough support from Sackville about these difficulties? 'One would have to trace the matter back a long way to arrive at the source of the trouble,' he wrote enigmatically. Certainly Sackville was said to have washed his hands of the commissariat problem, which later drew the more gullible Lord Granby into murky waters.

Whatever his merits, Sackville lacked the art of ingratiating himself; and the terms in which one of his generals was writing about him suggest that all was not well with his relationships even in his own British force. Jolly Jack Mostyn was at the pinnacle of his excitement about the colonelcy of Bland's Dragoon Guards, and feared that if Bland died Sackville might be the first to apply for the regiment.

I believe our great commander Ld. G.S.'s prick don't stand quite so stiff at it as mine [he wrote in his usual choice imagery], yet for the dignity of the thing and for that he has (as I hear) said he should not ask for it, I have taken it into my head that he *has* or will, and therefore happen to get into it before me, which will be the devil: debauching my daughter, fucking my wife, and buggering me.

This was written before the operations had really begun, but the deepening crisis of the campaign did not deflect the amiable Noll Bluff from pursuing his own interests. On 18 July on the Weser he followed up with heavy irony to his go-between, Newcastle's nephew Lord Lincoln. He guessed that Newcastle would hesitate to offend the Lieutenant-General of the Ordnance for fear that business would suffer.

I owe it to my *attachment* to the Duke of Newcastle [he wrote] that *nothing* can or will make Lord George Sackville the Duke of Newcastle's friend but his not *daring* to be otherwise. In the next place, the withdrawing himself from the business he is so able and necessary in, take it from me the want of him . . . may be most amply and fully supplied from the blindest choice among the War Office clerks; and yet *that* is his forte. Then as to his station *here*, he has *more* pay and less *duty* than I have. . . . Don't think me a bragger, but I must own to you that I have the vanity to believe that if the Regiment in question was to be at the disposal of the *real Commander* of the King's army here [presumably a reference to his friend Lord Granby] I should have it.

It was just now that Lord George Sackville learned that he had received a legacy from General Bragge, the colonel of the regiment in which he had served at Dettingen, showing that he was not without friends who regarded him well. Yet reading Mostyn's abuse, one feels that it was not thus that the close subordinates of Marlborough and Wellington, or Nelson's captains, would have written about their commander. But perhaps they were better men than Jack Mostyn, with a better cause.

The French army had had a month of methodical success, and the careful advance of Marshal Contades had reaped its harvest. Prince Ferdinand's army had been pushed back towards the lower Weser, abandoning the Westphalian fortresses of Münster and Lippstadt to be besieged by d'Armentières' force from the Rhine. Contades' plan was now to sit down in a secure position where he could contain the allied army and prevent it from interfering with his sieges. When the fortresses fell, d'Armentières would join him and he would resume his offensive with still stronger forces. Ferdinand would be driven inexorably across the Weser into Hanover, on the road that had taken Cumberland to Kloster Zeven.

Contades had if anything advanced further than necessary. His position behind the mountains at Herford had been perfectly satisfactory for his immediate purpose. There he had been able to paralyse Ferdinand by threatening both Minden and Hameln; and if Ferdinand had ignored the threat and stayed in Westphalia to defend Münster and Lippstadt, Contades could have struck into his flank and rear. There had been no immediate need to press forward as far as Minden.

But the success of the raid on Minden tempted him on. When the place fell unexpectedly on 10 July to Fischer's assault, Contades pushed a cavalry brigade and four infantry brigades forward from Herford to secure the prize, and he arrived at Minden himself with the rest of the army on the 15th, the day after Ferdinand reached the Weser seventeen miles further down the river at Stolzenau. At Minden Contades' long advance finally came to a halt. He had stretched his supply lines by advancing from Herford, and now depended on a single road through the river-gap in the Wiehengebirge. But his tactical position was very strong. His right rested on the Weser, his left on the steep wooded heights of the Wiehengebirge; and his front was protected by the fortress of Minden, the little river Bastau, and the marshes of the Grosses Torfmoor. The only point where he could be attacked was a gap of 2,000 yards of firm going between Minden and the marshes, though even this involved a crossing of the Bastau. On his left there was a gap of 1,400 yards between the marshes and the hills; but to reach it Ferdinand would have to make a flank march across the marshes and uncover his magazines on the Weser. On the far bank of the Weser the duc de Broglie's corps protected the pontoon bridges which the French engineers had thrown across so that the army could forage beyond the river in Hanover. Behind the army a small flank guard of two battalions commanded by the comte de Saint-Germain covered Contades' communications against raids by the Hameln garrison and the German light troops.

To Ferdinand it was not yet clear that the enemy's remorseless advance had halted, and it was still possible that Broglie's corps beyond the Weser might lay siege to Hameln while Contades covered that and the other sieges in his strong central position. The campaign was calculated like a game of chess, and if Contades were allowed to develop his operations slowly and surely as he had planned them, the allies would become steadily more helpless, and Contades would win without even risking a battle. Münster and Lippstadt would capitulate; d'Armentières' thirty-six battalions and twenty-two squadrons would join Contades; and Hanover would fall prey to the French. The logic of the situation was spelt out by Westphalen. Ferdinand had to fight Contades before the Westphalian fortresses surrendered; and must therefore attack him quickly before he had time to strengthen his Minden position. The same advice arrived from Frederick, who was deeply uneasy about Ferdinand's state of mind since Bergen. The worst thing you can do is to take no decision, he told him: you cannot escape from your situation without a battle.

The increasing brutality of Frederick's letters reflected his own desperation. Soltikov was bearing down with 70,000 Russians after defeating a covering force at Züllichau, and 80,000 Austrians under Loudon were marching to join him. Frederick warned the British government that he could not send help to Ferdinand until he had defeated the Russians; but in reality his own situation was worse than Ferdinand's, and soon he might himself depend on Ferdinand's help.

The best moment to attack Contades was the day when he reached Minden, and Westphalen urged Ferdinand to attack him at once before he had time to settle into the position. The French army was divided. Broglie's corps on the further bank of the Weser had moved off to the east; and four or five brigades of Contades' grand army had advanced across the protecting Bastau and encamped in front of Minden where they were exposed to attack. Ferdinand accepted Westphalen's advice. The army closed up to Petershagen, and on the following night advanced to surprise the outlying French brigades. But moving forward in the dawn with the pickets, Ferdinand found that the French had slipped away from him during the night and withdrawn behind the Bastau.

The chance had gone, and Contades' force was now behind the marshes in a position which Ferdinand described as unassailable. Broglie's corps beyond the Weser had been drawn in close to the river and could join Contades in a matter of hours. And worse still, intelligence indicated that Münster had fallen, and that d'Armentières with part of the besieging army had joined the grand army while another force of 9,000 men was pushing towards Ferdinand's rear base at Bremen. Matters were not in fact quite as black as they seemed. D'Armentières was still occupied at Münster, where the failure of an attempted *coup de main* had obliged him to wait for siege guns to arrive from Wesel; and the force reported on the Bremen road was merely a foraging detachment, one of whose parties had picked up the English courier. Again Westphalen urged Ferdinand to seek a decision quickly, even though the best chance had gone: 'I see no other remedy than a battle.'

But how? Contades had superior numbers in an impregnable position, and there was a general feeling of bafflement in the allied camp. 'I see little hope of mending our situation,' Lord George confided to Bute. 'The enemy will not fight as long as they can carry all their points without a battle, and I confess, in my poor opinion, Marshal Contades has fairly outwitted us.'

Yet Prince Ferdinand had still one superiority: the quality and discipline of his army. This was what Sackville stressed in his official letters, whatever he might write privately to his friends about the outlook. 'We hear no grumbling or complaint,' he told the Secretary of State, 'but the finest spirit and cheerfulness appear upon every occasion. Prince Ferdinand often expresses the satisfaction it gives him to see such a disposition in all the troops under his command.'

Such troops, if the French could be lured from behind their barrier, might overcome the disparity of numbers.

A LURE FOR CONTADES

Contades, however, did not intend to give Ferdinand an opening; and to most onlookers it must have seemed, as it did to Sackville, that nothing could break the deadlock except disaster. The dam would burst and the torrent would rush down into the plains of Hanover.

But Contades' strong situation had two weaknesses: his vulnerable communications and the difficulty of advancing from the French camp to attack. Westphalen immediately put his finger on the first of these. Contades had advanced just too far. The fortress of Hameln blocking the navigation of the Weser meant that all the French supplies, apart from what their foragers could collect beyond the river, had to come up the long road from Paderborn and the bakeries at Herford and Bielefeld. The slow wagon convoys from Herford crossed the river Werre by the Gohfeld bridge, turned eastwards for four miles between the Weser and the mountains, then plunged between the frowning buttresses of the Porta Westfalica to reach the French camp on the northern slopes. If the road were cut, Contades could no longer sit passively in his safe position defying attack. He would have to send back part of his army to clear his communications and bring up his bread, or else advance across the Bastau and attack Ferdinand. If he did neither, his army would starve, and he would be forced to withdraw through the bottleneck of the Porta Westfalica.

Four days after Sackville's assertion that the allies had been outwitted, Westphalen produced the first part of the plan which saved them: a raid on the French communications. He proposed that a detachment from Ferdinand's army on the Weser should sweep round to the west, cross the mountains by the Lübbecke gap, and threaten the French bakeries at Herford. Contades would be forced either to send back a force from Minden, or raise the siege of Münster and summon d'Armentières to save his magazines and bakeries.

Thus far the plan was not particularly hopeful, though better than doing nothing. Ferdinand raised his usual doubts: Contades could send help back faster than Ferdinand could reinforce his raiders by the circuitous Lübbecke route. Of course he could, replied Westphalen, but that would be to the good: the allied raiders had only to fall back a little to receive their reinforcement, and the war would be removed from the Weser. Perhaps Ferdinand would have gone on doubting and hesitating, but in the late afternoon of 23 July two French deserters confirmed the precariousness of Contades' supplies. Even with the road open the French bread and meat were rotten, and local supplies were too scarce and expensive for the soldiers to buy. The same day the need to act quickly was brought home to Ferdinand by a message found on a prisoner indicating that siege trenches had been opened at Münster four days earlier. The time to save the fortress was running out.

Ferdinand took the plunge; and on the 24th he issued orders for the Hereditary Prince to attack the enemy's communications. The plan followed Westphalen's suggestions. The Erbprinz was to seize the pass at Lübbecke and cross to the south side of the mountain barrier. In the meantime the force under Dreves at Bremen, which had been sent forward to relieve Vechta, would advance to Osnabrück, drive out the French, and send on forty hussars towards Münster, spreading the report that they were the vanguard of a relieving army. That should fix the attention of d'Armentières, while Dreves himself moved eastwards to join the Hereditary Prince at Riemsloh. From there the combined force would send on its light troops towards Herford and the enemy convoys. Contades would be forced to send back troops from Minden to deal with the thrust, and if they were not superior in numbers the Hereditary Prince was to attack them without a moment's reflection: if the enemy force was too strong, he should wait for reinforcements to enable him to fight a battle. If Münster fell and d'Armentières advanced on him, he was again to fight without hesitation: 'Our only hope is a successful battle.'

These orders required that Ferdinand should reinforce the Hereditary Prince if necessary. But here lay a problem. Ferdinand's army had to be near enough to the Lübbecke gap to support the raiders; yet it had still to cover the magazines on the lower Weser and the line of retreat into Hanover. It could not do both without a dangerous division of force.

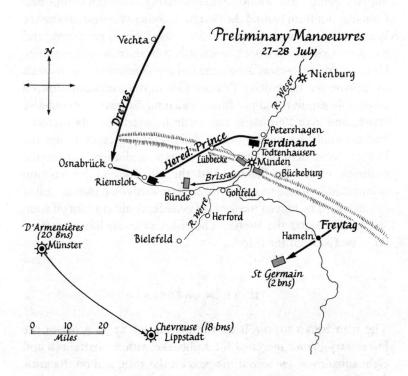

Preliminary Manoeuvres
27–28 July

But in this very difficulty Ferdinand saw his chance: a chance to exploit the second weakness in Contades' situation. The French camp was unassailable; but it was difficult for them to take the offensive. To attack the allies, Contades would have to pass his army through that narrow 2,000-yard gap between Minden and the marshes before he could deploy it. This meant that to avoid being counter-attacked while they were deploying, the French would have to achieve surprise by making their initial advance across the

Bastau by night, with the risk of confusion and delay in the dark. And the French, whom the future General Burgoyne described as being by the admission of their own officers the worst-disciplined troops in Europe, could be relied on for confusion.

Suddenly the mists in Ferdinand's mind began to clear, and he formed the daring plan which one of his staff described as a work of military genius. He would divide his army deliberately and lure Contades out from behind the Bastau. Leaving Wangenheim on the Weser with some 10,000 men to cover his inner flank and magazines, he would march westwards with the rest of the army to Hille, where a causeway across the Grosses Torfmoor enabled him to support the Hereditary Prince. This movement would open a three-mile gap in the allies' front, which might tempt Contades to attack, and give Ferdinand the battle he needed so desperately. Success would depend on the speed of his army's reaction when the French were defiling across the Bastau; and therefore on the swiftness of his intelligence and the efficiency of his column commanders. There was room for friction in his own plan as well as Contades'. If he moved too slowly Contades could cut him off from Wangenheim and the Weser. The risk was great, but he saw no other escape from the trap.

THE PLAN UNROLLS

The plan began to unroll on the evening of 27 July, when the Hereditary Prince marched for Lübbecke with six battalions and eight squadrons. He seized the pass on the 28th; and on the same day Dreves' force from Vechta burst into Osnabrück after four forced marches and drove out the French. On the 29th the two forces met beyond the mountains at Riemsloh, and the ten allied battalions were in a position which threatened the French bread convoys and the depot at Herford.

Ferdinand intended to take the next step on the 28th, by moving westwards to Hille to support the Hereditary Prince; but on Westphalen's advice he allowed another twenty-four hours for the threat of the enemy's communications to become apparent to

Contades. His westward movement, which was to open the tempting gap in the allied front, began in the small hours of the 29th. The first people astir were the regimental quartermasters and camp colour men, who assembled in the darkness at the head of the right-hand regiment of the line, whence the quartermaster-generals led them to the rendezvous where they were due at one o'clock, ready to mark the new camp at daylight. At three the rest of the army roused to the drums beating the *générale*; half an hour later the regiments fell in; and at four the army marched off to its right. It was a flank march in the enemy's presence, and the army moved in its order of battle, with the first and second lines forming two parallel columns which could instantly form a battle front to their left if the French attacked them. Between the two lines marched the heavy artillery, followed by the headquarters' baggage wagons. This wheeled column was headed by Prince Ferdinand's carriages

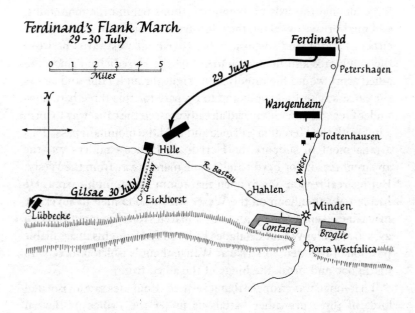

Ferdinand's Flank March
29–30 July

and his six kitchen wagons, to prepare his new quarters in Hille. On the flanks of the columns patrols moved out to prevent a surprise.

The first troops to file off were the cavalry of the right wing, the British and German dragoons leading the two snaking columns out of the camp and across the level fields in the summer dawn, with the guns and carriages following the dusty track between them, and the peasants staring at the dock-tailed wasters of their winter keep. At Detz Kamp the regiments filed into the spaces marked with their camp colours by the advance parties, and two lines of tents rose ranged in order of battle fronting towards the enemy five miles off at Minden: cavalry on the flanks, infantry in the centre; and behind the centre the guns of the British and Hanoverian heavy batteries. To their right was Hille on the edge of the marsh, where two British battalions guarded the causeway and Ferdinand's headquarters. The front was covered by the Lander brook, and beyond it the plain of Minden stretched away towards the distant enemy at the foot of the Wiehengebirge.

By now Contades would be aware of the Hereditary Prince's force moving towards his communications behind the mountains, and might react by taking the offensive with his main army against either of Ferdinand's wings. If he moved out westwards between the mountains and the marsh to cut off the Hereditary Prince, the allied army would file rapidly to its right through Hille and across the causeway to Eickhorst; and to prepare for this three battalions under General von Gilsae had already crossed the causeway to form a link with the Hereditary Prince and hold the mountain pass. This arrangement to support the Hereditary Prince's raiders was the apparent reason for Ferdinand's flank marsh away from the Weser. But his real reason was to open that tempting gap in his front. He had left Wangenheim on the Weser with 13,000 men to cover the magazines, separated by an hour's march from his main force of 25,000 at Hille. Would Contades be lured out from his unassailable position at Minden, to strike at Wangenheim's isolated force with his 44,000 and break the hinge of the allied front?

That hinge was stronger that it seemed. Contades saw an isolated force of three grenadier battalions under the Prince of Bevern in front of Todtenhausen; but that was merely the picket line, guarding a strong, prepared line of entrenchments. Concealed behind a low crest 4,000 paces to the rear was the rest of

Wangenheim's force. If the enemy advanced, Wangenheim was to march rapidly forward and occupy the entrenchments with his infantry and twenty-four Hanoverian heavy cannon, deploying his cavalry on his right towards Ferdinand. He would give the French a harder fight than they expected.

Wangenheim's force was the anvil, Ferdinand the hammer. For Ferdinand had prepared his counterstroke. The delays the French were sure to suffer as they crossed the Bastau in the darkness would give him time to close the gap in his front: not by marching back to his left towards Wangenheim, but by a rapid oblique advance into the plain of Minden towards the enemy. Ferdinand planned to wheel his force forward so that its left joined the flank of Wangenheim's battle position at Stemmern, with his right pushed forward and anchored on the village of Hahlen on the edge of the marsh. From this line he could launch a counterblow into the flank of the deploying French.

As usual Ferdinand kept his intention to himself. Till the last possible moment his generals knew no more than they could infer from certain warning orders. As the regiments filed into their new camp, orders were issued to clear the ground on their front so that they could get forward quickly into the plain. Nine routes into the plain were cleared of obstacles, and the generals were ordered to reconnoitre them so that they could lead their columns forward instantly if the order was given to advance. These arrangements, however, did not mean that the next move would necessarily be to the front. It could equally well be a march to the right across the Hille causeway to support the Hereditary Prince.

The success of the plan depended on the army reaching the Stemmern-Hahlen line before the French had completed their deployment. To secure the anchor at Hahlen when the moment came, the general of the day was stationed in front of the right of the army at Hartum, ready to advance with the pickets and seize Hahlen before the enemy reached it. The rest of the troops were kept in constant readiness. The first news that the French were moving across the Bastau was likely to come towards the middle of the night, and the army was under daily orders to be ready to march at one o'clock in the morning. From that hour of the night the cavalry were to be saddled and the gun teams harnessed, while the infantry lay in their tents dressed in full equipment. On some the pace was beginning to tell, after the weeks of marches, skirmishes and retreats. 'I assure you,' the colonel of the Blues wrote of a cornet who wanted sick leave, 'gooseberries within a common pie crust may safely defy the vigour of his arm.'

On his patrols' superiority Ferdinand could still rely. 'The French know nothing about skirmishing,' he had told Colonel Durand on a reconnaissance a year earlier; and throughout the recent retreat from the Lippe his light infantry and cavalry had had the upper hand. It was tiring work. 'It's impossible to describe the fatigue we have suffered,' a British cavalry officer wrote after the arrival on the Weser, 'we are scarcely ever in bed.' In the Minden plain the cavalry vedettes of the two armies were within a hundred yards of each other, and patrols passed closer, the officers bowing to each other but forbidden to talk to the enemy. 'Our light troops do marvels,' Ferdinand declared as the daily reports streamed in from his patrols. The French generals had reconnoitred the allied left . . . much dust had been seen at Minden . . . the enemy's forward posts had been strengthened . . . a deserter reported an issue of four days' bread . . . Saint-Germain's force was still near Hameln. Hour by hour Ferdinand and Westphalen studied the intelligence and peered into the fog of war.

Ferdinand was ceaselessly alert and active. One morning at four o'clock in Petershagen he was writing to Sackville for confirmation of a report that the French had thrown ten bridges across the Bastau; twelve hours later at Hemmern he thanked him for his reply, sent a further query about enemy movements, and implored him to procure news of the enemy as often as possible. Sackville remained pessimistic: Contades would not fight, and Frederick could spare no aid – 'I cannot conceive that his campaign can end successfully,' he told Newcastle. But of the prince himself he wrote warmly. 'Our great comfort is that everybody is persuaded of the ability of our Commander in Chief, and we all have the fullest confidence in his doing all that can be done.' He assured Lord Holdernesse that there was no danger of a surprise, for the prince kept the army alert. These letters were addressed to members of the

Cabinet, and may have been written with an eye to what would please them; but there is unlikely to have been a hidden motive in what he wrote to his father:

> Prince Ferdinand continues acting with that alertness and attention to his business, as few men but himself could undergo; but the present situation of his army must give him great anxiety; yet he preserves the same good manner and cheerfulness, and I believe it seldom happens to him to sleep two hours together; he corresponds himself with all his outposts, and when I was the other night advanced with the picquets of the army, I had no less than three letters from him, wrote all with his own hand. How he goes through such work I cannot comprehend.

The writer of that letter was not trying to undermine confidence in his commander.

But beneath the carapace of equanimity which Sackville saw, Ferdinand was feeling the six weeks of strain and tension. He received a blow to his hopes on the day of the march to Hille, when he learned that Münster had fallen. He had relied on the fortress detaining d'Armentières for another four or five days while he settled with Contades. Zastrow's surrender of the Münster citadel on the 25th after a token resistance meant that time was running short; though in fact d'Armentières had marched away to besiege Lippstadt, and not towards Contades and Minden. Ferdinand and his staff were shaken by Zastrow's capitulation, and their confidence was not restored by a flow of ungracious criticism from Frederick. 'I do not understand how with such a large army you could have such a great fear of the French . . . by your retreats you are creating your own bad situation . . . no professional soldier will approve your continual retreats . . . you have taken an aversion to battles since Bergen. . . .' Ferdinand replied to one of these letters on the eve of the battle of Minden, when he was hourly expecting Contades to attack him: 'I do not in the least fear to fight; but I do not want to do it except when I see a chance of success.'

He was showing signs of tetchiness. Like many secretive men, he expected his plans to be executed exactly, without fully confiding them to his subordinates. He was dissatisfied with the effort of the Hameln garrison to hold Saint-Germain to his ground, and angry

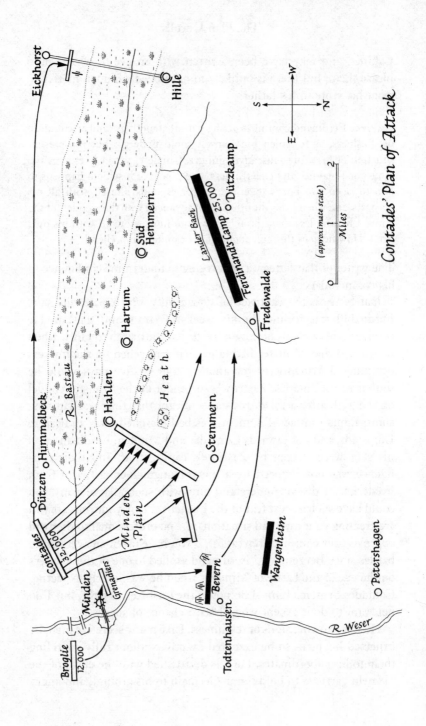

Contades' Plan of Attack

Eickhorst

Hille

Contades 32,000

Dützen ○ Hummelbeck

R. Bastau

○ Hartum

○ Hahlen

Minden Plain

Heath

Süd Hemmern ○

Ferdinand's Camp 25,000

○ Dützkamp

Lander Bach

○ Fredewalde

○ Stemmern

Minden

Broglie 12,000

Grenadiers

Bevern
○

Wargenheim

○ Todtenhausen

R. Weser

○ Petershagen

(approximate scale)
Miles
0   1   2

N ← → S
(compass: E, W)

with Zastrow for surrendering Münster. Sackville, who seems to have advised against the flank march to Hille, was the victim of an unjustified complaint that the British pickets were under strength, though he disposed of it promptly by reminding Ferdinand that two of his battalions were guarding the Hille causeway and providing their own pickets. A further irritation for Ferdinand was a quarrel between Wangenheim and the army's artillery commander, the Count of Schaumburg-Lippe. The count informed the senior officer of Wangenheim's powerful heavy artillery that he was not under Wangenheim's command, and ordered him to withdraw his cannon from a redoubt. Wangenheim challenged the order and won; whereupon Schaumburg-Lippe retaliated by forbidding artillery officers to fire without his orders, and arrested a Hessian captain who opened fire on orders from Ferdinand. Wangenheim demanded to know what would happen if he were attacked, or if he ordered his batteries to open fire on enemy parties entrenching or bringing up cannon. The count retorted that the dispute was too trivial to cause reasonable people to quarrel, and that Wangenheim was making mischief. It was an affair which needed patience and diplomacy; but Ferdinand can have had little of either to spare on the eve of a general action, and the quarrel promised friction in his complex plan for the battle.

THE EVE OF BATTLE

The news that the Hereditary Prince was across the mountains in his rear drew the expected reaction from Contades: he sent back the duc de Brissac with 3,000 men to deal with the raid. Brissac marched back through the Porta Westfalica, and turned west behind the mountains to meet the Hereditary Prince. On 31 July beyond Bünde his advanced troops encountered the enemy's, and held them up while an important convoy of supplies and money passed up the road to Minden. Brissac then fell back to cover the bridge at Gohfeld, without realizing that he was in the presence of a force three times as strong as his own.

In the meantime Contades at Minden observed the main body of

Ferdinand's army moving across his front to Hille. He saw the gap opening in the allies' front, and the exposed left flank of the Hille position. Ferdinand's army had been weakened by detaching the Hereditary Prince, while his own detachment of Brissac would be replaced on the 31st by Saint-Germain's force from near Hameln, which had been relieved by some battalions coming up from Hesse. Contades would therefore be ready to attack the allied army on 1 August with superior force.

His outline plan was an orthodox one dictated by the enemy's apparent mistakes. Ferdinand had moved away from the position which protected his communications, leaving only a small covering force on the Weser to hold the hinge. If Contades could overwhelm this covering force with a sudden attack, he could wheel on to the flank of Ferdinand's position at Hille, and drive him off his communications and line of retreat. This plan was based on two false assumptions: that the covering force on the Weser was only the Prince of Bevern's outpost of grenadiers; and that Ferdinand would wait in his camp to receive the French attack.

Contades' orders were issued in the early evening of 31 July at a conference with his generals; and a British general later described them as 'the best digested I ever saw'. The staff had a complicated problem. Broglie's corps had to be brought across the Weser and forward through the town of Minden to its start line; and the main body of the French army had to cross the Bastau in the narrow mile-wide gap between Minden and the marshes. All this in the darkness of the night, followed by a deployment in the dark for a surprise attack at dawn. Broglie was to march at dusk, cross the Weser by the stone bridge at Minden, and pass his column through the town and out by the northern gate, where he would join eight battalions of grenadiers camped in front of the walls. For the main army the French engineers had thrown nineteen bridges across the Bastau. The troops were to cross in eight columns guided by staff officers, and advance to deploy into order of battle at an angle oblique to the allied camp with their left on Hahlen, almost on the very line where Ferdinand also planned to deploy. On the right Broglie would launch a swift and sudden attack on the Prince of Bevern's force at Todtenhausen, sweep it away, and wheel to envelop Ferdinand's left while the rest of the French advanced obliquely against his front. To deter Ferdinand from advancing to meet the deploying French, a brigade would launch a false attack against the Hille causeway from beyond the marshes at Eickhorst, threatening Ferdinand's communications with the Hereditary Prince.

In one respect, however, the French deployment plan was unorthodox. It placed the cavalry in the centre of the line instead of its normal position on the flanks. This odd arrangement was dictated by the terrain. On both flanks the ground was unsuitable for cavalry. On the left were the villages along the edge of the marsh, with their hedges and enclosures; and on the right Broglie had to clear an entrenched infantry position with a village and enclosures before he could wheel in to envelop the allied left. In the centre, however, was the open Minden heath where cavalry could move freely, filling the space between the relatively weak French left and the stronger right, which had been strengthened to deliver the decisive stroke against the allied flank. It was true that unsupported cavalry had no fire power and were vulnerable to attack; but their front was to be protected with cross-fire from artillery batteries on their flanks.

This arrangement was criticized by German officers as totally 'contrary to sound tactical principles. It was a rule of the day that infantry must remain in a cohesive body and never be separated by cavalry, which had no defensive power and if attacked must either charge or retreat. Cavalry should be stationed on the flanks of an attack if the ground was suitable, or behind the infantry to support it and exploit a breakthrough. Mauvillon took the criticism further. Contades' ignorance of the groundwork of tactics and of the use of the different arms was the cause of the muddle. It was vain to study only the higher reaches of the art of war without understanding the rudiments.

These criticisms made with hindsight did not take full account of Contades' expectations. It might have been better if the cavalry could have been stacked in reserve behind Broglie, ready to exploit his success and complete the envelopment of the allied line; but Contades had a long front to cover, and could not afford a gap in the open Minden heath in his centre. The risk in an enveloping operation was always that the front would be overstretched; but Contades relied on Ferdinand waiting to receive the attack in his camp at Hille.

In the allied camp 31 July was much like any other day in the past fortnight. The usual routine appeared in general orders: the password Augsburg; the Prince of Anhalt to relieve Lord George Sackville that evening as general of the day. Sackville, who had spent the previous night in Hartum in command of the pickets, did his rounds in the morning and sent a brief report to Ferdinand: '*J'ai visité les postes ce matin et n'ai rien trouvé d'extraordinaire.*'

But in Ferdinand's mind there was much that was out of the ordinary, and everything was dropping into place. The intelligence reports of the past three days had indicated that Contades would be ready to attack him on about 1 or 2 August, and that unless he did so his shortage of supplies would force him to withdraw behind the mountains. To increase the pressure on the French supplies Ferdinand had ordered the Hereditary Prince to attack the bridge at Gohfeld on 1 August and cut the road from the south. On the 31st Ferdinand himself rode out to the westward across the causeway from Hille to Lübbecke, and from the crest of the Wiehengebirge examined the enemy camp. A generation later in the French Revolutionary wars it would have been more difficult to survey and count a French army in the irregular shelters and bivouacs of divisional columns; but here laid out below the prince were the neat lines of an army camped in its order of battle. Peering and counting through his telescope, he saw that the enemy had called in all his small detachments, and read the signs of a coming change of position. Back he rode to his headquarters in Hille, confident that the night would bring on the crisis; and any remaining doubt was cleared by a message that evening from Lückner's light troops beyond the Weser reporting the sound of the 'March' in Broglie's camp and the dust of marching men. Ferdinand made a last-minute check with his adjutant-general Reden that all was ready. The guides had been briefed and the routes from the camp into the Minden plain had been cleared, with footbridges laid across the Lander brook and the walls and hedges gapped for marching

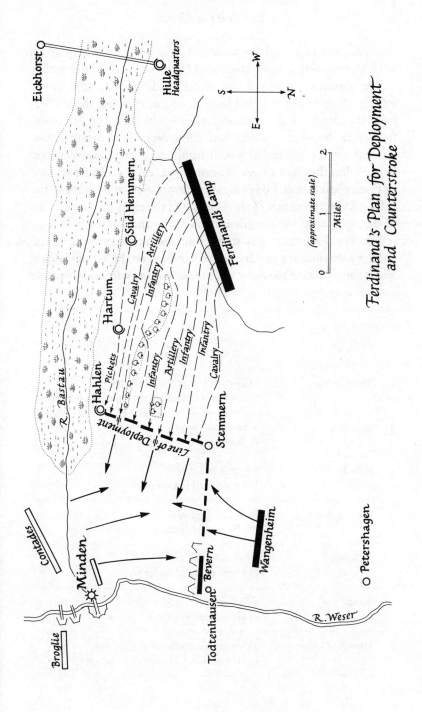

Eickhorst

Hille
Headquarters

R. Bastau

Hartum

Süd Hemmern

Hahlen

Pickets

Cavalry

Infantry

Artillery

Line of Deployment

Infantry

Artillery

Infantry

Infantry

Cavalry

Stemmern

Ferdinand's Camp

Contades

Broglie

Minden

Todtenhausen

Bevern

Wangenheim

Petershagen

R. Weser

W
S   N
E

0   1   2
Miles
(approximate scale)

*Ferdinand's Plan for Deployment
and Counterstroke*

columns. At five o'clock his orders were issued from headquarters at Hille, revealing at last a glimpse of his intentions to the generals.

The moment he heard that the French were on the move, Ferdinand intended to push his army forward about three miles from the camp in eight columns, wheeling half left and deploying for attack between Hahlen and Stemmern. The whole allied strength on the battlefield would be about 37,000 against 44,000 French; but they had 181 guns against 162, and Ferdinand trusted to French confusion. His orders laid down the composition of the columns and the names of the guides. On the right was the cavalry of the right wing, commanded by Sackville and guided by Meyer senior. No destination was stated, but the intention given to the guide was to form the cavalry by the windmill on the left of Hahlen, where the pickets of the army were to occupy the village and protect

Column		
1.	Sackville	24 squadrons cavalry of the right wing (14 British, 10 Hanoverian)
2.	Major Haase	Heavy artillery of the right wing (28 British and Hanoverian guns, 2 howitzers)
3.	Spörcken	8 battalions infantry (6 British, 2 Hanoverian)
4.	Scheele	6 battalions infantry (1 Hessian, 5 Hanoverian)
5.	Colonel Braun	Heavy artillery of the centre (26 Hanoverian guns, 3 howitzers)
6.	Wutginau	6 battalions infantry (1 Hanoverian, 5 Hessian)
7.	Imhoff	6 battalions infantry (4 Hessian, 2 Brunswick)
8.	Holstein-Gottorp	19 squadrons cavalry of the left wing (4 Hanoverian, 6 Hessian, 9 Prussian)

the right flank of the deployment. In succession to the left came four columns of infantry, and the cavalry of the left wing. Between the columns of infantry and cavalry marched the artillery: on Sackville's left the heavy artillery of the right wing, twenty-eight guns and two howitzers including a British battery; and to the left of Scheele's infantry the twenty-six guns and three howitzers of the heavy artillery of the centre (see table opposite).

Compared with the orders which Contades issued at about the same time, Ferdinand's seem incomplete. They did not explain that he expected an attack on Wangenheim, nor that he intended to advance and attack the French in the flank; and no explicit order of battle is shown, as the British complained. Contades gathered his generals that afternoon for a personal briefing; Ferdinand sent out written instructions to his column commanders which revealed nothing of his mind or calculations. This was the more strange because Ferdinand was well known for his briefings before a battle. Colonel Durand had admired them in the Krefeld campaign; and before the battle of Bergen he had sent for all his lieutenant-generals and explained his plans. Lord Granby had been present, and knowing Ferdinand's reputation for clarity, noted the lucidity of his briefing. Nothing of the kind was staged before Minden.

Nor did the written instruction provide enlightenment: it was a bare order of march, though a little more could be inferred from it. For the first time the line on which the army was to deploy was named; and the column commanders, who had already been warned to familiarize themselves with their approach routes, were ordered to reconnoitre the deployment area between Hahlen and Stemmern in person. The army was ordered to be ready to march at one o'clock, with the cavalry saddled, the gun teams harnessed, and the infantry dressed and accoutred; but this was no more than the routine for several nights past, and gave no special reason to suppose that a battle was expected. Nor did Ferdinand take an opportunity to drop a personal warning. When Sackville was relieved as general of the day at five o'clock in the afternoon, and rode back to headquarters at Hille to report all quiet on the forward positions, Ferdinand received the information without comment, though his orders for the battle were even then being distributed.

Sackville was allowed to return to his own quarters with no warning that Ferdinand had seen signs of an attack, or that the night's precautions were more than the routine of the past fortnight. The written instructions might have been no more than an elaboration of the existing arrangements, designed to meet one of several contingencies. On the morning of that very day an order had been received for the British troops to be ready to march, supposedly westwards to their right across the Hille causeway.

By chance however Lord George had heard as he was coming in to headquarters that orders were being issued to reconnoitre the deployment area. He had been hampered in obeying the earlier order to reconnoitre the routes by the fact that he was general of the day. He had spent the whole morning of the 30th at Ferdinand's headquarters, and in the afternoon had gone forward to Hartum to command the pickets. Here as it happened he was on the ground where his column was intended to operate; and on the morning of the 31st when he visited his forward posts he reconnoitred the ground as much as his duties allowed, riding out into the Minden plain beyond the cavalry vedettes and on as far as the hussars. Accompanied by his aide-de-camp Captain Smith, he went far out beyond the Hahlen windmill where the cavalry were to deploy on the following morning, and could see forward into the plain where they could expect to advance. What Sackville did not do was to explore a strip of woodland on the left of his forming-up position, or the heath which it concealed beyond it.

When he learned of the fresh orders to reconnoitre the ground that evening it was already full late to do so; but while he was making his report to Ferdinand, which took about half an hour, he sent back his aide-de-camp Captain Smith and his deputy quartermaster-general Colonel Watson to reconnoitre the approach routes which he had been unable to visit while he was on duty. The guide Meyer who was to lead their column showed them the Hahlen windmill, which he said they were to pass on their left if they were ordered to advance into the Minden plain.

Sackville reached his own quarters between seven and eight o'clock in the evening to find the British adjutant-general Colonel Hotham waiting with the orders he had received that evening. The custom in the allied army was for Ferdinand's adjutant-general Reden to give out orders for the German contingents in German, passing them directly to the brigade-majors and aides-de-camp; but he delivered the orders for the British in French, to the British adjutant-general, who then gave them out in English to the British brigade-majors and aides-de-camp. Hotham had already passed down the orders to be ready at one in the morning to the brigades, which had received many such orders in the past fortnight, and he drew Sackville's attention to the order for the generals to reconnoitre the ground, which Sackville had already done what he could to obey. The order of march of the columns had been received earlier; but this, as Hotham later pointed out in evidence, was nothing more than the ranging of the army in order of battle in case Prince Ferdinand should order it to advance, or the enemy advanced on the allies. It contained no plan for the conduct of the battle. General Kingsley contrasted Ferdinand's procedure with the 'well-digested' orders of Contades: 'We received none from Prince Ferdinand, nor did he seem to put that confidence in generals to be so explicit, as he seldom or never entrusted any with the order of battle.'*

Orders to stand down for the night arrived from Ferdinand, and the army settled down to rest. The cavalry unsaddled, the gun teams were unharnessed, the infantry unbuckled their equipment and boiled their kettles. The generals, in the absence of special orders to the contrary, withdrew as unusual with their staffs to their quarters in the villages behind the camp. Evening faded into a dark blowing night. The hidden moon in its first quarter would set at about eleven, and dawn would begin to stain the sky between two and three, with sunrise at 4.20 a.m.† At one, the men of the cavalry division turned out to the picket lines and saddled their horses, and

*In the Hanoverian archives is a note of 31 July from Ferdinand for Reden that the column commanders should familiarize themselves with the approaches, and reconnoitre them in person. This supports the impression given in Hotham's evidence that, although the battle orders as published later contain both the dispositions and the warning orders, they were originally issued separately.

†Local times for the meridian of Minden. I am grateful to Mr M. F. Ingham for this astronomical information.

returned to their tents to doze or sleep in their boots and clothing.

Out in front of the camp beyond Hartum the sentries of Anhalt's forward pickets peered into the darkness towards Minden. The grand guard of cavalry, half of whom had been dismounted at a time in daylight, were now all on horseback, silent in their saddles through the long dark hours, dozing to the chinking and stamping of the horses while patrols watched the roads on the flanks. Germans and British peered and listened, but if anyone was on the move in the direction of Minden the wind carried the sound away.

At about ten o'clock two French deserters came in from the night to the British picket at Hartum and reported that the French army was advancing. The picket commander sent them straight in to the general of the day; but Anhalt was not much interested. Deserters brought in these tales, and like Sackville he had probably been given no special warning to expect an attack. The Frenchmen hung about his quarters till two in the morning before being sent back to headquarters three miles away in Hille.

The news might still have been held up, for the adjutant-general Reden did not believe it and hesitated to wake the prince. But the Frenchmen were pressing, and eventually he went into the room where Ferdinand was lying fully dressed on a bed. The prince leapt to his feet, alert in an instant. The enemy were on him. All the planning and precautions of the past days had been wrecked by Anhalt's stupidity. Ferdinand and his army had been surprised.

FOUR

THE ALLIES SURPRISED

THE SOLITARY HORSEMEN

A groom was at the door with a horse, and as Ferdinand mounted he fired off orders to the staff officers assembling in the yard: to Reden, to rouse the army and start the columns on their march; to von Taube to find the Count of Schaumburg-Lippe. A scurry of aides-de-camp and orderlies galloped off to the lines to wake the troops. Soon the drums would be rattling in the dark among the rows of tents, and sleepy men would stumble out to form in their companies. The left-hand columns had 5,000 paces to march as the crow flies to reach their battle positions on the Hahlen–Stemmern line; but the columns on the right, which had to wheel round the outside of the arc, had 7,500 paces to traverse, or three and a half miles.

It would be a long time before the troops reached their deployment positions, and much could happen before then in the plain of Minden. Would Wangenheim's force on the left hold till Ferdinand's counterstroke fell on the attacking French? Could Hahlen be occupied before the French reached it, to secure the right flank of the deployment line? Out there at Hartum 4,000 yards in front of the camp Anhalt was supposed to gather his pickets on the first alarm and advance to seize the village of Hahlen. But was he doing it, or would the French be there before him? Ferdinand set off at a gallop to make sure.

Clattering past the Hanoverian picket at Süd-Hemmern, he pressed on to Hartum three miles from his headquarters, where Anhalt was quartered with the British picket. All was quiet. He found Anhalt and asked him for news: nothing changed, was the reply. Ferdinand ordered him to call in his pickets and advance to occupy Hahlen, and left a couple of officers to help him gather his force – the Hanoverian picket from Süd-Hemmern, the Hessians from the wood to the east of Hartum, the cavalry beyond the Hessians. While this was being done Ferdinand rode on towards Hahlen, with only a groom and a peasant guide. Near Hahlen he met a cavalry patrol who warned him that the French were in the village. His groom went forward to look, and came back to confirm that it was full of the enemy.

At this point Ferdinand was joined by his assistant adjutant-general Estorff, and thought again of his left, where he expected the main French attack. Not a word had come from Wangenheim, and Ferdinand feared that he would be caught napping like Anhalt. Off went Estorff to find out, and the prince and his groom rode on into the deserted plain, two solitary horsemen riding out to seek the enemy in the greying morning light. Soon they saw them. Brigade on brigade of white-coated French infantry were advancing towards Wangenheim's flank at Kutenhausen.

Wangenheim was evidently under attack already, for thick smoke was rising from his battery positions in front of Todtenhausen, blowing before a strong wind which carried away the sound of the guns. But now from behind Ferdinand came the sudden thudding of a violent cannonade. The French had begun their diversion on the Eickhorst causeway against Hille. But it was too late to distract Ferdinand now that he had seen the French army ranged for battle in the plain. He sent orders for two more guns to reinforce the two already in the battery commanding the causeway, and scribbled a note on horseback to General Gilsae's detachment beyond the marshes at Lübbecke to attack the enemy at Eickhorst from the rear. At the same time he sent a message to tell the Hereditary Prince what was happening, so that he would launch his own attack scheduled for that day on Contades' lines of communication.

These were probably the last messages that Ferdinand had time to commit to paper. From now on his orders would be given verbally to young staff officers, British, Hanoverian, Hessian and Prussian, who would have to memorize the words and gallop through the shot and smoke to interpret them to some confused or puzzled general. Ferdinand kept no record of these verbal orders. It was said that Prince Eugene had carried a pencil in battle to write his orders in the aide-de-camp's notebook. Ferdinand did not do this, and there was no one beside him to take notes of his instructions. It is no wonder that his later memories of the battle were unreliable.

Ferdinand was tempted to push on and continue his reconnaissance; but he was already too far out in the plain for safety, and decided to fall back on his debouching columns and direct their deployment. The first troops he met were the grand guard of the cavalry of the left, whom he ordered to push on towards the enemy and keep Holstein's cavalry informed of the situation. Soon he encountered Holstein himself trotting at the head of his German squadrons, and advised him to deploy as soon as possible and watch for the right moment to charge. Returning towards the right, he met Imhoff's infantry and repeated the advice he had given Holstein, and sent orders to the other column commanders to speed their march across the wider arc they had to traverse. So far things were going better than Ferdinand had a right to hope after the night's surprise. But moving onwards to the right he found that Anhalt had failed him again. The pickets were still on their own side of Hahlen, and a message from Anhalt reported that the village was in enemy hands and asked whether he should attack it. What did he suppose had been intended? Ferdinand replied that he should attack without further hesitation, and followed in person to ensure that the assault was launched.

From the left there was till no news, but there too the beginning had been shaky. In front of Wangenheim's position on the Weser Broglie had managed to form his troops in the dark without being detected. The blowing gale extinguished the sound of his movements; but it is strange that no patrol from the grand guard discovered twenty-two battalions and sixteen squadrons forming within half a mile of them.

That, however, was to be the end of Broglie's success. Driving in the allies' pickets with his advance guard, he breasted a low rise and for the first time saw Wangenheim's entrenchments and his infantry hurrying forward to occupy them. On the flank of the entrenchments eighteen squadrons of German cavalry blocked the open gap between Kutenhausen and Stemmern, where (though Broglie did not know it) Ferdinand's wheeling columns were to find their hinge with Wangenheim's force. Broglie did realize, however, that he was in the presence of a much larger force than he had been told to expect. On his left, eight French battalions under Nicolai which were coming up from beyond the Bastau to link him to Contades' main army had not yet arrived; and instead of launching the swift attack with which Contades had planned to sweep away Wangenheim's post on the Weser, he waited for Nicolai to come up and laboriously brought foward his artillery to engage Wangenheim's batteries. Then he went off to consult Contades, leaving his troops pinned under a heavy cannonade in which the Hanoverian batteries soon dominated the fire of the French.

While Wangenheim held off Broglie's corps, Ferdinand's cast was moving purposefully on to the centre of the stage. The columns were wheeling up in succession towards the deployment line from which he intended to launch them obliquely into the flank of the French assault. Holstein's horse were already in possession of the Stemmern hinge, and in succession to the right were coming Imhoff's dark-blue Brunswickers with their yellow drummers, the dark-blue battalions of Wutginau's Hessians, and Scheele's scarlet Hanoverians. Further to the right the scarlet of Spörcken's British and Hanoverian brigades was emerging from the belt of woodland which screened the allies' camp. To Spörcken Ferdinand sent word to deploy on to a half-battalion front as he advanced. Beyond him the column of the extreme right, Sackville's cavalry, was concealed by the woodland which ran parallel with its line of advance. Ferdinand sent him an order to deploy into squadrons, and warned him that the pattern of the battle was not yet established. He might have to extend his infantry across Sackville's front as far as Hahlen, in which case the cavalry would form a third and fourth line to support them. Later Ferdinand remembered giving this order to Captain Malortie. In fact the bearer was Estorff.

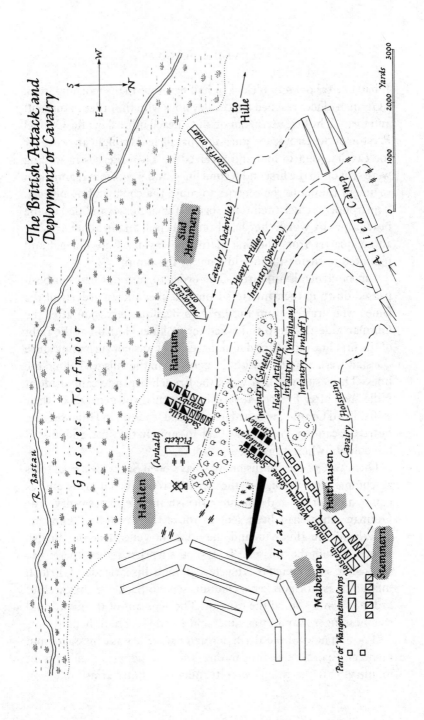

The British Attack and
Deployment of Cavalry

R. Bastau

Grosses Torfmoor

Hahlen

Süd Hemmern

Hartum

(Anhalt)

Pickets

Sackville Granby

Infantry (Scheele)

Heavy Artillery (Scheele)

Spörcken Waldegrave Kingsley

Infantry (Waldegrave)

Holstein Imhoff Scheele

Malbergen

Holthausen

Infantry (Wutginau)

Infantry (Imhoff)

Cavalry (Holstein)

Part of Wangenheims Corps

Heath

Eichorst's order

Cavalry (Sackville)

Heavy Artillery (Spörcken)

Infantry (Spörcken)

Malortie's order

to Hille

Allied Camp

Stemmern

W
S — N
E

0   1000   2000   3000
Yards

It had been about four o'clock or half past four in the morning when a German officer reached the cavalry lines with the order to turn out and form. The brigade-major on duty heard him asking for Colonel Preston of the Greys, and guessing that he had brought an order for the cavalry went to him and received it. The orderlies in waiting were sent off to the first and second lines, and went from regiment to regiment calling to the sentries to rouse the commanding officers. The troopers struck their tents, bridled their horses and tied up the head-ropes by which they had been tethered; and in about an hour and a quarter from the first alarm the cavalry were formed and mounted in their two lines in front of the camp.

But no generals appeared. The order to turn out had not been passed down to their quarters from the line; and an orderly of the Blues who arrived from Ferdinand's headquarters soon after the German aide-de-camp and asked for Colonel Hotham at the right of the first line did not find him there. This was not surprising since the staff were quartered with the generals in the villages behind the lines. The result was that when the French began to cannonade at Hille soon after five not a word had reached the generals or their staffs. Lord Granby, who had just dressed, rode off to Hille when he heard the cannon, lost his way back to camp in the dust, and missed the column when it marched.

One cause of the confusion may have been Sackville's dual roles as commander-in-chief of the British troops of all arms and as commander of a mixed column of British and German cavalry. The German officer had been sent to rouse the cavalry column; the orderly of the Blues to find the adjutant-general of the British troops, whom he missed. It is not surprising that there was confusion; and General Kingsley, though his brigade of British infantry was in Spörcken's column, sent to Sackville in search of orders when he heard the cannon. The sergeant of the guard told the messenger that all was quiet and Lord George in bed.

The first news of the alarm to reach Sackville was a message from General Spörcken, commanding the neighbouring column of infantry, that the troops were turning out under arms; and soon after, while his horses were being bridled, the brigade-major cantered into the yard to report that the line was formed and waiting for orders. He found Lord George in the yard between the house and the stables. Lord George called for his horses, a groom led one round to the door, and without waiting for his aides-de-camp he galloped up to the line with the brigade-major. When he reached the cavalry the line had been formed for about half an hour, and Spörcken's infantry on its left were just breaking into column and beginning their march. A message arrived from Spörcken himself that the infantry were on the move, and Sackville immediately formed his own column by wheeling the files to the right in quarter ranks (a quarter of the squadron fronts) and ordering the first line to march. Led by the guide Meyer, the horsemen filed off at a walk-march into the lane which led to Süd-Hemmern.

Soon General Jack Mostyn, the British brigade commander of the first line, caught up with Sackville at the head of the column, but they had not gone far when an officer came up from the second line saying that no general had joined it and asking for orders to march. Sackville ordered them to follow him, halted the first line till they caught up, and sent back word to the generals that the line had moved off.

The morning had not begun auspiciously, and communications between Ferdinand's headquarters and the cavalry had not stood the test of a surprise. But in spite of the confusion Sackville had been the first general to join the cavalry, and had ordered it to march on his own initiative before the order to march eventually found its way to Hotham. The cavalry were well up with the neighbouring infantry. Yet later Ferdinand was to charge Lord George with disobeying the order to saddle and with being late at his post and in beginning his march.

Behind the generals and the guide at the head of the cavalry rode the drummers of the regiments in their squat grenadier caps, each with a side drum on the left side of his horse's withers: for kettle-drums were still a rarity. They were Sackville's signallers, for the trumpet was only beginning to replace the drum as the cavalry's means of passing orders. The squadrons followed in quarter ranks, each squadron twelve files deep, till they emerged from the lane into the open fields of Süd-Hemmern. Here Captain Estorff rode up to Sackville with Ferdinand's order to form squadrons on the march. He also brought the message that the infantry might have to extend to the right as far as Hahlen, in which case the cavalry were to form in line behind the infantry so as to be at hand if the situation required them. Estorff's memory of this transaction differs slightly from Ferdinand's account. His 'form in line' is materially different from Ferdinand's 'form a third and fourth line', but is nearer to the later orders which Sackville received; and while Ferdinand recorded his intention as having been to anchor (*appuyer*) his infantry at Hahlen, implying an extension of his front, Estorff's '*porter l'infanterie sur Hahlen*' could have referred to the pickets' impending attack on the village, and not to a change in the general order of battle.

On receiving this order Sackville halted the column, and began to form a column of squadrons, each squadron three ranks deep with a front of about forty-five men. When the leading five or six squadrons had formed he resumed the march. But the rear of a column, whether of men or vehicles, moves faster than the front, and two messages came up that the rear squadrons were hurrying and that the horses would be blown. Sackville made one short halt; but to the second appeal he replied that he would halt no more; though he would move slower to give the squadrons in the rear time to form and catch up. Naturally the head of the column could not see the hurry of the rear, and there was some impatience at the slow pace which Sackville was setting. At the head of the leading regiment Colonel Sloper described it as not above half stepping out. A slow pace seems to have been characteristic of Sackville's movements: at his trial Colonel Pitt was to remark that he 'always marched very slow', a habit not usually admired by cavalry officers. But in this instance Lord George was rightly observing the duty laid down for a column commander to preserve order in the rear. There was no need to hurry, for he was well up with the neighbouring column; and if he met the enemy's cavalry his squadrons would need to be closed up in good order and not blown.

Sackville Deploys

Squadron upon squadron the cavalry walked up across the dusty fields between the woods and the marshland towards their deployment position by the Hahlen windmill, where Sackville expected to emerge from the defile and form his battle-line in the plain. But as the leading squadron approached Hartum, still 2,000 yards or more from Hahlen, Captain Malortie arrived with another order from Ferdinand. The cavalry was to halt short of Hahlen and deploy in two lines because the village was still in enemy hands. Malortie led Sackville on till the head of the column was just past the level of Hartum, and stopped him. '*Vous êtes bien ici, milord,*' he said, and rode away. Sackville gave the order to deploy in two lines; the leading squadron of each line stood fast; and the squadrons behind doubled up to their left at a trot, extending the front towards the woods. The position chosen by Malortie between the woods and the hedges of Hartum proved to be too narrow for the whole line to form; but an aide-de-camp returned from reconnoitring the ground ahead and reported that it opened out to the right beyond the village. The lines therefore moved forward, the right-hand regiments inclined to the right to find more room, and the cavalry drew up on a correctly extended front of about 700 yards. The officers took post half a horse's length ahead of the front rank, and the cornet carrying the standard of each regiment reined back into the front rank. The force was now deployed and ready for battle.

The twenty-four squadrons, fourteen in the first line and ten in the second, formed a massive array of 3,300 horsemen, 1,900 of them British and 1,400 Hanoverian. The squadrons were three ranks deep; and allowing four feet to each man, the front of each squadron was about 100 or 112 feet, with an interval equal to a squadron front between the squadrons. They were still probably in 'order', with a space between the three ranks equal to a third of the squadron front. If they advanced to attack the enemy they would move up into close order, with just enough space between the ranks for four men to wheel; and as the charge crashed home the rear ranks would pack forward to a solid mass 'close to the croup', nose to tail, to push the front rank on as it met the shock of the enemy.

The Allies Surprised

Sackville's eye could now sweep the fourteen squadrons of his first line, the British regiments all mounted on black horses. Nearest the marsh on the right of the line were the three squadrons of General Bland's regiment, the former 2nd Horse but for the past fourteen years the 1st Dragoon Guards; and in succession on their left the two squadrons of the 6th Inniskilling Dragoons. These five squadrons formed a solid block of scarlet coats, Bland's distinguished by their blue facings, waistcoats and breeches, the Inniskillings by yellow facings and waistcoats with red breeches. Beyond the Inniskillings were the Blues, the old 1st Regiment of Horse but since 1746 Household troops, their blue coats set off with red facings, waistcoats and breeches. Then came three Hanoverian regiments, comprising a single squadron of the Horse Grenadiers and four squadrons of Max Breidenbach's Dragoons in white coats; and one squadron of grey-coated Life Guards. The eight British squadrons of the first line were commanded by General Mostyn, the six Hanoverian squadrons by Colonel Breidenbach acting as Major-General.

Three or four hundred yards behind the first line, the ten squadrons of the second line were drawn up under Lord Granby. On the right were six scarlet-coated British squadrons: Howard's (3rd Dragoon Guards) in white facings, waistcoats and breeches; Mordaunt's (10th Dragoons) with yellow distinctions; and conspicuous in the centre of the line the grey horses of two squadrons of the Scots Greys, distinguished also among the universal tricornes by the troopers' low grenadier caps with the thistle and motto of Scotland. These British regiments were commanded by Major-General Granville Elliot. On their left Colonel Bock commanded the white-coated Hanoverian regiments of Veltheim and Bremer.

There in the defile between marshland and wood the two lines waited in battle array, still 1,200 yards short of the expected deployment position by the Hahlen windmill. On their left the long wood hid the heath where the infantry columns were beginning to debouch. To their front open stubble-fields rose scarcely perceptibly to where the windmill raised its arms against the sky; near

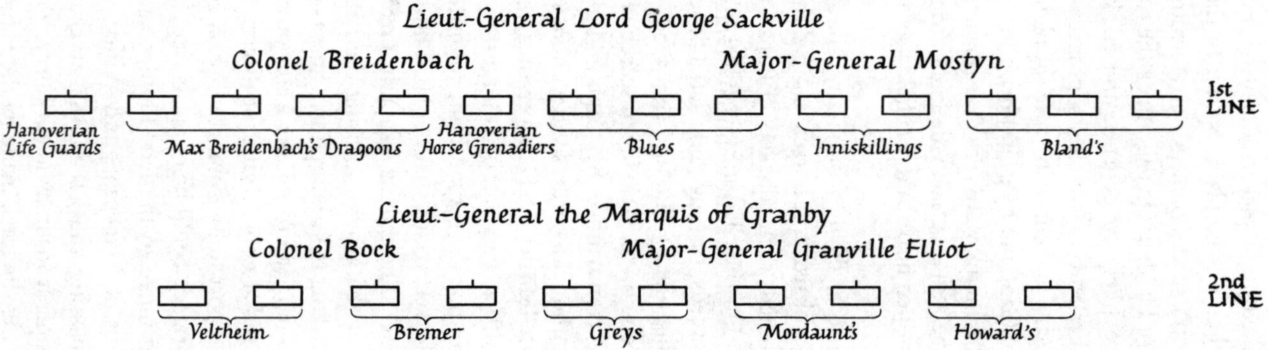

Lieut.-General Lord George Sackville

Major-General Mostyn

Colonel Breidenbach

Hanoverian
Life Guards

Max Breidenbach's Dragoons

Hanoverian
Horse Grenadiers

Blues

Inniskillings

Bland's

1st
LINE

Lieut.-General the Marquis of Granby

Major-General Granville Elliot

Colonel Bock

Veltheim

Bremer

Greys

Mordaunts

Howard's

2nd
LINE

The Cavalry Battle-Lines

it a battery attached to the pickets was firing furiously at an unseen enemy beyond them in the plain. Nearer to the right front of the cavalry the infantry of the pickets were forming up to attack and clear the village of Hahlen. On this attack the future movements of the cavalry were likely to depend, and Sackville sent forward Lieutenant Sutherland to watch its progress. Two other staff officers rode forward to reconnoitre into the plain, but were stopped by the gunners of Captain Foy's light brigade by the windmill, who told them that the enemy were very near through the smoke. In the smoke beyond the guns, as Sackville knew from the previous day, the level plain of open heath and cornfields stretched away towards Minden.

There was little to do now but wait. The men returned their swords to their scabbards; the horses stamped their feet, shook their heads and switched their docked stumps of tail against the tormenting flies. On their left grey-coated Hanoverian gun-teams were moving forwards, turning to the left a little in front of the first line and vanishing one by one into the wood. Presently a British artillery officer rode up to Sackville in search of orders. The heavy artillery brigade commanded by Captain Phillips had marched from the camp without any orders and without a glimpse of a guide, who was probably leading the Hanoverian artillery ahead of them. Sackville guessed that they had been forgotten in the confusion of the morning, and took the responsibility of ordering them forward as fast as possible, remarking that 'we shall find something for you to do in the front'. The gunner, Captain Griffith Williams, rode forward to look at the ground, passing the British battery by the windmill and speaking to Captain Foy who was too busy to answer. Williams could see that Foy's guns were warmly engaged with a French battery; and after observing the direction of the enemy shot he rode back to report to his commanding officer Captain Phillips that the heavy brigade could be of no service there, and suggested that they should move to the left. Phillips agreed, and soon the seven-horse teams of Macbean's and Williams's twelve-pounder batteries were passing the left of the cavalry and through the intervals of the squadrons in a violent hurry. They turned left into the wood, following the track made by the Hanoverian gun-teams.

1. Lord George Sackville, 1759. An engraving of the portrait by Reynolds, painted about five months before the Battle of Minden

2. An engraving of Lord George Sackville
for the *Grand Magazine*, 1760

3. Romney's portrait of Sackville, 1778

LORD GEORGE
SACKVILLE
1760.

4. Sackville's obituary engraving in the
European Magazine, 1785

5.-8. Cavalry Trooper painted by David Morier, *c.* 1751.

5. Royal Horse Guards (The Blues) 6. 1st Dragoon Guards (Bland's)

7. 2nd Royal North British Dragoons
(The Scots Greys)

8. 3rd Dragoon Guards (Howard's)

9. The Marquis of Granby giving alms to a sick soldier

10. A sketch of the Marquis of Granby

11. A grenadier of the 12th Foot (Napier's) by David Morier, c. 1751. The grenadier companies were grouped into a separate battalion of British Grenadiers

12. A Brunswick grenadier, Regiment Imhoff, by David Morier, c. 1751

13. The Battle of Minden with staff officers reporting to Prince Ferdinand

14. A cartoon showing Sackville on the left refusing to advance, and on the right staff officers reporting to Ferdinand

15. Prince Ferdinand of Brunswick by Johan Georg Ziesenis

16. Colonel Robert Sloper as a General in 1787, in a miniature by John Smart.

Sackville's mind was on the enemy, whom he knew to be in the plain to his front; but he would have done well to use the period of waiting to investigate the wood into which the artillery was moving, and discover what was happening beyond it on the left. Had he sent some of his staff to do this, they would have found that the woodland opposite the front line and to the front was three or four hundred yards deep, with tall thick trees and a dense underbrush of thorn and holly which grew thicker in the direction of the enemy. The Hanoverian artillery had forced a passage through the trees in single file, but Captain Williams regarded that part of the wood as impracticable for cavalry in tactical formation; and Sackville was firmly convinced that the whole wood was a barrier to movement. To his rear, however, opposite the second line, the wood narrowed to about a hundred yards. Here the trees were more scattered, the ground was clear of undergrowth, and cavalry could pass through easily on a squadron front by opening out if they did not have to preserve their order. Sackville was right to regard the woodland as an obstacle to tactical movement in the enemy's presence; but if tactical precautions could be abandoned, cavalry could quickly cross the waist of the wood opposite the second line.

This period of waiting was trying for Lord George's temperament, with his liking for 'keeping his time' and his impatience of delay or disappointment. Now he began to fume. Bottled up between woods and marsh, with the way ahead blocked by the enemy infantry in Hahlen and no notion of what Ferdinand intended, he felt caged with his massive force of cavalry; hemmed in on the flanks and likely to come under cannon fire from the front while he waited for orders. Some cannon shot grounded near by, killing an artillery horse; and he complained to his aide-de-camp Captain Smith of being 'put in a hole' and hoped they would not be kept there long. He sent for General Elliot from the second line, and asked him why he thought they had received no instructions from the prince. Elliot replied that he assumed the battle had not been expected and the plans not yet settled, and that Sackville would receive orders as soon as the cavalry's destination had been fixed. As the random shot fell Lord George caught sight of his staff chaplain, Colonel Hotham's brother John, twenty-four and newly ordained.

'Are you yet here?' he exclaimed. 'You have no business here, it is time for you to take care of yourself. Fare you well, we shall be in action before long.'

All that he knew of Ferdinand's present intentions was that the infantry might extend across his front and push the cavalry into reserve. What he could actually see were the pickets forming up and marching to assault Hahlen village. His eyes and thoughts were fixed to his front: on the open country beyond the windmill where he still expected to find the French cavalry, which he could reasonably suppose to be on the flank of the enemy line. In this frame of mind he saw a German aide-de-camp galloping towards him with orders from Ferdinand.

THE ATTACK OF THE BRITISH FOOT

As Ferdinand watched the heads of his columns emerging into the plain, he must have felt some welling back of confidence after his initial dismay. If his army had been surprised, its training and discipline were paying off. The columns had assembled and moved off with speed. They had every chance of outpacing the French to their deployment line, and would form smoothly when they reached it. The less well-drilled French infantry had taken too long to cross the Bastau in the dark, and too long to deploy. The infantry of their left wing were only now coming up behind the force which had seized Hahlen; and Contades' opportunity was slipping through his fingers.

Spörcken's right-hand column of infantry, with the furthest to march, was now debouching from the woodland. The six British battalions had roused in the dawn to the urgent beat of their drums. In eight minutes they were under arms, and soon the column was filing off through the dusty morning towards the Minden plain. For three miles they marched in the silence prescribed by the articles of war; then, as the scarlet column emerged from the woods the leading British brigade deployed into line with brilliant speed and marched on towards the enemy.

Ferdinand watched their progress, and as the lean General

Waldegrave deployed his brigade he sent an order that (as he recorded it later) 'if the troops advanced, they were to do so with drums beating'. It sounds an empty and even fatuous message from a busy commander; and von Taube, who delivered it, remembered it differently: he was 'to tell General Spörcken to advance with the regiments he had, with drums beating, and attack whatever he might encounter'. Whatever Ferdinand may really have said, he complained that his order had been badly delivered or misunderstood. Only Spörcken's first line had deployed, the three battalions of Waldegrave's brigade; but these launched themselves towards the enemy at a rapid pace, followed by the two battalions of Hanoverian guards, which formed as they marched and pushed up to join the line on Waldegrave's left.

Ferdinand, however, was not yet ready to launch his attack. On the right, French troops in Hahlen still blocked the advance of Sackville's cavalry, and were backed by batteries and strong divisions of French and Saxon troops flanking the line of advance of the allied infantry. He needed a little longer to complete the forming of his line and secure his flank: Waldegrave's battalions must not launch themselves into the void towards sixty-three squadrons of French cavalry, flanked by enemy infantry and enfiladed from both sides by cannon. They had to be halted.

Off went Taube and the Duke of Richmond to stop them; but again Ferdinand's memory of his order differs from that of the bearer. According to Ferdinand he sent an order to halt, so that the British foot would not outstrip the columns of their left and their own second line, nor be out of breath when they came into action. But Taube remembered the message as merely to slow the pace to avoid being out of breath. Probably Taube went to Spörcken and the English-speaking Richmond to Waldegrave; but what Richmond may have said is not recorded.

Ferdinand saw Waldegrave's battalions halt in the rear of an isolated rectangle of fir-wood which screened them from enemy fire; and he turned his attention to his artillery, as the head of Major Haase's Hanoverian brigade began to emerge rather late from the woodland on the right. As they came out on to the cornfields the gun-teams deployed into line, and Ferdinand ordered them forward to the point of the woodland to engage the enemy. He also sent the Duke of Richmond to bring up the British artillery which Sackville had sent on behind the Hanoverians. The inexperienced young man found the British on the far side of the wood and about to enter it; and addressing no one in particular told them that the artillery were to go through the forward end of the wood and engage the French. Captain Williams replied that it was impossible to take the guns through that way, Phillips and Macbean agreed, and the three artillerymen pursued their own way through the wood, which they had made it their business to reconnoitre. Emerging on to the heath, they wheeled to the right towards the enemy.

Siting his cannon was a burden which Ferdinand should not have been carrying; but his artillery commander Schaumburg-Lippe had been absorbed by Wangenheim's artillery duel on the left and was seen no more by his commander-in-chief during the battle. Even while Ferdinand was deploying his batteries, the British battalions which he had halted behind the fir-wood suddenly shouldered arms. Their drums began to beat, and under the amazed regard of Ferdinand and his staff they set off at a rapid pace in the direction of the enemy. It was too late to stop or slow them now. Their swift advance inclined towards the left, pushing across the front of General Scheele's Hanoverian column and blocking its line of advance.

Three ranks deep, the scarlet line of General Waldegrave's brigade marched on. The grenadier companies of its three battalions had been removed and grouped into an élite battalion of British Grenadiers stationed on the left of the army with Wangenheim, so only the eight battalion companies were present with each regiment. According to custom the senior regiments were stationed on the flanks with the junior one between them: on the right Napier's, the 12th Foot, their red coats lined and faced with light yellow, with red breeches and grey marching gaiters, tricorne hats on their powdered and pigtailed hair. On the left flank were the blue facings of the Welch Fusiliers, who, fourteen years earlier, had been in the attack at Fontenoy; in the centre, Stuart's, the 37th Foot, with yellow facings. Behind Waldegrave's brigade Kingsley's followed in second line, with his own regiment the 20th Foot on the right and Home's Scottish 25th on the left, both regiments in yellow facings and both veterans of Fontenoy. In the centre of the second line were the deep-green facings of the youngest of the six British regiments, Brudenell's 51st, only raised in 1756 and now going into the first battle of its long and glorious history. The drummers of each regiment in their low caps of grenadier style wore coats in the colour of their regiments' facings, except in the Welch Fusiliers where the drums wore the royal livery of red faced with blue. On the flanks of the companies marched officers carrying the short pike called a spontoon, and in the rear were the watchful sergeants with their halberds. Above the heads of the senior company of each regiment flapped the pair of colours.

At first all was quiet as the lines moved off. Then as they left the shelter of the wood cannon began to thud in the distance, and an eighteen-pound ball rolled gently across the heath towards them. On they strode, and in another quarter of a mile the shot was sighing through the files as they came into range of eighteen heavy French eighteen-pounders. Heads and limbs began to fly, and in the second line a single shot dashed a file of three men of the 20th to pieces and spattered Lieutenant Thomson with their blood. For a while he felt shaken. Then the blow of a spent musket ball on his arm pulled him together, and forgetting his own fear he began to feel anger and concern for the men he commanded.

Thinned by the shot, the line marched unwaveringly on, closing ranks as the dead and wounded dropped. Soon they had advanced so far that the batteries were firing into their flank; further still, and the shot was striking through the files from the rear. The two battalions of Hanoverian foot guards caught up and came into the first line on their left, and Hardenberg's regiment from Scheele's column found room to extend the line. But Scheele's other five German battalions were pushed out by the leftward incline of the British and dropped back to the rear.

Spörcken's brigades had outmarched their three-pounder battalion guns; nor had the Hanoverian heavy artillery brigade in the centre of the army yet come into action. For a time the infantry were at the mercy of the French cannon. Then on their right Major Haase's Hanoverian artillery deployed out of the woodland, followed by Phillips's British twelve-pounders. Coming into line with the Hanoverian cannon, the British unlimbered by removing the forewheels from the gun-carriages, loaded rapidly and opened fire. After a few shots at the French cavalry they found that they were under fire from a French battery. They lifted their trails and swivelled their guns on to the new target, and in five or ten minutes the French artillery were battered into silence. The guns were trained back on to the enemy's horse and foot and resumed their fire.

The French cavalry, ranged in two lines with two more brigades in reserve behind them, had watched Spörcken's scarlet column winding forth from the distant woodland. The infantry advanced into the fire of the French cannon, deployed with incredible speed and marched forward towards the cavalry's left. The cavalry, drawn up so unconventionally in the centre, depended on the cross-fire of their flanking batteries to protect them. But the allied infantry advanced through their fire, and then the British and German cannon which had moved so boldly across the open to the point of the woodland battered the guns on the French left and silenced them. On the cavalry's right Colonel Braun's Hanoverian guns and the Bückeburg artillery were coming into action; and thus partly protected by their own artillery fire the redcoats came inexorably on towards the waiting mass of horse. Soon they would be in musket range. The scarlet lines would halt and level their muskets, and deadly white ropes of smoke would ripple from platoon to platoon. The cavalry could not reply to their fire. If they stayed still, the 7,000 horsemen would be shot down helplessly by the rolling volleys. They had to charge or be destroyed. The duc de Fitz-James gave the word, and out from the left of the front line moved the marquis de Castries at the head of eleven squadrons of the Royal Cravates and Mestre de Camp.

THE CALL FOR CAVALRY

The crisis of the morning had come; and at the very moment when Ferdinand's plans seemed to be falling into place the lunatic behaviour of the British infantry had thrown the whole army into danger. It was like Bergen again, where a precipitate attack had drawn the army piecemeal into battle. From now on Ferdinand was no longer implementing a design, but improvising as he reacted to the rapid shifts of the battle. No wonder that his memories of the confused and changing scene in the drifting smoke were uncertain. He was often wrong in his recollections of the words of his orders – about the situation when he issued them, about who delivered them.

As Spörcken's infantry moved off from behind the fir-wood and headed for the massed ranks of the French cavalry, inclining to their left and widening the gap on their right flank, it was apparent that the allied line was in danger. If the French cavalry broke through, Spörcken's battalions would be totally destroyed and a huge gap would be torn in the allied front. Ferdinand thought of Sackville's twenty-four squadrons waiting inactive somewhere beyond the woodland. Though less than half the strength of the French cavalry, they might save the day. If they could be brought across to the rear of Spörcken's infantry they could charge the disordered French squadrons after their attack and give the foot a chance to rally. Ferdinand turned to Winzingerode and ordered him to fetch the cavalry. The message he gave him for Sackville (Winzingerode's evidence makes it clear, though Ferdinand's account is confused) was to advance with the cavalry of the right wing and sustain the infantry, which was going to be engaged. These words appear to mean that Sackville was to advance past Hahlen, which was just then being cleared of the enemy, enter the plain by the route originally intended, and sustain the infantry either from the rear or perhaps better still from the flank. But no sooner had Winzingerode galloped off than Ferdinand had an afterthought and sent the Duke of Richmond in pursuit with a vital change or clarification – it is not clear which. Winzingerode was to hasten the arrival of the cavalry, and tell Lord George to form on the heath as a third line behind the infantry. Richmond passed the message to Winzingerode, who raced on in search of the cavalry.

Winzingerode galloped across to the belt of woodland in the

direction of Hartum, rode through the trees at the narrow neck where they were thinnest, and emerged to find that he was opposite the second line of cavalry, nearly a quarter of a mile in the rear of the first line. Riding across the front of the second line and asking for Lord George, he was met by Lord Granby, who told him that Sackville was at the head of the first line. Winzingerode explained that the cavalry were to advance and form on the heath behind the infantry to sustain them; but when his evidence to this effect was read over to him at Sackville's court martial, he added that he had mentioned that the cavalry were to pass through the trees to their left. This Lord Granby confirms; yet though this interpretation of the order was not challenged, there is no evidence that Ferdinand had said anything of the kind, though he may have meant it.

Leaving Granby, Winzingerode galloped on with drawn sword, and found Lord George on the right of the first line at the head of Bland's Dragoon Guards. What happened next was a matter of dispute. According to Winzingerode he delivered his orders, but Sackville did not seem to understand him and asked how it was to be done. He tried to explain, saying that the cavalry was to pass through the trees on the left, form on the heath, and advance to sustain the infantry.

Sackville denied that this explanation was ever given. Winzingerode, he said, had come up to him at a full gallop, and delivered an order in hasty breathless French which Lord George made him repeat. As Lord George and Colonel Hotham then understood him, he said in French that it was the prince's order to form the cavalry into a single line, making a third line to sustain the infantry, and to advance. This fitted in with Sackville's preconception. He could see the infantry of the pickets attacking Hahlen, and hear the heavy cannon fire ahead; he knew that the country in front was open; he remembered Estorff's message that the infantry might be extended across his front, in which case the cavalry would form a third and fourth line behind them. To Sackville and Hotham the word 'advance' meant to move forward. Three other officers of Sackville's staff agreed that the order was delivered as Lord George and Colonel Hotham claimed to have heard it, and when Captain Lloyd rode up a moment later he gathered the same from the others:

none of them had heard Winzingerode's explanation. If Sackville was puzzled about how to execute the order, it could have been simply because he had no room to extend into a single line between the woods and the marsh. In Ferdinand's mind the word 'advance' no doubt related to the forward position of the infantry, but Sackville had no means of knowing how far and how rashly they had pushed on. This Winzingerode never claimed to have explained; and indeed he had no clear general picture of how the battle was developing. At the court martial he disclaimed knowledge of the enemy cavalry's position and refused to answer questions on the point.

But against Sackville and all his staff there was one witness with a different story. Colonel Sloper of Bland's Dragoon Guards was close by at the head of his regiment; and according to him Winzingerode said twice in French that the cavalry was to advance *to the left* and form in a line behind the infantry. This was not part of Ferdinand's order, and Winzingerode himself did not claim to have delivered the order in this way to Sackville. According to Sloper Winzingerode then said in English that Sackville was to form the cavalry in a line behind the infantry. '*Mais comment? Mais comment?*' asked Sackville. With a wave of his hand the German explained: 'You must pass through those trees, you will then arrive upon the heath. You will then see our infantry and the enemy.' With that Winzingerode rode off, and Sloper heard Sackville say: 'I do not comprehend how the movement is to be made.' Sloper broke in with his unsolicited opinion. It seemed very clear to him, he said, that the movement was to be made to the left by the right wing of the cavalry. Sackville replied that he would do so, and rode away.

If Sloper's story is to be believed, Sackville's assumption that he was to advance to his front should now have been shaken. But Sackville's staff denied that they had seen Sloper, or that Winzingerode had spoken in English. Sloper also put it about in London (though not in his sworn evidence) that Winzingerode had spoken in German to Sackville's Hanoverian aide-de-camp Captain Hugo: this Hugo also denied.

What Sackville actually did when Winzingerode left him was to prepare for an advance to the front. Winzingerode had not suggested that the move was critically urgent, and he decided to resolve the question of how to form a single line by reconnaissance. If he formed the line in his present position his force would have to extend beyond the belt of woodland and become divided; and he intended, if reconnaissance justified it, to advance in two lines till he was clear of the wood, and form a single line when he had room to do so in the open plain. While Winzingerode was still with him Sackville had sent off Captain Joseph Broome, his ordnance aide-de-camp, to reconnoitre to the front; and now he sent Captain Keith and Captain Lloyd through the woods to locate the infantry. In the meantime he cleared the ground ahead for the cavalry's advance. A few hundred yards in front the way was blocked by an infantry battalion, the Saxe-Gotha Regiment, which had been detailed as escort to the artillery. Sackville sent forward his German aide-de-camp to move the regiment off to the right. All this was rather deliberate; but Anhalt's pickets had still to finish clearing the enemy from Hahlen.

That Sackville believed that the infantry he was to support were in front is suggested by what Captain Smith heard when he rode up as Sackville was ordering Hugo to move the Saxe-Gotha Regiment. Sackville remarked that the regiment was not the second line, implying that he was looking ahead and beyond the Saxe-Gotha troops for the line of infantry which he was required to support. And indeed a line of infantry was now on the move close to the windmill, and might be the right flank of the line he was to support. Granby shared his belief. 'I thought', he told the court martial, 'that infantry was in front of the cavalry. I did not know what infantry, but I thought there was infantry in front of the cavalry.'

While Sackville was making these preparations, Lord Granby had put the second line in motion as a result of what Winzingerode had told him. He was observed by the chaplain John Hotham, who had walked his horse back to the second line after being sent away by Lord George, and was talking to General Elliot when Winzingerode arrived and said something to Granby in French. Granby then spoke to Elliot, who returned to Hotham with his sword drawn saying, 'We are going to move forward, fare you well.' The second line then moved forward towards the first line. If Winzingerode had really told Granby that the move was to be to the left, Granby's direction was curious. He may have been closing up in preparation for forming a single line, but if that was so his movement was not well judged, since the practicable passage of the wood was opposite the second line's rearward position. In any case Sackville stopped him by sending for General Elliot, whom he ordered to stand fast, saying that he would send him orders immediately.

FIVE

THE TARNISHED VICTORY

A CONFLICT OF ORDERS

Even while Winzingerode galloped in search of the cavalry the battle was developing with incredible speed, as de Castries' squadrons moved off to charge the exposed salient formed by the advance of the British foot.

For cavalry to charge unshaken infantry was hazardous, and Spörcken's lines halted and prepared confidently to receive their attack. This was the moment for which the British battalions had drilled through their year of service in Germany, learning the new practice of aiming their muskets individually and rehearsing their alternate firing. As the French horsemen trotted up stirrup to stirrup to the charge the first British volley rolled down the line. Horses staggered and saddles emptied, and the French reeled back smashed and defeated, leaving the ground in front of the infantry strewn with a piteous litter of men and horses. The infantry closed their ranks, distributed the ammunition of the casualties, passed their wounded to the rear, and resumed their advance.

Fitz-James had no choice but to attack again. As the flotsam of the first attack was sucked back through his ranks, he ordered his second line to charge. Out through the debris came twenty-two squadrons of the Royal Étranger, Bourgogne and the Brigade du Roi. Again the volleys crashed, and again the shattered cavalry retired. The infantry shouldered arms and marched forward through the smoke, red coats brown with dust, faces blackened by burnt powder. Between the first and second lines the wounded were sheltering behind dead horses, or helping each other through the shot to the rear in search of the surgeons who had disappeared in the confusion of the morning. Lieutenant Thomson of the 20th, wounded at last after three hits from spent balls, was being helped by a slightly wounded soldier when he was spun completely round by the wind of a cannon ball, and found his helper dying beside him with his leg gone.

Ferdinand in the meantime had gone off towards the centre to bring forward Wutginau's infantry and close the gap on Spörcken's left. Taube carried the order; and on rejoining the prince he heard him exclaim as he rode up, '*Mais est-ce que cette cavalerie n'arrive pas encore?*' Considering that Winzingerode had had a mile to gallop to deliver the order, and had been gone only a few minutes, it was scarcely reasonable to expect twenty-four squadrons to have formed column and passed through the wood on to the heath. But in the critical state of the battle Ferdinand's impatience was natural.

About now, when the first or second cavalry attack had been broken, the prince sent a second summons to Sackville. This time the bearer was a British aide-de-camp, Captain Ligonier; but again Ferdinand's later memory of sending him was confused. He believed that he had sent Winzingerode and Ligonier simultaneously and with identical orders. In fact both the time and circumstances were different. Winzingerode had been sent off before the infantry had advanced a hundred paces, to bring up cavalry in anticipation of a French breakthrough. Ligonier was dispatched when the French horse had been beaten off in confusion, to bring up cavalry to exploit the success.

Captain Edward Ligonier was the most experienced and least excitable of Ferdinand's British aides-de-camp. A cavalryman aged about thirty, he was several years older than Richmond and Fitzroy; but in spite of being the nephew and heir of the commander-in-chief of the British army he was still only a captain, while Richmond and Fitzroy were lieutenant-colonels. Perhaps his illegitimate birth had held him back. Perhaps too the fact that his rise had been less easy than that of Fitzroy and the Duke of Richmond had taught him to behave with more discretion, and made him more capable of imagining the situation of a man in difficulties. He was, however, a warm admirer of Ferdinand, whom he had seen in action at Bergen. 'The calmness of Prince Ferdinand in the hottest fire,' he wrote to Hotham after that battle, '*the distinct manner of giving his orders*, in short his conduct and courage deserved better success.' Ligonier bore his orders to Sackville with utter confidence in their originator, and was unlikely to see the situation through the eyes of Sackville.

As Ligonier reached the wood he met Captain Lloyd, whom Sackville had sent to reconnoitre. Guessing that Ligonier had brought fresh orders Lloyd turned back to lead him to Sackville, and together they galloped out of the wood and across the stubble towards the front of the cavalry. In front of the left squadron of the Inniskillings Major Marriot saw Ligonier coming on a small black horse, which was blowing hard from the gallop, and rode forward to ask for news. Glorious! he remembered Ligonier replying: the enemy were giving way, and he was coming to order up the British cavalry. Whether Ligonier really said *British* cavalry or Marriott only imagined it in retrospect one cannot know: it was certainly not part of Ferdinand's order, which was to bring up the whole of the cavalry of the right wing, but it indicates the ease with which confusion could creep in. Marriott rode across to his commanding officer in front of the other squadron, and asked for permission to clear his men for action by throwing away their corn and picket poles.

Ligonier rode on towards Sackville, and delivered the order to advance with the cavalry (no mention this time of the British). Captain Lloyd heard him add ('but it was no order; it was only conversation,' said Lloyd) that the enemy was in confusion and he hoped they should profit from it. Hotham's version of this remark represented it as a message from Ferdinand: the enemy were in confusion and the prince '*vous prie d'en profiter*' – an extraordinary way for a British officer to deliver an order to a British general even in that polyglot army, but Ligonier's father was French.

The new order was immediate and urgent, and realizing this Hotham suggested that he should go back to see to the second line and rode off. Just at this moment Sutherland returned from Hahlen to report that the pickets' attack had succeeded in clearing the village. The way to the front was thus opened and Sackville, without answering Ligonier, turned about to face the troops, drew his own sword, and gave the order to draw swords and march. The drums rattled, and the first line of cavalry moved off to the front.

Ligonier was disconcerted, and before the cavalry had advanced more than a few paces he told Sackville, riding by his side, that he was meant to march to the left. Sackville maintained afterwards that he did not hear this. Nor did any of his staff. Lord George himself was intent on executing the expected order to advance to his front; and with the drums beating behind him, he agreed that Ligonier might have said something of the kind without being heard. The line marched on; but a moment later yet another messenger from Ferdinand reined up beside the British commander.

At the moment when Ligonier rode off to summon the cavalry, frontal attacks by thirty-three French squadrons had been shattered by the first line of Spörcken's infantry, whose exposed flanks had hitherto been left unmolested. But soon after that the immunity of their flanks came to an end. As the first French charge was beaten Contades himself had arrived on the scene, and began to co-ordinate that part of his front. On the right of his cavalry he ordered forward Beaupréau's two brigades of infantry with eight guns to occupy the hamlet of Malbergen (nowadays called Maulbeerkamp) and its surrounding hedges and from there assail the flank of Spörcken's column. On the French cavalry's left the comte de Guerchy, whose infantry had been standing passively three-quarters of a mile away behind Hahlen, decided to intervene at the crisis point of the battle, and advanced towards Spörcken's right flank with eight battalions of his front line. Though they had already faced two attacks the right-hand battalions of Waldegrave's brigade, the 12th and 37th, wheeled to face the new threat, while behind them Spörcken wheeled up Kingsley's brigade half right to extend their line. Kingsley's three battalions volleyed into Guerchy's attack while the British and Hanoverian batteries in front of the wood blasted its flanks. Almost simultaneously Fitz-James committed the last of his cavalry, the two reserve brigades. Two thousand troopers of the Carabiniers and Gendarmerie, the élite of the French monarchy in men and horses, fell on the left of Spörcken's line and lapped round its flank and rear. There was nothing now behind it, for the second line had wheeled away to meet Guerchy's attack. But the battalions of the left, the Welch Fusiliers, Hanoverian Guards and Hardenberg's, faced their rear ranks about and fought off the horsemen, while two of Wutginau's battalions coming up on their left fired into the flank of the attack. The Carabiniers and Gendarmerie fell back with the loss of half their men, and on the right Guerchy's broken infantry withdrew covered by three Saxon battalions.

When this storm burst on Spörcken's flanks Ferdinand began to shift his order of battle to meet the crisis. Five of Scheele's battalions, which had been pushed out of the line on the left by the oblique advance of the British, were shifted across the rear of the battle to fill the void on the right. As the attacks grew fiercer Ferdinand also summoned two of Wutginau's battalions to the right. These two battalions, Wangenheim's and the Hessian Guards, seem to have arrived as the final tempest struck Kingsley's line. Saxon infantry stormed forward led by the comte de Lusace. Kingsley's horse was shot in four places and fell and died on him, and he was twice marched over by Saxon infantry. For the first time the British infantry wavered, and after sustaining heavy losses Kingsley's regiment fell back.

Seeing some of the scarlet line yielding ground, Ferdinand sent yet another summons to Sackville. Ferdinand afterwards remembered sending Lieutenant-Colonel Charles Fitzroy, and telling him to fetch only the British cavalry in order to avoid delay. But again the messenger's account differs from the general's. While Ferdinand was moving Wutginau's battalions to meet the Saxon attacks, he did indeed send the Prussian Derenthal to urge Sackville to hurry. But Fitzroy was sent off much earlier; not when the final crisis of the battle was erupting, but while the French cavalry were still in the confusion of their first defeats. According to Fitzroy it was only a moment after Ligonier's departure that he was sent. The Duke of Richmond rode back from the infantry and reported the enemy's confusion; and Ferdinand, riding forward through the fog of battle to see for himself, exclaimed: '*Voici le beau moment pour la cavalerie.*' On hearing this Fitzroy asked his leave to go and fetch the British cavalry. Ferdinand answered simply, '*Courez-y.*'

If this is true it was Fitzroy, not Ferdinand, who suggested bringing up only the British cavalry. He knew that Winzingerode had been sent off to fetch the cavalry, and sensed Ferdinand's impatience. But till Richmond appeared Fitzroy did not know of the enemy's disorder; and he did not know that Ligonier had been sent off moments earlier to bring up the whole of the cavalry of the right wing. By suggesting that he should bring up the *British* cavalry Fitzroy may unwittingly have introduced confusion. Was he even aware that Sackville had Hanoverian cavalry in his column? And did Ferdinand grasp the implications of his words, or did he take him to mean 'the cavalry commanded by the British general'? If Ferdinand did grasp what the words meant it was senseless of him to agree. Even if one supposes that for some reason (which no one explained) Sackville would more readily have brought up the British squadrons than his whole command, the British squadrons were further away by some hundreds of yards than the Hanoverians. But off went Fitzroy with his general's assent.

Sackville turned to see beside him an excitable and self-important youth of twenty-two, out of breath from galloping and bursting with a message from the supreme commander. What he seemed to be saying sounded wildly improbable. March the *British* cavalry? To the *left*? Lord George raised his hand and gave the order 'cease the drums'; then 'halt the line'. The drums fell silent, the horsemen drew rein, and he said to this sprig of the Graftons beside him: 'Why, sir, Mr. Ligonier says the whole. Don't be in a hurry, Fitzroy.' Fitzroy replied crossly that he had spoken indistinctly because he was out of breath, and repeated that the British cavalry were to advance towards the left. He added that it was a glorious opportunity for the British, and that Sackville would win immortal honour by leading them on.

On top of the confusion of orders this puppy's presumption was affecting Sackville's temper. Remembering the French superiority in cavalry, he replied that he could not believe that the prince meant to divide the cavalry: Ligonier's order made better sense. 'My lord, we bring the same order,' Fitzroy insisted, and asserted that he and

Ligonier had left the prince at the same time with orders to bring up the British. Two days later he was capable of asserting this in writing, though he had neither heard Ligonier receive his orders nor seen him leave the prince.

At this Sackville called out for Ligonier and said, 'Captain Ligonier, your orders are contradictory.' On what followed the evidence is divergent. According to Ligonier and Colonel Sloper, Ligonier replied: 'In numbers, my lord, but their destination is the same.' If he did say that, it should have partly resolved Sackville's dilemma: the movement was certainly intended to be to the left, and the British cavalry were certainly wanted even if the Hanoverians were not. But Sackville denied that Ligonier had said it. According to him Ligonier asserted that his own orders were right and that he would answer for them with his commission and his honour, but said nothing about how they agreed or disagreed with Fitzroy's. Sackville's story was confirmed by Lloyd, Smith and Sutherland. 'Did they both continue positive in their orders?' Sutherland was asked. 'They certainly did,' the laconic Scot replied.

Fitzroy continued to insist that he and Ligonier had brought the same order and that his version was correct, and at last Sackville said angrily, 'I wish you would agree what your orders are; I am ready to obey either.' Still Fitzroy urged that he was right; and Sackville was impressed enough by his eagerness to ask him which way the cavalry was to march, and who would guide them. Both Fitzroy and Ligonier claim to have offered to lead the way through the wood as well as they could; but still Lord George hesitated. His doubts were reasonable. The two aides-de-camp seemed to the group around the general to have left the prince at about the same time with identical orders, and to have arrived separately by different routes (because Ligonier had come straight through the woods from the front while Fitzroy had gone more circuitously to the rear). Which of them had delivered his orders correctly? Or if their orders were really different, which of them had been the last to leave the prince? Neither of them knew. If Ferdinand did mean to separate the fourteen British squadrons from the ten German in the presence of a superior force of French cavalry, why did he send for the British, who were the furthest away?

A Conflict of Orders

It was argued in retrospect at Sackville's court martial that it was better to do anything that to do nothing. This is a military doctrine still heard today; but when the time-scale of the decision is in minutes rather than hours, the maxim may be more pertinent to a troop-leader than to the commander of the wing of an army. Undoubtedly Ferdinand wanted the British squadrons, and it was argued that they at least should have marched immediately while Sackville verified the orders. But in which direction? Sackville and his staff still seem to have believed that Ligonier's order was to advance to the front (the tautology is necessary in the context). If the cavalry advanced and it turned out that they had been intended to move to the left, the density and depth of the wood in front would prevent them from correcting the error. If they moved through the wood to the left and turned out to have been wrong, more time would be lost in remedying the mistake than would be lost in verifying the order.

From the Olympian viewpoint of history we can see that the fighting had receded and that it probably made little difference which course Sackville chose, with the balance slightly in favour of a move to the front rather than a tortuous retrograde march with broken formation through the wood behind them. But Sackville did not know how far out into the plain the infantry had advanced, and had no quick means of discovering. Ferdinand's messengers gave him no help; and Captain Broome, who had gone forward to reconnoitre, and saw great numbers of the enemy about a mile away to his left, apparently cavalry, was unable to see the enemy immediately in front through the smoke. Would Sackville uncover the right flank of the army if he moved to the left?

These considerations jangled in his mind. Whatever action he took could lead to a serious miscarriage, and he decided that he must clear up the confusion. 'Where is the prince?' he asked in a loud voice. 'Is he far off?' 'I left him just on the other side of the wood, coming this way,' Fitzroy answered. 'How far?' 'About one or two brigades.' Lead me to him, said Sackville; and off he went with his aides-de-camp, following Fitzroy's lead to the rear till they reached the narrow neck of the woodland, and through to the heath beyond at a half-gallop.

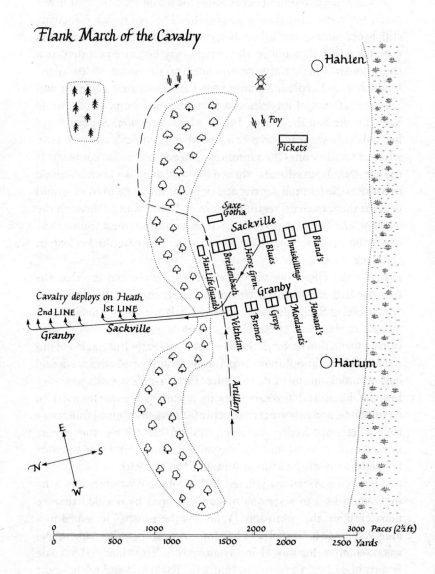

Flank March of the Cavalry

Hahlen

Foy

Pickets

Saxe-Gotha

Sackville

Bland's

Innsikillings

Blues

Horse Gren.

Breidenbach

Han.Life Guards

Granby

Howard's

Mordaunt's

Greys

Bremer

Veltheim

Cavalry deploys on Heath

2nd LINE   1st LINE

Granby   Sackville

Artillery

Hartum

E

S

N

W

0   1000   2000   3000 Paces (2½ ft)

0   500   1000   1500   2000   2500 Yards

As Sackville's cavalcade cantered through the wood Fitzroy continued to assert that he was right, and the now worried Jack Smith, who thought his manner was more pressing that Ligonier's, made him repeat his orders twice. They seemed so clear and positive that Smith said so to Sackville, and offered to go back and bring on the British squadrons so that no time would be lost while he spoke to the prince. Lord George replied that Ligonier was quite as positive, and Ferdinand could not possibly mean to split the cavalry. Smith argued that if the whole of the cavalry were wanted on the left, the British were at least part of the force; and they could easily be sent back to rejoin the German squadrons if Fitzroy were wrong. At that moment the trees began to open on to the heath, much sooner than Sackville had expected from what he had seen of the thick woodland near the front line. To pass cavalry through this part of the wood was less difficult and irreversible than he had supposed, and he changed his mind. 'Then do it as far as you can,' he told Smith, who turned back through the wood to fetch the British cavalry. While they had been talking, Fitzroy pushed his horse into a gallop across the open heath, and raced ahead to Ferdinand. He was with him in time to tell his story before Sackville rode up. Sackville, he said, had refused to believe his orders or move the cavalry, and was coming to speak to the prince himself. Ferdinand received the news with a gesture of astonishment, and rode on to meet Sackville.

Captain Smith rode back through the wood, and as he emerged from the trees he was astonished to see the entire second line of cavalry, both British and German, entering the wood. It was Winzingerode's doing. As he was returning to Ferdinand after delivering his orders to Sackville, he had met Fitzroy coming at full gallop towards the wood. Fitzroy asked why the cavalry had not yet appeared – an unreasonable question since Winzingerode himself had scarcely had time to repass the wood after delivering the order. Winzingerode turned and followed him, shouting that the cavalry was coming, but Fitzroy galloped on without answering; and to help him speed the cavalry Winzingerode rode back to the second line and found Granby where he had left him. 'For God's sake,' he asked, 'how come the cavalry not to have marched?' He told him it was absolutely necessary for the cavalry to form a line behind the infantry and support them. Granby's reply was to remove his sash and bind it tightly round his waist in readiness for a charge, and to order the line to march. While Winzingerode rode back to the left and led the Hanoverians, Granby placed himself at the head of the Greys and led his six British squadrons at the walk in a disorderly column of squadrons through the trees and on to the heath.

More confusion! Granby was obeying Winzingerode's summons to all the cavalry, while Smith was going back to fetch only the British cavalry on the later orders brought by Fitzroy. Telling Granby that the orders had been changed and only the British cavalry were now wanted, Smith spurred on to the first line as fast as he could push his horse, telling the officers of the Blues as he passed to wheel their men to the left by quarter ranks to form the column. General Mostyn walked his horse to meet him; Smith delivered his order; and Mostyn pushed his horse into a trot to lead the column. Smith asked him to go faster, to which Mostyn replied that the rear would already be hurrying. But never fear, he added, I will bring them up fast enough. While the Hanoverian squadrons on the left stood fast, the ten British squadrons trotted behind them across the stubble, inclining still further to the rear as they entered the wood to avoid an underbrush of holly and blackthorn, the files dividing as they passed between the trees. Near by a shot struck a wagon of the artillery train.

In the meantime Sackville and his staff had pushed on across the heath, several cannon balls passing over or grounding near them as they rode. They found Ferdinand at the corner of the rectangular fir-wood from which the infantry had launched their attack. Ferdinand had recovered from the effects of his conversation with the angry Fitzroy and the mask of princely courtesy was in place again. He received Sackville, as far as the British staff could see, with his usual politeness, and showed no disapproval in word or manner. '*Voilà la cavalerie qui avance*,' said Sackville, pointing to the leading squadron emerging from the wood; and Ferdinand ordered him to form a single line and sustain the infantry. Then something passed which Sackville and his staff did not record. Sackville was probably still upset, angry and rattled by the confusion of the orders. Evidently he remonstrated at the order, or explained his misunderstanding by saying that the orders of the previous day had given him a post on the right and a line of advance by Hahlen. Two German officers heard Ferdinand reply in French: 'My Lord, the situation has changed, my dispositions of yesterday can no longer have effect; and in any case it is enough that I want it so, and I beg you to do it immediately.'

With that snubbing rebuke Ferdinand turned his horse and rode off towards the left. Beneath his courteous mask smouldered fires stoked by weeks of strain and brought to a blaze by the miscarriage of his battle plans. Anhalt had allowed him to be surprised, had bungled the occupation of Hahlen and delayed its capture, and when he did take it halted his troops and did no more. From Wangenheim Ferdinand had had not a word. Schaumburg-Lippe had vanished at the static end of the battlefield, leaving him to deploy his artillery himself in the confusion of an army surprised and hurrying piecemeal into battle. The British infantry had plunged forward before the line was formed or their flanks secured. And now this unpleasant British general, who had been making difficulties in the weeks before the battle, was withholding the cavalry he desperately needed to repair the errors of the British foot.

At the moment Ferdinand had a battle to fight; but in due course he would repay the injury.

'HIS LORDSHIP ALWAYS MARCHED VERY SLOWLY'

When Sackville joined Ferdinand for their brief interview the crisis of the battle was already past. As Kingsley's infantry began to give way under the Saxon attacks, the German battalions had arrived from the left. The British rallied, and the Saxons fell back battered by the allied cannon. Contades' effort was spent, and he had lost the battle irretrievably. On the left of Spörcken's brigades, Imhoff's Brunswickers and Colonel Braun's Hanoverian guns struck into Beaupréau's eight battalions just when Contades was launching them against Spörcken. Holstein's nineteen German squadrons burst into their rear, and they were driven on to the jumbled mass of the defeated French cavalry. Spörcken, who had feared that his infantry were about to crack under the final French and Saxon attacks, saw the turning-point of his combat as the moment when the Hessian General Urff at the head of the second line of Holstein's cavalry charged the right of the French horse and drove them back with the loss of a twelve-gun battery.

The battle, incredibly, was won. In the space of about an hour nine British and Hanoverian battalions, supported by the superb allied artillery and towards the end by seven more German battalions, had defeated more than fifty squadrons of enemy cavalry and thirty-one battalions of foot. In the centre of the French army an enormous gap had been torn, in which fifty or sixty squadrons were intermingled in frightful confusion, with so many senior officers killed and wounded that no order could be restored. Contades realized that the battle was lost, and was pulling back his troops as fast as possible, partly covered by the still intact forces of Broglie and Nicolai on his right.

Captain Derenthal rode back from Kingsley's brigade to report that the battle was probably won, and joined Ferdinand shortly before the arrival of Sackville. Now was the moment to turn Contades' defeat into catastrophe: to send Sackville's twenty-four squadrons crashing into the chaotic mass of the French centre as it coagulated towards the defile of the Bastau bridges, while Holstein's cavalry drove in from the flank and Wangenheim sallied from his entrenchments against the retiring Broglie. A great battlefield commander would have seized the flying moment and thrown every man into the attack, driving his subordinates mercilessly to exploit the victory and make a second Blenheim.

But Ferdinand was not the man to do it. He was not in close touch with the changing feel of the battle. From the fir wood where he spoke to Sackville the distant allied infantry could be identified only by the glitter of their arms; but the French had vanished. A succession of aides-de-camp galloping to and fro were no substitute for Ferdinand's own eye and voice at the critical point, nor could they convey the flavour of the changing situation.

Ferdinand had already lost precious time by moving Sackville's cavalry laterally through the woodland, so that instead of advancing by Hahlen to swoop into the flank of the defeated Saxons they had been moved to the rear and through the woods behind the front, changing formation and reforming again. That movement had been ordered in the emergency when the infantry were exposed by their sudden advance. It was too late to undo it; but now that the cavalry were emerging from the woods and forming on the heath they should have been sent forward with urgency, even perhaps by ordering a pursuit by squadrons as they formed. At the least Ferdinand should have explained the situation to Sackville and ordered him to advance and attack the enemy with all speed as soon as his line was formed. Instead Ferdinand coolly repeated his order to form a single line and sustain the infantry, and even ordered Sackville to leave Breidenbach's six German squadrons of the first line in their old position behind Hahlen, where they remained unused till Sackville sent for them at the close of the battle. Then with a cold rebuke he turned his back on his cavalry and rode away.

Left thus to interpret his orders, which Ferdinand had not altered from those he had sent at the moments of crisis and impending defeat, Sackville had not the smallest reason to suppose that the battle had been won in the past hour by the incredible valour of nine battalions or that the French cavalry were no longer a formed fighting force. He could not conceive that six British battalions assisted by three of Hanoverians had routed the whole right wing of the French Army. The leading infantry were a mile away and scarcely distinguishable, the French were invisible. He could not read the situation with his own eye, and received no guidance from Ferdinand.

Nevertheless he should have sensed the urgency in the air, as Granby did. But Sackville was not the soldier to redeem Ferdinand's insufficiencies. He had been told to form a line behind the infantry to support them, and he settled down deliberately to execute his orders according to the rule-book as though it were a field-day. Up to a point his actions were defensible. He expected to charge a formed line of enemy horse or foot, and would need the special quality of the British cavalry, their weight. To produce their full shock these heavy squadrons had to charge in close order. Army instructions were to advance to charge at a slow trot, and at a point sixty yards from the enemy to trot out to deliver the charge. The revolution in cavalry tactics inaugurated by Frederick the Great, who insisted that cavalry should attack at the gallop, had not reached the British manual and regulations and was barely beginning to creep into practice. Ferdinand's voice and words gave no hint that order should be sacrificed to speed, and Sackville formed his line and moved on at a steady pace as prescribed by the Duke of Cumberland's regulations, halting occasionally to dress the line as he judged necessary to preserve the order of eighteen squadrons advancing on a front of 1,300 yards.

On parting from Ferdinand he sent off aides-de-camp to discover the situation to the front, and rode back to meet his troops emerging from the wood. The second line had already formed on the heath and was trotting on. He halted them to wait for the first line and form the single line which Ferdinand had ordered, but found that the Hanoverians leading the second line had formed too near the wood to give room for the whole line to form. As the cavalry moved forward again he sent Captain Smith to order the Hanoverians to incline to their left as they advanced; but instead of inclining the Hanoverians wheeled to their left. Smith tried to explain, but they ignored him and continued with their wheel at the halt. Sackville reproached Smith with mistaking his orders. No, said Smith, but he thought the Hanoverians did not practise inclining, and begged Sackville to send the German Hugo to the Hanoverians in future. Sackville went to execute the order himself, and being finally satisfied that the line was formed he advanced towards the fir-wood where the battle had begun.

Another officer arrived from Ferdinand. The prince, riding off towards the left after leaving Sackville, had been asking, '*la cavalerie ne paraît-elle pas encore?*', and sent Graf von Oeynhausen with the words, '*Courez à my lord Sackville et faites donc au nom de Dieu que la cavalerie avance.*' Oeynhausen had difficulty in finding the cavalry, but eventually found them halted behind the fir-wood and delivered his message. Sackville replied that he would come; and seeing Granby advancing with the second line and passing the first, Oeynhausen joined him. But an order arrived from Sackville to halt, and Oeynhausen went off to rejoin the prince.

The cause of the further delay was the fir-wood, which blocked the passage of the right of the line and forced Bland's and the Inniskillings to drop back. To make room for them Sackville sent word to Granby to march to his left. But while Granby was doing so, Fitzroy reappeared with a direct order from Ferdinand. The prince was now on the right, engaged in moving Captain Phillips's batteries forward to silence some French guns which were covering their infantry's retreat. He had remarked that even now it was not too late for the cavalry to advance. Fitzroy, never diffident, again volunteered to fetch them, and the prince agreed. Fitzroy then asked pointedly to whom he should deliver the order, and Ferdinand replied: 'To Lord Granby, as I know he will obey me.' Fitzroy hurried gleefully off, and found Lord Granby about forty yards ahead of the left of the cavalry on the Minden side of the fir-wood. He delivered an order to advance as fast as possible. Granby replied that the delay was not his fault, since Sackville was in command and they were marching to the left by his orders. 'I was vexed that we had halted in that manner,' he was to explain at the court martial. 'I believe that I found fault with Lord George's manoeuvres, thinking we had lost time.' Certainly some of the regimental commanding officers agreed with him. The ground was clear and level, the heath a bare dusty soil with little vegetation, and they thought the pace was slower than was necessary to preserve a reasonable order. The regiments which had been pushed out of the line by the fir-wood could have been hastened forward again when they were clear of the obstacle, instead of laboriously marching the whole line to the left.

Granby, after his outburst, told Fitzroy to deliver his order to Sackville. No, replied Fitzroy, he had already brought orders to Sackville which he had not obeyed: this time he had been told to deliver them to Granby. On that Granby rode over to Lord George and told him that Ferdinand's orders were to advance directly, to which Sackville replied that he was only forming the troops into a line. Granby had by now lost all patience. He declared that as the orders were to advance he would order his own squadrons to march on; and ordering Elliot to follow him with the second line he galloped on fifty or sixty yards ahead of them. For three or four hundred yards his squadrons advanced uninterrupted at a full trot, with some cantering to keep up. Then Granby saw that they had halted again, and sent back his brigade-major to ask Elliot why he had halted without his orders and tell him to advance as fast as possible. Back came the reply that they had halted on orders passed from the right by Lord George. And now Major Keith rode up from Sackville to ask whether Granby had any special orders which would explain why the second line was ahead of the first; to which Granby replied that his orders were to march and sustain the infantry, and by God he would follow them. He ordered Elliot to advance and not to halt except by his own orders: nevertheless there was a further halt to dress the line by Sackville's order before the cavalry drew up behind the infantry.

In the meantime Captain Smith had been sent forward to warn the batteries on the skirts of the woods not to fire on the cavalry as they advanced. From the guns he could see some hats go up into the air in the distance, and rode forward into the plain to investigate; but before he had gone far he came on so many wounded men and horses that he turned back to warn the cavalry. He met Sackville at the head of the line, many of the squadrons going briskly on at a full trot, and gave his warning. Sackville gave orders to take care how they went over the wounded, and they slowed their pace. Perhaps battle-hardened troops would have ridden on without regard.

Other members of Sackville's staff who had ridden forward to reconnoitre found that in front of the cavalry all fighting had already ceased. Captain Lloyd, galloping forward immediately after delivering Sackville's orders for the cavalry to form a single line, saw the French cavalry at a great distance, 'going off as a cloud . . . quite out of musket shot and the firing of small arms was over . . . the action was quite over'. From the time when the cavalry passed through the long wood, he said, no enemy was within their reach.

Lloyd reckoned that the allied infantry were more than a mile from where the cavalry first formed on the heath; Sutherland that the British infantry further forward in the enclosures 800 or 1,000 yards from Minden were nearly two miles off. Captain Roy's survey of the battlefield shows that if anything these were underestimates. Two staff officers went right up to the British foot. Bisset found them in a single line among the hedges near Minden with no enemy in sight; and his own regiment, Brudenell's, were so short of officers that he went back and obtained Sackville's permission to serve with them. Jack Smith, after warning Sackville about the wounded, went forward to the British infantry among the first hedges, about a quarter of a mile beyond a line of German infantry and just out of effective cannon shot of the fortress guns of Minden. The British were indignant that they had not been supported, and four officers asked Smith where the rest of the army was. Smith told them that he had just passed a line of infantry in their rear, and they complained that the only troops they had seen all day were the Hanoverian Guards. 'How could you?' replied Smith. 'You run so fast they could not keep up with you.'

The British battalions were utterly spent and had come to a halt in a line with the regiments mixed together and not quite formed. When the 12th Foot rallied the commanding officer found that he had only four officers and thirteen files of men with him. The six battalions had gone into action 4,434 strong and had lost 79 officers and 1,252 men, about thirty per cent of their strength. Even now they prepared to return to the attack; but 'to our unspeakable joy no opponents could be found'. The French had melted into the dust and smoke towards Minden.

THE BATTLE DISSOLVES

Sackville trotted on across the heath looking for the infantry. Ferdinand's order to form behind the infantry invited further confusion. Which infantry? The British who had first needed support had disappeared among the hedges of Minden where mounted troops could not operate; and the German battalions which had started the morning on their left were somewhere to the right or rear of them. Eventually the cavalry came up behind a line of foot and halted. The prosecution was to suggest at Sackville's trial that these were merely the pickets of the army and that by halting behind them Sackville did not fulfil his orders; but this was not so. They were a line of seven or eight formed battalions commanded by Scheele, and were the only infantry to be seen in that part of the battlefield; though whether they were the troops Ferdinand had meant the cavalry to support it was impossible to say. As for the enemy, they could literally not be seen for dust.

There was clearly no work for the cavalry here; and at that moment Smith rode up to report what he had seen. On the right of the British infantry's position in the hedges large, open, stubble fields sloped gently down to the Bastau marshes; and over the fields were moving a line of infantry with whom he thought he could see Ferdinand. He suggested that the action there was not yet over; and Sackville sent him to Ferdinand to report that the cavalry were useless in their present position and to ask for orders. Ferdinand, said Smith, 'received me with great joy', as well he might. He was bringing forward the pickets which Anhalt had halted in Hahlen. Those 1,200 men drawn from many regiments were, since the cavalry had been moved to the left, the only troops in that vital quarter where the French were crowding across the Bastau bridges, apart from Breidenbach's six German squadrons which Ferdinand had clamped to their original position behind Hahlen. He ordered Smith to bring the cavalry down to him, and they moved across to their original position at the right of the line. The missing German squadrons were at last sent for and brought forward by Captain Hugo. But apart from some long-range bombarding of targets beyond the Bastau, the fighting was over. The allied batteries had moved down to the edge of the marsh where they continued to the end to harass the French withdrawal.

Whether Sackville could have brought the cavalry across the heath fast enough to engage the enemy is doubtful: he maintained that the fighting on his front was over when the cavalry first formed on the heath, and brought evidence to support him. Granby believed that if the cavalry had marched as fast as possible without blowing the horses, they could have come up with the infantry fifteen or twenty minutes sooner; but he admitted that the action had been over for some time when they did come up, and did not claim that they could have engaged the enemy.

But the charge which Sackville must answer is not that he failed to support the infantry: it is that he did not do his utmost to do so. Why he manoeuvred as he did on the heath must ultimately remain a matter of opinion. There is evidence that he habitually moved cavalry slowly to maintain order; and we shall see him argue eloquently in his defence that to move eighteen squadrons in a single line in a fit state to charge required a steady pace and occasional halts to dress the line. It was a matter of judgement, and Granby maintained that the cavalry could have moved much faster – 'we could not have kept so exact a line as upon the parade; but yet keeping a proper line'.

Was there more to it than that? Was Sackville still rattled by the earlier confusion? Was he perhaps, after the rebuke he had received, seething with an angry determination to execute only the strict letter of Ferdinand's last order? Or did his conduct reflect no more than a lack of flair for cavalry tactics, and inexperience in moving large bodies of horse on the battlefield? Whatever the reason, Lord George displayed a deafness to urgency which earlier orders should have conveyed to him even if his personal conversation with Ferdinand did not. In some degree he fell short of the occasion, though he could put up a logical defence of his actions.

SIX

DISGRACE

THE ORDER OF DISHONOUR

By eleven o'clock Contades' ruined left wing was safe behind the Bastau, and Broglie's corps which had covered the retreat was under the walls of Minden. But the allied artillery continued to harass the defeated French, and to save his men Broglie withdrew them through the town. The French were then out of reach of further harm, and towards the end of the day the allies drew back and pitched their camp on the battlefield, and began to bury the dead. An officer was sent in with a trumpeter to summon the fortress of Minden.

So ended this extraordinary battle. Short and bloody, it had inflicted a stunning moral defeat on the French. But as far as Ferdinand could see it had not resolved his strategic difficulties. The enemy were again immovably lodged in their impregnable position. To Contades, however, matters looked different. While his force was resuming its defensive positions, refugees in still greater disarray came streaming across the mountains from the south. They were the fragments of Brissac's battalions which had been sent to deal with the Hereditary Prince. That very day while Contades suffered disaster in front of Minden, the Hereditary Prince had enveloped Brissac's inferior force on the Werre near Gohfeld and scattered it in total ruin.

While Contades was contemplating this fresh misfortune Broglie appeared, having completed the withdrawal of his corps through Minden. He found Contades planning to retreat through the gorge of the Porta Westfalica and force his way back down the lines of communication to Herford. This was probably the right decision, since the Hereditary Prince had not maintained his position athwart the French communications after his victory but had withdrawn westwards, ignorant of the French defeat at Minden and conscious of d'Armentières' force in his rear. But this Broglie did not know. The Hereditary Prince's force was believed to be 12,000 strong and masters of the Werre bridges, and if this were true it would be too dangerous for the French to try to force their way back on the route by which they had come. Broglie urged an alternative. The French still had three bridges across the Weser at Minden. They should put the river between themselves and the allies, retreat by the far bank, and stand in the defile of Hameln. The majority of the council of war supported him.

So it was decided, and there was no rest for the confused and exhausted French in the night after the battle. By dawn they were across the Weser and the bridges destroyed. That day confusion continued. Part of the heavy baggage had already been sent off up the left bank of the river towards Herford; and the army itself made only six miles eastwards to Klemenbremen, where it spent the second night under arms and reorganizing.

But there was no pursuit. Minden blocked the direct road to the south by which Ferdinand expected the French to retreat; and though Lückner, commanding the light troops beyond the Weser, reported the enemy's true direction he was not believed. The day after the battle the allied army paraded to fire a *feu de joie* and sing a Te Deum, and arrangements were made to receive the capitulation of Minden, whose garrison of 300 men had only been left to protect the mass of wounded in the hospitals. Ferdinand moved his headquarters into the town: and not till the second day did he even send off support to Lückner's light troops beyond the Weser, by which time the enemy had restored some order and begun their second march.

In this leisurely fashion the allied army contemplated the miracle of 1 August. In the short, four-hour battle it had inflicted 7,000 casualties on the French, including six generals, at a cost of 2,762 killed and wounded. If the French performance is measured by their losses they had fought hard; but in Paris Marshal Belleisle marvelled at the extraordinary spectacle of sixty squadrons in an open plain failing to break nine battalions, while a few Hessian squadrons overthrew four French brigades. At all levels the French had failed to co-ordinate their attacks. Contades' divisional commanders had operated with little regard for their neighbours, nor did the infantry and cavalry articulate their attacks; and their artillery was beaten down and silenced as soon as the allied guns came into action. The technical performance of the French had not been impressive. But having said that one turns to the comment of the allied adjutant-general Colonel Reden: 'Never did an army fight more sluggishly and with less confidence and dash than the French on that day.'

But what of the allies' performance? The distribution of their casualties tells the story. Half the losses had fallen on the six British battalions, which lost thirty per cent of their strength. The miracle of the victory was theirs. They had been involved in the most bewildering blunder of the day – it is still unexplained – by advancing into the enemy's front without their artillery and with their flanks unsecured. The Hereditary Prince was said to have done the same thing at Bergen with disastrous results; but at Minden the error was redeemed, and redeemed solely by the courage and fire-drill of the British infantry.

The victory, so far as it was not due to French errors, belonged to the British battalions. It is true that Ferdinand had probably calculated that the French would execute their plan incompetently; but the allies' performance at the higher levels had been shaky too. Both wings of the army had been surprised; the column commanders had not been fully briefed; the artillery commander had left the moving wing of the battle to devote himself to the static left flank; Spörcken's column had attacked prematurely; Sackville's cavalry had not intervened in the battle at all; Wangenheim had done little to interfere with Broglie's withdrawal. The battle was won by the British and German regimental officers and soldiers, a triumph of training and discipline. Ferdinand had not revealed himself as a master of the battlefield. His plan may, as Mauvillon claimed, have been a 'masterpiece of art', though it owed much to Westphalen. But in the fluid battle Ferdinand failed to impose his will on the shifting kaleidoscope. He failed to control Spörcken's advance, to bring Sackville's cavalry into action, to galvanize Wangenheim into a timely counterstroke. He commanded a mixed army from two nations and half a dozen sovereign states, a difficult force to command: but does the blame for errors lie wholly with his subordinates?

The most glaring failure in the battle was the absence of Sackville's cavalry. If those twenty-four squadrons had crashed into the French left wing as it disintegrated, Contades' army might never have escaped across the Bastau. So at least most of the chroniclers of the battle assure us. If our cavalry of the right had intervened, wrote Westphalen a few days after the battle, the left wing of the French army would have been lost without resource. It would have been another Blenheim, claimed Mauvillon. Later historians have echoed them: another Rossbach, said Waddington in his *Guerre de sept ans*. The blame for the failure to annihilate the French army has down to the present day almost invariably been heaped on Sackville. 'Seldom, if ever,' writes Sir Reginald Savory, 'has there been in battle such disgraceful disobedience . . . one of the greatest opportunities for cavalry in the whole of military history was lost for ever.'

The British troops and most of their commanders did not, however, blame Sackville immediately; and General Kingsley, whose unsupported infantry suffered so much, never did blame Sackville though he was critical of Ferdinand. Puzzled and disappointed the cavalry certainly were at having had no share in the victory, and they are said to have stayed silent when the Te Deum was sung. The cavalry subalterns were young men, most of them facing their first test in battle, and eager to get at the enemy; impatient of the calculation and prudence derived from experience. They would have been quick to join in blaming their unpopular general, who was known to move slowly, if there had been any rumour that he had prevented them from sharing in the victory. Yet until the middle of the day after the battle Lieutenant Hartnell of the Inniskillings heard nothing of Sackville's part in holding back the cavalry, and Captain Chauncy made no mention of Sackville's conduct in his letter about the battle on 2 August.

Disgrace

One officer, however, was hotly critical of Sackville from the first moment: Colonel Sloper of Bland's Dragoon Guards. When Colonel Harvey of the Inniskillings rode into the camp with a detachment on the early afternoon of the day after the battle, he met Sloper and expressed his strong concern that the cavalry had had no part in the battle, and asked how it had happened. Sloper replied instantly that it had been due to the misbehaviour of Sackville. He related his version of how Sackville had received the orders, and added that he had observed personal confusion in Lord George.

Sloper carried the same story to Lord Granby. Whether he was actuated by malice was a question to be raised at the court martial; but tempers had run high among the officers around Sackville when Ligonier and Fitzroy brought their confusing orders. At the end of the battle Sutherland had reproached Ligonier for mistaking his orders so dangerously at a critical moment. Ligonier, furious at the suggestion that he had brought wrong orders, complained to Captain Smith who brought him straight up to confront Sutherland. One word brought on another till they became so heated that Smith reminded them that no harm had been done and begged them to keep their tempers.

Another officer who was seething with suppressed anger on the evening of the battle was Ferdinand himself. He felt let down by his subordinates; and in the recent torrent of advice from Frederick, had been this apt remark – 'a general who misunderstands an order or executes it badly exposes your enterprise to great risks'. Months later, in the long account of the battle which he wrote to support the prosecution of Sackville, Ferdinand complained of Wangenheim, Schaumburg-Lippe and Anhalt; and he sent Lückner an angry letter about his failure to press an attack near Hameln on the day of the battle. Not all these complaints were just. He blamed Anhalt for failing to press on after capturing Hahlen; but what Anhalt's 1,200 pickets could have done against forty battalions of the French left wing is not clear, especially after Sackville's cavalry were removed. Nevertheless Ferdinand's displeasure was duly marked, and the names of Anhalt and Wangenheim were omitted from the general order in which he thanked the army for the victory.

For the other delinquent lieutenant-general a harsher fate was in store. Though Ferdinand had controlled his feelings when Sackville rode up to him during the battle, he gave vent to them later when he told Fitzroy to deliver an order to Granby 'as I know he will obey me'. It was a reflection on Sackville not really warranted by what had happened. But Ferdinand did not wait to inquire before he punished. He accepted without question Fitzroy's version of how Sackville had received his orders; and he was also convinced, wrongly and without a shadow of serious evidence, that Sackville's column had disobeyed the order to saddle in the early morning and had been late at its destination. When Sackville took his place among the generals dining with Ferdinand on the evening after the battle he is said to have exclaimed, 'there is that man as much at his ease as if he had done marvels'. His treatment of Sackville seems to reflect a settled distrust and resentment.

If that was so it was necessary to get rid of Sackville, whatever the true facts of the case might be, for a commander-in-chief must have confidence in his subordinates. But how was it to be done? To complain to the British government about its general would be awkward at the very moment when the British troops had won a brilliant victory; and it might raise a suspicion that Ferdinand's real motive was to remove the man who had guarded British interests against the German commissaries and Ferdinand's Prussian-oriented strategy. Ferdinand therefore sent no complaint to London in his official dispatches to Holdernesse or even his private letters to Pitt; but confined himself to praising the leadership of Waldegrave and Kingsley, the infantry's 'prodigies of valour', and the marvels performed by the artillery.

The other course open to Ferdinand was to make Sackville's position in the army untenable and force him to resign. But he dared not risk affronting the touchy pride of the British contingent by a direct reflection on their commander. Mauvillon interprets his thinking on the problem. Imagine, he says, the thoughts of a general whose unparalleled victory had been reduced to an ordinary one, and what feelings must rage inside him. But Ferdinand controlled his anger: the course he adopted was a triumph of policy over passion. He would make Sackville's conduct known to the whole army without naming him, and would couple veiled censure of the British general with glowing praise of the British troops.

The general order issued on the day after the battle reached the British regiments in the afternoon. Sackville was not named; but after thanking numerous officers by name the order continued:

His Serene Highness further orders to be declared to Lieutenant-General the Marquis of Granby, that he is persuaded, that if he had had the good fortune to have had him at the head of the cavalry of the right wing, his presence would have greatly contributed to make the decision of that day more complete and more brilliant.

The order ended with this admonition:

His Serene Highness desires and orders the Generals of the army that upon all occasions, when orders are brought to them by his aides-de-camp, that they be obeyed punctually and without delay.

For these devastating blows at Sackville the admiring Colonel Mauvillon found a word: *bewunderswürdig*! 'Marvellous is the sharpness and delicacy with which he punished Sackville's disobedience.' The order would mollify the humiliated British cavalry by providing them with a scapegoat, and show that Ferdinand did not view all British generals with disfavour. To Sackville it delivered an unparalleled insult which was difficult to answer because he was identified only by the praising of another man.

A BATTLE OF WITS

Sackville was thunderstruck. He had received no hint of Ferdinand's displeasure, and the order of 2 August fell upon him out of a clear sky. Earlier in the day when he had written an account of the victory to Lord Bute, he had been one of the happiest men in the world; now he wrote that he was one of the most miserable. It was in character that he immediately explained the blow in terms of a personal vendetta which he attributed to his earlier suggestion that the British troops might be recalled as a result of Ferdinand's decision to abandon Westphalia. But even if this were not so, said Sackville, and if Ferdinand's sole motive for issuing the order had been Sackville's conduct in the battle, he had condemned him without trial or inquiry or giving him any opportunity to defend himself. Sackville had grounds for this complaint. Ferdinand had censured him without personal knowledge of his situation beyond the woods, and on the interested word of Fitzroy. This was immediately apparent to Sir Joseph Yorke when Fitzroy passed through The Hague a few days later, though Yorke was no friend of Sackville. Fitzroy's youth and high spirits had given rise to a good deal of the trouble, he reported to Lord Hardwicke;

for Lord George was pretty sharp with him when he brought the orders, and he in his heat reported it all to the prince; I had some serious talk with Mr. Fitzroy upon the subject, and bid him take warning for the future, and instanced many things that had happened to me whilst I was aide de camp. The young man is good natured tho' full of life, and took my advice like a man of sense and birth.

But Yorke's advice was too late to avert the consequence of Fitzroy's indiscretion. What was Sackville to do? He might accept the rebuke quietly, lie low and wait for the cloud to pass. That was what Imhoff chose to do in the following year when he was peremptorily and perhaps únfairly relegated to the command of a garrison for giving up the line of the Ohm. But for Sackville that course was impossible. Imhoff was not pilloried in public orders, while Sackville's disgrace was copied into the order book of every regiment in the allied army, and would be published in England. If he let it pass his position in the army would be impossible, his pride destroyed, his honour lost; and the verdict of history would be handed to his enemies. Being the man he was, he had to reply.

His first attempt was an appeal to Ferdinand to retract the order. Hotham was sent off to put Sackville's case verbally; and Lord George asked Granby to come to his quarters, and tried to enlist his support by inviting him to sign a paper which stated the facts of the case as he saw them. Granby refused. He had not himself heard Ligonier and Fitzroy deliver their orders and could give no opinion about what had happened; and with regard to the advance across the heath he told Sackville that he differed from him in several respects and could not put his name to what Sackville had written. Sackville then asked him to write to Ferdinand in his own words to clear him of the charge of unnecessary delay on the heath. But Granby regarded writing as a bore, and anyway he thought the advance had been too slow. He replied that he had already told Sackville several times all he could say about the orders he had received from him to halt. If these facts were of any use to Sackville he was prepared to state them in person to Ferdinand; but he did not know French well enough to explain himself in a letter. Would he then allow a letter to be dictated for his consideration, asked Sackville. A letter was begun, but it was so contrary to Granby's views that he stopped it.

No joy was to be had from Granby, and Sackville then composed his own appeal to Ferdinand. 'The order it pleased your Serene Highness to issue today struck me like a thunderbolt,' he began. 'I feel it so much and see myself so deeply concerned by it that for my own peace I must take the liberty of relating the matter simply as it happened.' He explained briefly the conflict of orders which had caused him to come to Ferdinand while the British cavalry began its detour through the wood. He defended the halts on the heath, and claimed that Granby was prepared to testify to the facts in Ferdinand's presence. These explanations were brief, temperate and in accordance with the facts as Sackville saw them. He concluded by appealing to Ferdinand to retract the order.

Lord George was not optimistic about the effect of this letter. He supposed, he told Bute, that if Ferdinand found himself in the wrong he would 'have an awkwardness in owning it'. Before he finished writing to Bute his fears were confirmed. Ferdinand had cornered his prey and was stealing in for the kill. His reply was icy, contemptuous and weary. It was mortifying, he wrote, to have to enter into fresh explanations when he thought he had already exhausted all that could be said on the subject in his talk with Hotham. So he would now say simply that he could not see with indifference what was done with the British cavalry on the right. He had given Sackville a splendid opportunity to decide the fate of the day if his orders had literally been obeyed. He begged Sackville to dispense him from entering into longer detail, or from revoking an order of whose truth he was convinced. 'I have grounds,' he concluded, 'for being ill satisfied with the non-execution of my orders. To what I should attribute it I do not know, and I suspend my judgement on it.'

It is a curious suspension of judgement that is coupled with a refusal to hear the evidence; and in two other respects Ferdinand's reply was disingenuous. He complained that as commander of the British contingent Sackville's post was not fixed with the cavalry, and that he should have led the whole British force according to the needs of the moment, keeping the situation of the infantry in view in his handling of the cavalry. This was a shabby blow. Ferdinand's order of battle had fixed Sackville to the command of the right-flank column, a mixed force of British and German cavalry; while the British infantry formed part of a mixed force commanded by a German lieutenant-general, operating beyond Sackville's area of vision, and the British artillery formed part of yet another mixed column operating under the direction of the army's German artillery commander. To claim that Sackville's administrative command of the British troops was a tactical command overriding the general order of battle almost warrants the warmth of Sackville's indignation: 'I never knew anything so unfair, so unjust and I must say so wicked.' Nevertheless, whether through the gossip of ignorant aides-de-camp on passage to England or the propaganda of Westphalen, Sir Joseph Yorke at The Hague formed the impression that Sackville's proper post in the order of battle had been at the right of the infantry, and that he had neither orders nor leave to post himself with the cavalry.

Equally disingenuous was Ferdinand's contention that the praise of Granby did not imply criticism of Sackville – 'it is not a rule that because I praise the one I blame the other.' Ferdinand was to use this argument again, mixing it cleverly with criticism of Sackville's actions while smearing him for taking the criticism amiss. 'Sackville,' he was to write in his narrative, 'who was insensible to the fine opportunity he had had to gain glory, was offended by the observation I had made in favour of Lord Granby. He saw in it only, according to his way of thinking, an indirect censure of his own conduct.' How else was Sackville to see it?

Prince Ferdinand's rejection of Sackville's appeal was written and received two days after the battle. Clearly Sackville's reputation was not going to be saved by recanting the censure in general orders, and he had to think quickly about its impact in London. Ferdinand's British aides-de-camp Ligonier, Fitzroy and Richmond were all being sent off to England, and he must try to prevent them from extending the damage. Richmond had been asserting that the cavalry could have intervened in the battle; and Sackville wrote him a long letter defending his actions and begging the favour of a visit to his headquarters before Richmond left for England. Whether the duke replied or visited Sackville I do not know; but the letter had no effect. Richmond went home and talked; and a quarter of a century later in the House of Lords he was still asserting that he had had his watch in his hand during the whole period when the cavalry was expected, and that it had taken an hour and a half to bring them up. At the age of twenty-four the Duke of Richmond must already have contained the embryo of the difficult and angry politician he later became.*

Richmond had not been a witness of Sackville's behaviour in the battle. Fitzroy, however, was a first-hand witness and the source of much of the trouble; and to him Sackville wrote a highly personal letter appealing for the truth: 'The orders of yesterday, you may believe, affected me very sensibly. His Serene Highness has been pleased to judge, condemn, and censure me, without hearing me, in the most cruel and unprecedented manner.' He briefly recounted his version of how he had received the conflicting orders and gone to Ferdinand, though curiously enough he transposed the order of arrival of Fitzroy and Ligonier; and he related the manner of his advance across the heath. He appealed to Fitzroy to confirm this narrative – 'for it is impossible to sit silent under such reproach, when I am conscious of having done the best that was in my power. For God's sake, let me see you before you go for England.'†

There is a note of desperation in this letter; but it is improbable that Fitzroy called on Lord George before his departure. He replied in writing, however: a cool statement of Sackville's refusal to

---

*A copy of Sackville's letter to Richmond is in the Royal Archives, but I have not found a reply.

†These letters were printed in the pamphlet *Lord George Sackville's Vindication of Himself* . . ., where Sackville's is misdated 2 August.

believe or obey his orders. 'I hope', he concluded, 'your Lordship will think I did nothing but my duty as aide-de-camp in mentioning to His Serene Highness my orders being so much questioned by your Lordship.'

Evidently Ferdinand's entourage would concede nothing. But if they were being sent off to retail Ferdinand's version of the story in England Sackville could at least send home some of his own staff, and Keith and Smith were dispatched to England. Keith carried a letter of resignation and a private letter for the Secretary of State, Lord Holdernesse; but he was to seek Lord Bute's advice on whether to deliver them.

To deliver them instantly was my first thought [Sackville explained to Lord Bute]; I am now advised if things are not misrepresented to the King etc. to delay them if practicable till the end of the campaign, nothing should make me stay longer after that, but I own I should be happy beyond expression if I could hereafter upon a future occasion make the Prince ashamed of this scandalous behaviour of his, and at the end of the campaign at least I might tell him freely my real opinion of his attempt upon my character.*

The rancorous tone of this letter was natural; but a wise friend might have warned Lord George to play his cards coolly, and that retaliation should wait. Nothing was more likely to play into Ferdinand's hands than conduct shaped by resentment.

On the day when these letters were exchanged with Richmond and Fitzroy, orders were being issued for the army to march; and on 4 August, three days after the battle, the allies did at last move southwards through the mountain chain to Gohfeld, still on the left bank of the Weser, with Sackville as usual leading the second line which formed the right-hand column of the army. On the following day he received a severe and apparently unmerited rebuke from Ferdinand, expressing his 'sovereign disapproval' of an arrangement made without his consent for the trains of the British light artillery. On Sackville's behalf Colonel Hotham denied that any such arrangement had been made, and evidently Ferdinand's rebuke had been administered, like the earlier one concerning the

*I owe this quotation to the kindness of Mr Ewan Fraser.

British pickets, without proper inquiry; but no retraction was made or regret expressed. On the same day Ferdinand inquired of Reden, hopefully perhaps, whether Sackville was to lead the second line again because, if not, Granby should do so. That Ferdinand was not incapable of undoing the ill effects of an order was demonstrated two days later when Reden pointed out that Captain Macbean had been omitted from the compliments to the British artillery commanders in the orders of 2 August. Ferdinand instantly undid the humiliating omission with a personal letter of thanks.

In his appeal to Fitzroy Sackville had indicated that he would make use of the reply if it were favourable during Fitzroy's absence in England; and in the days when the army was following the retreating French he pursued his plan of justifying himself in the army. A paper was drawn up vindicating his conduct in the battle, and most of the field officers of the cavalry were invited to sign it. Evidently he had no success in committing senior officers to this sensitive document, but in England Newcastle was affrighted by a report that General Mostyn had been persuaded to sign it. That Mostyn should have involved himself with paper was improbable, and Granby reassured the duke: 'I can assure your Grace our friend Jack never signed any paper, he even contrived not to read any.'

Whether or not Sackville's efforts to enlist support were what Ferdinand had hoped for, he reacted with a display of real or pretended indignation. On 13 August he wrote a letter on the subject to George II which Lord Hardwicke described as the strangest he had ever read in his life. This was Ferdinand's first complaint to the British government about the events of Minden, and he demanded Sackville's removal with a strong hint that he would resign if Sackville stayed. He founded his complaint solely on Sackville's conduct in the battle, and made no mention of the subsequent attempts to rally support in the army. But he let it be understood that those attempts were the real reason for his complaint, both in a letter to Sackville himself and in unofficial letters which Westphalen sent off to The Hague, where they were seen by Sir Joseph Yorke, and to the Hanoverian minister-in-attendance in London, who was sure to inform the king. Sackville, wrote Westphalen, 'put to work those talents for which he is known . . . he stirred everything up . . . and seeing that he was tending to disturb the harmony in the army the Duke asked for his recall'. Ferdinand even considered making a solemn declaration to the army on the subject, which suggests that his concern about Sackville's machinations was genuine; but from this extreme measure he was dissuaded by Westphalen. After such a declaration, the secretary argued, any relations with Sackville would be impossible, to the detriment of the service; and Sackville could make capital with it by accusing Ferdinand of imputing conversations to him which had not taken place. Ferdinand and Westphalen rated Sackville's tactical cunning highly; but in this battle of wits the cool-headed friendship of Westphalen gave Ferdinand the advantage.

SACKVILLE RECALLED

In London the first week of August had seen anxious days for the ministers. It was known that Ferdinand had intended to launch an operation on 27 July to force the enemy to fight or retire; and the critical state of affairs on the Weser caused the Prince of Wales to lament the military confusion created by his grandfather's partiality for 'that horrid electorate'. The first news of the victory came by a German messenger, who had cut across enemy-held territory by the shortest route to The Hague and was sent over to England by Yorke in a Dutch fishing boat. He arrived on 8 August, and that night London was in an uproar of celebrations. 'It has wrought a deliverance like Cressy or Blenheim,' Lord Mansfield rejoiced. The official world congratulated itself on its victorious German general, and the mobs round their bonfires were drinking to their own marquis, Lord Granby, who they were sure had won the battle. No one was toasting Sackville.

Two days later Edward Ligonier and Estorff arrived with Ferdinand's dispatches, and the delighted king rewarded Ligonier with a lieutenant-colonelcy in the 1st Guards in addition to the usual £500. Ligonier gave his uncle the commander-in-chief an account of the Sackville affair but seems to have guarded his tongue in public; and it was not till Fitzroy and Richmond arrived a day or two later that the story became public. Richmond talked even more freely than Fitzroy, and the line-up of Lord George's enemies began. 'Disgraced in public orders,' crowed the plundering army agent Calcraft. 'As he was greatly hated the officers are greatly rejoiced.' Pleasure at his fall was a natural reaction of the small and envious. 'You have seen enough of the world', General Robert Napier commented to Hotham, 'to know how willingly and even eagerly people swallow and propagate everything that tends to hurt one who happens to be in any conspicuous light.' Copies of Ferdinand's general order were circulating in profusion, and had raised 'the most cruel and violent reflections in the lower parts of the town'.

But Sackville's fate depended on the men in power. The king was in the seventh heaven about his German general's victory, and off went the Order of the Garter and £20,000 to Ferdinand: there would be no support for Sackville at St James's. At the young court at Leicester House the Prince of Wales pitied Sackville's misfortune and thought it 'pretty pert for a little German prince to make public any fault he finds with the English commander, without first waiting for instructions from the King on so delicate a matter'. But from that quarter Sackville could not expect much more than sympathy. Even if Bute were disposed to help, his relations with the key figure in the ministry, Pitt, had been chilled by the king's rejection of a request from the Prince of Wales for an active command in the army. 'This insolence of Pitt's', as the Prince of Wales termed it, did not promise well for any intervention by Bute on Sackville's behalf. Not that Bute was likely to risk much for him. Their relations had been cool for some months, and Sackville's cause would not be a popular one to support. When Major Keith arrived with Sackville's letter of resignation, Bute passed it straight on to the Secretary of State.

Now indeed Sackville's fate was in the hands of the twin pillars of the ministry, Pitt and Newcastle: the cunning showman and the slippery old chatterbox. Newcastle would not stand up to the king for an unpopular cause; but he was never unpleasant to anyone until he felt sure that it was safe. Sackville was a tough and able politician who might yet hit back, so Newcastle kept his head down and stayed in the country till the resignation issue was settled, and was able to assure all and sundry that 'all was over before I returned here from Sussex'. 'I am truly sorry for Lord George Sackville,' he snivelled to Granby.

As for Pitt, personal friendship was a phrase with no meaning in his life; but he was a master of the art of seeming to help. Sackville's resignation would be accepted, he told Bute as though this were a favour contrived by himself.

I have the satisfaction to acquaint your Lordship that the King has *given leave* to Lord George Sackville to return to England. . . . This mode of returning, your Lordship will perceive, is a very considerable softening of his misfortune. The torrent in all parts bears hard upon him. As I have already, so I shall continue to give him, as a most unhappy man, all the *offices of humanity*, which our *first, sacred* object, my dear Lord, the public good, will allow.

This sanctimonious masterpiece ('all oratory and no substance', to borrow the phrase with which Shelburne characterized Pitt's orders to General Bligh for the Cherbourg expedition) tells the outcome of Sackville's application. On 14 August he was sent leave to quit his command, and Granby replaced him as commander of the British forces in Germany. Newcastle would have liked to claim the credit for Granby's promotion, but had the sense to see that it could not be plausibly coupled with his disclaimer of responsibility for Sackville's recall.

The letter of recall crossed with Ferdinand's demand for Sackville's removal, and reached the British camp south of Kassel on 21 August. Lord George was shocked by its arrival: either he had not expected Bute to pass on his letter of resignation, or he had not expected the ministry to accept it. He appealed to Ferdinand to declare in what way he had failed so grossly as to earn this 'punishment a thousand times worse than death'. Cold as ever, Ferdinand replied that he had not complained of Sackville in his letters to England in the fortnight after the battle – 'so you see it is not I who gave your affairs the twist of which you complain'. He admitted that he had written to the king when he saw that Sackville was disturbing the harmony of the army, but that letter had not arrived till after Sackville's recall.

There was nothing left for Lord George but to withdraw as quietly as possible to England, and he slipped away unobtrusively from the camp. Rumour said more. 'He was disgracefully dismissed from our army,' a farrier of the Greys confided to his journal, 'his sword broke over his head, and sent by a strong guard through the whole front line and straight off to England' – which only proves how little the second line knew of what the first line was doing. An officer of the second line showed more wisdom: 'No judgment can be formed why the cavalry were not employed but from a knowledge of the facts, which I have not, and therefore can form no opinion.' But opinion would be more common than fact-finding in the coming months.

The waters closed over Sackville's head, and the army floated on with Granby at the helm, faintly pursued by the admonishing voice of Newcastle to 'look on yourself as a man of business, and attend to it'. A useless warning: Granby went his own way, and let the commissaries go theirs. The Treasury would have plenty to worry them in the future.

Ferdinand, however, was well satisfied with the exchange, and the British government was doing everything possible to sweeten him, in contrast with the criticism of him which had preceded the battle of Minden: 'we shall now see praises as much beyond the proper medium as the objections were,' Yorke predicted. In October Ferdinand was invested with the Garter by Granby, amid celebrations on a prominent hill in full view of the enemy camp. Granby managed some French for his address to the new knight: 'Among so many princes and sovereigns who have thought themselves honoured by the Garter, only Gustavus Adolphus and your Highness have received it at the head of an army.'

By this time the importance and limits of the battle of Minden could be measured. In Westphalia its effects had been less than decisive. Lippstadt was saved when d'Armentières raised the siege to reinforce Contades; but the key fortress of Münster, which had surrendered just before the battle that was meant to save it, remained in French hands and would require a distracting siege to recover it. The main French army under Contades (who was soon to be replaced by Broglie) made good its retreat, saved by an uninspired pursuit, though it lost its baggage. Contades' decision to cross the Weser and retreat by the right bank might have enabled the allies by vigorous marches to reach his base at Kassel before him, and cut his line of retreat by seizing the crossings of the Werre. But Ferdinand failed to do it.

The French army lived to fight again, though with reduced confidence, and would soon renew the threat to Hanover. Yet on the wider canvas of the war Minden was a saving triumph, for on 12 August Frederick the Great was defeated catastrophically by the Russians and Austrians at Kunersdorf with the loss of 178 guns and forty-eight per cent of his men. His appeals to Ferdinand for help and diversions became shriller. Ferdinand, as Mauvillon would have it, had an unselfish capacity to subordinate the needs of his own army to the general good of the alliance; or, as George II would have said a few months later, he was under Frederick's thumb. Bit by bit he leaked his force away to the aid of Prussia till, after the recapture of Münster at the end of November and the news of further Prussian defeats, the reinforcements totalled 12,000 men commanded by the Hereditary Prince. At the end of the year Prussia's situation was more desperate than ever. For England 1759 had been an *annus mirabilis* of victories; but in Germany Minden had been the only ray of light for the alliance.

SEVEN

APPEAL FOR JUSTICE

CLAMOUR

Sackville slipped away from the army as inconspicuously as possible, accompanied by Lloyd, Sutherland and the chaplain John Hotham. They seem to have been a cheerful party as they laughed and joked their way through the crowded towns of Holland; but to spare the British minister Sir Joseph Yorke the embarrassment of receiving him Lord George avoided The Hague and went home by Rotterdam. From there he wrote a letter of polite apology to Yorke in which he complained of his treatment by Ferdinand and his condemnation without inquiry.

Sir Joseph Yorke, third son of Lord Hardwicke and a member of a powerful political family, had already been primed with Fitzroy's version of the facts and Westphalen's story of Sackville's subsequent caballing in the army. Disliking Sackville, with whom he had served on Cumberland's staff in the previous war, and knowing that Ferdinand 'passes for a well-bred and generous man', he was puzzled how to reply to Sackville's letter; and after vainly fingering his pen for a quarter of an hour he took him at his word and sent no answer. But he remarked to his brother Lord Royston that Sackville seemed to have a mind to prove Contades a better general than Ferdinand and Sackville better than either. 'He falls as little to be pitied as anyone can do, for which he can only blame himself.'

Yorke feared that Sackville's friends were trying to throw mud at Ferdinand, and Sackville's letter contained a hint that his defence must necessarily discredit the prince. This was the core of the problem for the British government. Whatever private calculations might shape each individual minister's treatment of Sackville, the national interest required that the generalissimo of the allied army should be supported. This was felt even more strongly after the news of the Prussian disaster at Kunersdorf, which arrived on 22 August. It meant that in spite of Minden Hanover was still in danger, and the king predicted that his Electorate would be devastated by Russians and Austrians instead of the French. Ferdinand's future operations were therefore critical. If he could cut Contades off from his base at Frankfurt or defeat him again, 'we might be able to hold up a little for the present'.

Frederick could therefore rely on the British government's support against Sackville. As the hero of the hour his word would in any case 'bear down everything before it', as Hardwicke had immediately grasped when the Sackville scandal broke. 'To be sure Prince Ferdinand must be made easy,' Newcastle assured George II on learning that the prince had demanded Sackville's recall. Granby was warned to obey Ferdinand's orders and see that his generals did the same; and the king begged Ferdinand in a personal letter to inform him instantly if any British officer dared to hesitate in obeying him.

The public uproar against Sackville continued, and was still in full spate when he arrived in London on 7 September five weeks after the battle. The anonymous Grub Street hacks were out in virulent force to bespatter him as three years earlier they had bespattered Admiral Byng. A few pamphlets defending Sackville appeared quickly. *A Seasonable Antidote* reminded the public that mistreating commanders had become a habit in the past three years. Byng had been shot and General Fowkes dismissed for the loss of Minorca; General Mordaunt had been forced by the popular clamour to insist on an inquiry to clear his name after the Rochefort expedition; and old General Bligh was ill-treated by the king on his return from Cherbourg. Another defence, *A Vindication of the Rt. Hon. Lord George Sackville*, was a confused and incompetent piece of work which inverted the points of the compass on the battlefield. 'Most absurd,' judged the clear-headed Lord Hardwicke, 'much in the style of some of Byng's.' So unsatisfactory were the efforts of these unsolicited defenders that on 22 September Sackville published a warning in the press that he would prosecute anyone who published an unauthorized pamphlet in his defence, and threatened to prosecute the printer of a pamphlet containing his exchange of letters with Fitzroy.

But attempts to defend Sackville were in any case outnumbered by the attacks, which plumbed the depths of laboured irony and scurrilous libel. At best they were wildly inaccurate: 'How could you see your countrymen and fellow soldiers, whom you was ordered to support, slaughtered within your view, and yet withold your assistance?' Cowardice, jealousy and disaffection were suggested as his motives for delay. Bribery was another popular explanation: 'I suspect there has been some French gold in the case.' That accusation had been made against Byng, and the parallel was drawn. 'Many have suspected my Lord G— of a fondness for French gold; and the late Admiral was thought to have been equally curious in it.' The two men were also said to share a taste for sodomy. 'It has been said of the Admiral, that he was addicted to a certain vice which seems highly incompatible with a military character; and it is well known that the gentleman to whom we are now comparing him, has been so much traduced by the vulgar upon the same head. . . .' The death sentence was demanded in a variety of tones, from the solemn 'let corporal punishment be inflicted' to the classroom sadism which drew on Virgil – '*tollere humo* . . . we cannot say that he has yet raised himself from the ground . . . but if the wishes of the public are not frustrated, he seems to bid fair for that elevation. . . . The name even of the lowest wretch never fails to make a noise in the world when he is going to be hanged.' All this abuse was served up with an insolent parade of deference to his social rank, concern for fairness and justice, and Christian pity for the delinquent.

As information became available Sackville's defenders grew better informed, and the respectable press attempted to present a fair balance. The more absurd misrepresentations were exposed. It had been written that an aide-de-camp had brought orders to pursue, that Sackville had replied that he was a stranger to the roads and unacquainted with the passes, and that the aide-de-camp had offered to guide him. This travesty of Lord George's conversation

Clamour

with Fitzroy was demolished, as was the common misunderstanding that Sackville had been ordered to attack. The *Gentleman's Magazine* printed Ferdinand's order of censure, and explained that the omission of Sackville from the thanks to the army reflected a belief that he had been late at his post and had delayed the execution of Ferdinand's orders; but it pointed out that there were answers to these charges. Some of Sackville's defenders suggested that there had already been ill-feeling on the part of Ferdinand. The dispute three weeks before the battle about the eastward retreat which had severed the British communications with Emden was revealed in a pamphlet which was quoted in the reputable *London Magazine*. Another author suggested (where he picked it up is a mystery, but he was right) that after the defeat at Bergen Ferdinand had 'shrunk into a diffidence of himself', and went on to argue that this had made him jealous of Sackville, sensitive to his criticisms, and determined to be rid of him.

The most persuasive answer to the attacks on Sackville was not published till after the end of the year. This was *The Conduct of a Late Noble Commander Candidly Considered*, written anonymously by John Douglas, D.D., a future bishop of Salisbury, who claimed that he did not know Lord George personally but saw him as a victim of the Grub Street hacks whom the misfortunes of Byng and Mordaunt had already brought out of their holes to make a quick penny. Douglas scrutinized the only attacks which he thought deserved an answer, the two *Letters to a Late Noble Commander*. Coolly and temperately he took these apart, pointing out the author's ignorance and misrepresentations, and the misunderstandings which he could have avoided if he had had the fairness to refer to Sackville's statement of his case.

Sackville's statement, *His Lordship's Apology*, denied the charges implicit in Ferdinand's order of censure: he had not been late, the orders he had received were contradictory, and there had been no delay in the advance across the heath. He attributed Ferdinand's censure to the fact that Fitzroy had reached the prince before him and had planted misunderstanding. All this, once again, was briefly stated, and Sackville rested his defence on a claim to be heard at a trial by court martial.

Lord George was sure that his best defence was the facts; but the facts could not be established by exchanging scattered volleys of pamphlets. Nothing short of clearly stated charges and a court martial would establish what had happened during those critical hours at Minden. He was confident that a fair trial would clear him, and was determined to seek it. But he knew that this might be difficult. From Rotterdam he had predicted that if the ministers thought he could clear himself they would try to prevent an inquiry and the airing of disagreeable truths.

As soon as he arrived in England he sent Lord Bute a draft of an application for a court martial, and asked for his support. The response was discouraging. In due course Bute might be able to use the affair as a political weapon, but at the present stage of the game Leicester House did not want to swim against popular opinion, and Bute replied merely that the affair was too delicate and he could not advise him. Sackville's pliant friends were bending before the storm; and he knew that the ministers in office must support Ferdinand. He did not even attempt to enlist the support of Newcastle, but wrote politely to announce his arrival and explain that he did not want to embarrass the minister while his case was still in a sense *sub judice*. He judged realistically. 'Newcastle,' wrote Horace Walpole, 'who never felt for a powerless friend, had abandoned him.' The Prime Minister was whinneying like an anxious mare for the approval of Ferdinand, who was not answering his letters as promptly as he answered other people's – Newcastle was easily alarmed by neglectful correspondents. Sir Joseph Yorke reassured him as one would a child, telling him that Ferdinand's writing more to others did not mean that he was hostile to Newcastle but the contrary, that he was sure of his support. No, replied Newcastle, Ferdinand *was* prejudiced against him: he had not answered his last letter as promptly as he had answered Holdernesse's.

Everyone knew that Newcastle was a coward, but perhaps Pitt would show more courage. His record in the Byng affair was not encouraging, for he had been among the first to condemn the admiral on the sole evidence of the French commander's dispatch; and though later he would have liked to save him he would not stand up and make it clear that it was the ministry which had been guilty of the loss of Minorca, for fear of driving Newcastle and Fox into alliance against him. At that time he had not been a minister, but now he was burdened with the responsibilities of office. Political considerations alone would determine his treatment of Sackville.

Lord George wrote to him, however, enclosing a copy of his letter demanding a court martial. Pitt's answer was phrased in that unique fusion of manly honesty with Uriah Heep which makes one's skin crawl as one reads his letters. He wanted, he said, to deal frankly on this unhappy and delicate occasion, when delusion might prove dangerous.

I find myself . . . under the painful necessity of declaring my infinite concern, at not having been able to find . . . any room (as I wish't) for me to offer support, with regard to a conduct which my incompetence perhaps to judge of military questions leaves me at a loss to account for.

This was accompanied by Pitt's usual claim to be doing his loyal best for a friend. He had seen to it that Sackville was allowed to come home from Germany by permission instead of by order, an intervention of common candour and humanity. 'I cannot enough lament the subject of a correspondence, so unlike everything I had wish't to a person for whose advantageous situation my poor endeavours had not been wanting.' Sackville may have smiled at the last sentence if he remembered one from the same pen less than two years earlier. 'The favourable and kind sentiments', Pitt had then assured him, 'with which your Lordship is so good to accompany your commands to your humble servant must ever be rank'd among my most valuable possessions.' The value of these possessions had now depreciated.

As he read this missive Sackville for the first time almost faltered in his faith in his own innocence. But Pitt had not written it simply to undeceive Sackville: that would have been too straightforward. He planned to use the affair as a weapon in his perpetual campaign of harassment against his colleague Newcastle. He told Newcastle that he would say nothing to encourage Sackville's dismissal, nor one word against it; that to grant him a trial was a matter of justice; but that if Sackville's supporters attacked Ferdinand he would defend him. He thus left the way open to make difficulties.

At any rate it was clear to Lord George that at this stage he could expect no firm support from Leicester House or any of the ministers. Moreover he had heard that the king in his present temper might dismiss him from the army as soon as he knew that he had arrived in England. If that happened his position would be weakened and his right to a trial put in doubt, for civilians were not amenable to martial law. He had to act quickly; and without waiting to hear from Pitt he had already sent in his request to the Secretary of State for a court martial. It was composed in one huge but eloquent sentence:

I am conscious of neither neglect nor disobedience of orders, as I am certain I did my duty to the utmost of my ability, and as I am persuaded that the Prince himself would have found that he had no just cause of complaint against me had he condescended to have enquired into my conduct before he had expressed his disapprobation of it from the partial representation of others; I therefore most humbly request that I may at last have a public opportunity given me of attempting to justify myself to His Majesty and to my country by a Court Martial being appointed, that if I am guilty I may suffer such punishment as I may have deserved, and if innocent that I may stand acquitted in the opinion of the world, but it is really too severe to have been censured unheard, to have been condemned before I was tried, and to be informed neither of my crime nor of my accusers.

DISMISSAL

The last thing the government wanted was a public trial, with its accompaniment of uproar, political disturbance and bitterness in the army. With the war going well the ministry had no need of a scapegoat, as they had had after the loss of Minorca: the news of the triumphs at Minden and Lagos had arrived, and soon the fall of Quebec and Hawke's battle in Quiberon Bay were to seal this year of victories. And to probe the truth about Minden might be dangerous. If Sackville justified his conduct, Ferdinand's position would be intolerable; and even if he were convicted the trial would probably air matters best left undisturbed and generate doubt and suspicion in Ferdinand.

The best thing for the country would be to let Sackville fall into oblivion. But this was not to be, since he insisted on a hearing; so the king and his ministers played for delay. Sackville should be promised a trial, but not till the end of the campaigning season when the witnesses could be spared from Germany. Time would be gained for public interest in the affair to cool; and in the interval Sackville might withdraw his application to be tried. In the meantime the king would prove his loyalty to Ferdinand by another measure which he had been planning: the dismissal of Sackville from the army by royal prerogative.

On 10 September, three days after his arrival from Germany, Sackville was informed by Lord Holdernesse that as he had not demanded a court martial while he was in Germany it must be deferred till witnesses could leave their posts in the winter, when the trial would be granted if Sackville still wished it. The reply was disingenuous since, as the ministers were aware, Sackville could not have been tried in Germany except by the British, and therefore not at all since he was commander-in-chief. The question whether he would be amenable to court martial when he was dismissed from the army was deferred, though Sackville and presumably the ministers were aware of the problem.

The duty of informing Sackville of his dismissal fell to the Secretary at War Lord Barrington who, according to Horace Walpole, called on Sackville and asked whether he preferred to receive his dismissal by word of mouth or in writing. Sackville asked for a letter. 'That will be easy,' Barrington replied, 'for I know but one precedent, that of the late Lord Cobham: I will send your lordship the same.'

This was highly entertaining. Lord Cobham had been dismissed from his regiment in 1733 by George II for opposing Sir Robert Walpole's excise scheme, an abuse of the Crown's military prerogative which had led to bills in both Houses to remove it. Sackville smiled at Lord Barrington and replied, 'I hope your lordship will send me a copy of Lord Cobham's answer too.'*

---

*Heaven knows whether this anecdote is true. One can attempt a rational assessment of most of one's sources, but what can one say of Horace Walpole's gossip from undisclosed sources except that it is pointed and amusing?

Barrington's letter was duly indited. It was succinct:

I have received His Majesty's command to let you know, that he has no further occasion for your services as Lieut.-General, and Colonel of Dragoon Guards; I am concerned that I have no better occasion to assure your lordship, that I am, My Lord, your Lordship's most humble and obedient servant.

Sackville's dismissal as Lieutenant-General of the Ordnance fell to the Master-General, Lord Ligonier, who felt no compunction about this sort of butchery and had treated his old friend General Bligh with unbending coldness on his return from Cherbourg. Once Sackville was down, however, neither Barrington nor Ligonier were disposed to kick him. Ligonier promised to take care of his aides-de-camp Lloyd and Smith; and on the following day Barrington called to offer his help to any particular officers Sackville might name.

The loss of his military positions deprived Sackville of about £7,000 a year, though he retained a sinecure in Ireland worth £1,200 of which he could not be deprived. 'With his parts and ambitions it cannot end here,' Horace Walpole predicted. 'He calls himself ruined, but when the Parliament meets, he will probably attempt some sort of revenge.'

For the present, however, Lord George was defeated. His power was gone, and it was uncertain whether he would obtain a hearing. The posts from which he had been dismissed went to men whose names would gratify Ferdinand: the colonelcy of the 2nd Dragoon Guards to Waldegrave, who had commanded the leading infantry brigade at Minden, and the Lieutenant-generalcy of the Ordnance to Granby. Sackville's dismissal and the promotion of Waldegrave and Granby were notified to Ferdinand immediately. Down at his retreat in Cambridgeshire Lord Hardwicke approved of the whole transaction. He had foretold that Sackville would demand a court martial to gain time and delay his dismissal. 'His Majesty has disappointed that scheme by his resolution.'

Whether the 'good old King' had made any such calculation is less certain than it seemed to Hardwicke in his rural retreat. Hardwicke's early Victorian biographer characterized the sovereign as 'not a gentleman, nor an Englishman': an illiberal and shocking truth. George's innate bad temper was becoming uncontrollable as he aged. After one outburst Newcastle vowed not to enter the closet again, and had to be soothed by Hardwicke and the royal mistress Lady Yarmouth, who assured him that such scenes were daily incidents in the lives of the courtiers and should not be taken seriously. Trivial things upset the king as much as important ones, and a valet's mistake could cast an alarming gloom over a levee. Germany was an important issue but was also the king's private passion, and the diminutive drawing-room tyrant was filled with vindictive animus against Sackville. He swore that if Jack Mostyn had signed a paper supporting Sackville, he would recall him. As for Sackville himself, he told Lady Yarmouth that he had persevered against Byng and would do the same with Lord George. To dismiss him without trial may have been clever policy, but it also suited the royal temper.

The name of Byng had an unpleasant sound for man who faced a charge of disobedience. The king had been determined to execute Byng, and was 'quite outrageous' with Pitt and Lord Temple when they tried to prevent it; and the ministers had done everything they could to inflame public opinion against him. He had been treated with the greatest harshness: dismissed on an extract from the French admiral's dispatch before his own report arrived; arrested the moment he landed in England with no charge preferred because the government did not yet know the facts; kept in strict confinement without comforts or resources. The membership of the court which tried him had been rigged by ordering admirals who were under an obligation to the First Lord, Anson, to hoist their flags at Portsmouth.

It was true that in 1759 the ministers no longer needed a scapegoat for the war, and the bread-riots which had disturbed the country at the time of Byng's arrest had died away. In Sackville's case they had no wish to promote a show trial. But if Sackville forced them to try him, could he trust them to treat him more fairly than Byng? Pamphleteers were screaming for his blood; and the king would use all his influence to secure a conviction and would execute any sentence of the court. Sackville, of course, was a political force to reckon with. But as Walpole wrote to his friend Horace Mann in Florence, 'if he finds more powerful friends than poor Admiral Byng, assure yourself, he has ten thousand times the number of *personal* enemies'. It was no light matter for Sackville to engineer a trial when he could have dropped into safe obscurity.

Yet that was what he proceeded to do. A week after his dismissal appeared his *Short Address to the Public*, pointing out that his dismissal had condemned him without trial and asking the public to suspend its judgement till the facts were known. For the time being he could do no more, but he asked Colonel Hotham to send him early warning when the army went into winter quarters so that he could renew his application for a court martial. He knew that he had a better case than the public guessed and could put up a fight for his reputation.

The delay in granting him a trial might even be beneficial, for he saw signs that the tide of opinion might turn. His steely reception by the ministry and the clamour of the mob did not mean that he was condemned universally. 'The cry thank God subsides,' he told Colonel Hotham on the day after his dismissal, 'and many feeling for themselves show compassion for my case.' The Duke of Argyll spoke out for him and sent him a friendly message; and at Knole, where he went down to stay with his father immediately after his dismissal, the house was full of company and the whole neighbourhood seemed to support him, including even election opponents. Two men who earned his special gratitude by insisting that they would believe nothing till they had heard his defence were Lord Cornwallis, father of a young man who had been on Granby's staff at Minden and would one day be a famous general, and the Duke of Richmond's brother Lord George Lennox, another future general who remained a friend for the rest of his life.

On the question whether he should be granted a court martial there were two opinions, the just and the worldly. 'This man has been condemned and punished while he is crying out to be heard,' wrote the naval biographer John Campbell. 'It must be an odd sort of crime that still wants a name and where the judgement precedes the indictment.' A letter to the *London Magazine* complained of the danger of dismissing an officer by royal prerogative without reason shown, and the abuses to which it could lead.

That was the just man's opinion; the establishment's view was naturally more pragmatic. Sir Joseph Yorke characteristically took this line of expediency in a long letter to Sir Jeffrey Amherst in Canada. The king, he argued, had done the best thing even for Sackville by dismissing him without trial, and had avoided putting the country into flames as had happened in the case of Byng. Besides, he continued, if the Sackville affair had been allowed to develop it would have been reduced to an option whether to give up Lord George or Prince Ferdinand, and the decision could hardly have gone in Lord George's favour.

This pragmatic view was shared by Sackville's able defender John Douglas, who reminded his readers of the safeguard won from the Stuarts that a civilian should not be tried by a military court. He went on to argue that the king's military prerogative was a necessary power. There might be reasons for dismissing Sackville which were not cognizable by a court martial and which it would not be in the public interest to disclose, such as a complaint from Ferdinand of continual disagreements. In that case Sackville's removal without trial would be necessary for the public good. 'There are certain situations so critical, that a particular hardship must be inflicted to obtain a general good.'

For some, however, there might be private profit as well as public good in Sackville's hardship, and others besides Pitt were hoping to exploit the affair politically. Though Lord Bute had told Sackville that he and the Prince of Wales could give him no effectual support, there were signs that he might use the case to stir the troubled waters of the ministry. He must have known that Pitt was being more than usually difficult with Newcastle. Pitt's brother-in-law Lord Temple had demanded the Garter and been refused, for the king detested him; and if the refusal were repeated, Temple intended to move closer to Bute and Leicester House, and Pitt would move with him. So far Pitt had been firm with Bute about Minden and had told him it was out of the question to help Sackville, and Newcastle hoped that Bute would not take the case up in public. But when Bute went into the City and used his

influence to prevent Sackville's conduct from being censured in the
address of congratulation to the king, it looked as though he and Pitt
could easily join hands on the issue. Newcastle smelt a general air of
disintegration around him. Both his Secretaries of State, Pitt and
Holdernesse, were making up to Leicester House, and he thought
that both were excluding him from their official business. 'I am kept
a stranger by both Secretaries to their business,' the Prime Minister
lamented.

As usual Newcastle was being unduly alarmist. Bute had shown
no confidence in Sackville's case, and when the busybody Sardinian
minister Count Viry asked why Sackville had not obeyed
Ferdinand's first order to support the infantry Bute replied, '*Ma
foi, vous avez raison.*' The truth was that the only support Sackville
had attracted among his political allies was on a squalid level of
intrigue. They might use the case for secret tunnelling, but dared
not stand up in the open for friendship or justice.

Without friends to manipulate the court and cabinet, Sackville
had to rely on the witnesses who would support him if he obtained a
trial. The most senior of those on whom he counted was General
Granville Elliot, who owed his transfer from the Dutch army to
Bute, and had defended Lord George in a letter to the Marquess.
'I think him highly ill used as to the manner of oppressing him,'
Elliot had written on the day after Ferdinand's order of censure.* The support of this much-liked and respected officer
would have been invaluable, and on 11 October Sackville wrote
to Hotham that he hoped Elliot would come home for his health
as he wanted his evidence, little suspecting that Elliot had died
on the previous day in Germany. This blow made Sackville still
more anxious to hasten his trial before other witnesses dropped
out.

Others on whose support he counted were the Hotham brothers,
Colonel Charles and his brother John the chaplain. 'I know your
exactness too well', he wrote to the colonel, 'to doubt your bringing
with you all the orders of this campaign.' Of all the witnesses
Sackville called in his defence Colonel Charles Hotham was the best

*A note of this letter from the Bute papers was given me by Mr Ewan Fraser.

connected. His family (they pronounced their name 'Hutham' with a soft *th*) had been squires in the East Riding since the Middle Ages, and the Hotham who had closed the gates of Hull against Charles I at the outbreak of the Civil War was an ancestor. The family were old friends of the Sackvilles, and Charles a personal friend of Lord George. But Charles was also friendly with Lord Ligonier, the commander-in-chief, whose aide-de-camp he had been and to whom he owed his appointment as deputy adjutant-general, and with Ligonier's nephew Captain Edward Ligonier of Minden, known to his friends as 'Leg'. In Germany Charles was on intimate terms with Colonel Reden, his German opposite number on Ferdinand's staff.

Thus Hotham had a foot in both camps, and since he was an ambitious man without a fortune and had not cultivated these connections for nothing, his position as a witness would be embarrassing. He was certainly not a simple protégé of Sackville, as his juniors Jack Smith and James Sutherland seem to have been. 'You and your brother have a nice game to play,' wrote his father when the news of the Minden scandal reached him. Hotham would not willingly antagonize Edward Ligonier, with whom he remained on close terms in Germany after Sackville's departure. Nor, if he wanted to remain deputy adjutant-general of the British force, would it be prudent to emphasize the failure of communications during the night before the battle, which might reflect on his friend Reden or even on Ferdinand.

Hotham's brother John, the chaplain, saw Sackville in November, and found him 'notwithstanding all things in very good spirits'. Lord George told him he would ask for a court martial again as soon as officers could come home for the winter, but did not think it would be granted. He had heard that Charles was against his having a trial, and commented kindly, 'I do not wonder at him for discouraging a thing in which his own reputation is not concerned, and in which however, he must be called upon as a principal evidence. But the case is very different between him and me.' So it was, and how Hotham would deliver his evidence was yet to be seen.

About 1 December Sackville learned that the army was going into winter quarters, and wrote to renew his request for a court martial. Now the ministers had to face the question they had shelved in September when Sackville was simultaneously promised a trial and dismissed from the army. Could he still be tried by a court martial, now that he was no longer a soldier? The question was referred to the law officers of the Crown.

The law officers of the day were an eminent pair. Charles Pratt, the Attorney-General, was the future Lord Camden, adjudicator of the general warrants issue and later Lord Chancellor. The Solicitor-General was Charles Yorke, son of Lord Hardwicke and another future Lord Chancellor. On reading the correspondence they raised a second question: whether an officer could be tried in Great Britain for a military offence committed outside the king's dominions. They replied on 12 January 1760, first that an officer who had committed a military offence whilst in service could be tried by court martial after he had left the army; and second, that for certain capital offences, of which disobedience was one, he could be tried in Great Britain regardless of where the offence had been committed.

Sackville therefore could have his trial. But for what offence? He had been accused of none. Holdernesse forwarded the law officers' report to him, and added the further question: 'As there is no specific charge exhibited against your Lordship, and as you have requested a court martial in order to justify your conduct, I am to desire your Lordship would acquaint me in what manner you propose to take the benefit of the same.'

This was extraordinary. An officer was being invited to name the capital charge on which he should be tried. The ministry appeared to be leaning over backwards to do justice. But perhaps its real hope was that Sackville was bluffing; and that if, as each successive difficulty in obtaining a trial was overcome, he were given the opportunity to withdraw his application, he would do so. 'I conjecture from the nature of the letter to his lordship,' wrote Hardwicke, 'that there will be no trial.'

Hardwicke was wrong. Sackville continued to behave like a man convinced of his innocence and determined to prove it. He replied on 17 January that Ferdinand would scarcely have reflected on his conduct in general orders without informing the king of his offence; a supposition confirmed by his immediate dismissal when he arrived in England. He could only repeat his request to be 'legally prosecuted for whatever crime I may have been thought guilty of'. Without a charge he could not defend himself. 'I have nothing so much at heart as the hearing my accusation and knowing my accusers, that I may be permitted to offer such proofs in justification of my conduct as may confute the many aspersions thrown upon my character.' He ended the letter with a sort of threat. He asked to be told whether he was to be charged, so that he could either prepare for his trial 'or endeavour by some other method to remove those prejudices which I have been obliged too long to labour under'.

So Sackville was obdurate. If he were denied a trial, he would find some other way to publicize his case, without the control which a court could exercise over the material he introduced, and with a greater likelihood that Ferdinand would be attacked. It was just as desirable as it had been four months earlier in September to protect Ferdinand from criticism; for the war in Germany had slid deeper into crisis. After his defeat at Kunersdorf and the loss of Dresden, Frederick the Great had launched a reckless attack on Marshal Daun which led to the capitulation of 12,000 of his troops at Maxen in November. 'Unhappy temerity!' Once again Prussia seemed about to be swallowed up by Austria, Russia and Sweden. In western Germany France was giving the war the highest priority, and was determined to compensate for the loss of Canada by seizing Hesse and Hanover. Ferdinand was suggesting peace with France before the next campaign to avoid being overwhelmed. 'Strengthen Prince Ferdinand' became the united cry of Pitt and Newcastle. But with what? And if reinforcements were found, were they to be accompanied by a campaign of vilification against their commander-in-chief?

A trial might therefore in the long run be less damaging than a publicity campaign in press and parliament. So it was resolved, and a warrant was circulated for Cabinet approval and issued on 26 January. 'We have been informed', it ran, 'that the said Lord George Sackville hath disobeyed the orders of . . . Prince Ferdinand of Brunswick, which charge we have thought fit should be enquired into by a general court martial.'

Thus Sackville brought on himself the capital charge of disobedience. People were astonished at his folly, assuming that his conduct was indefensible; and this presumption was strengthened by the arrival in the middle of February of the account of the battle which Ferdinand had been asked to provide. It was published in the English press, omitting for the sake of national vanity a passage which revealed that the British infantry had momentarily given ground. 'A very remarkable performance,' judged Sir Joseph Yorke, who read it at The Hague on its way to England, and Newcastle thought it did Ferdinand much honour and the contrary to Sackville. It was indeed a remarkable picture of a commander in battle, and still reads well today; but Newcastle might have reflected that the source which honoured Prince Ferdinand and damned Lord George was neither impartial nor omniscient.

Just as reassuring for Sackville's prosecutors were the views of Lord Granby, who arrived in England about the same time as Ferdinand's report. He was full of enthusiasm for Ferdinand and told Newcastle that he was not well served by his generals, naming Imhoff, Anhalt and Urff. About Sackville he was guarded, but it was clear that he thought him unwise to insist on a trial. 'Everyone is surprised at Lord George pushing so hard,' wrote Yorke after hearing of Granby's views and reading Ferdinand's story. 'People are apt to dazzle themselves with the perusal of the state of their own case, and imagine till it comes to be pulled to pieces that it is unanswerable.'

This accords with a quality which Lord Shelburne saw as inherent in Sackville's character, initial optimism coupled with a tendency to be disconcerted by difficulties and sink into despondency. Would this happen as he listened to the prosecution driving the nails into his coffin, and would his spirits still be bouyant when his own witnesses came under cross-examination? For the moment at any rate he settled down with enthusiasm to prepare his defence. A court martial was a curious institution, 'a court of honour and equity' rather than 'a court of strict law', in the words of Sackville's legal adviser. The great jurist Sir William Blackstone, who published his *Commentaries on the Laws of England* in this decade, regretted the unsettled and arbitrary nature of military law. A general court martial to try an officer required not less than thirteen judges, all of them soldiers and none expert in the law; and their director on law and procedure was the Judge-Advocate, who was also the prosecutor. The prisoner conducted his own defence, but was 'indulged' with counsel under the character of 'friends of the court', who were allowed to sit near him and prime him with questions for the witnesses.

Sackville's principal adviser and counsel was another lawyer on his way to fame: one of those Scotsmen-on-the-make who aroused the paranoid hostility of Horace Walpole. Alexander Wedderburn, a member of Bute's circle, had left the Scottish bar two years earlier after insulting the Lord President in open court, and had been called to the English bar at the Inner Temple. He was very able; and a tough and opportunistic career was to take him dazzlingly upwards through the highest legal offices to the Woolsack and an earldom.

Wedderburn showed no doubt of the strength of Lord George's case. The first object, he said, was acquittal; the second, an illustrious acquittal. He tutored his pupil in some elementary rules for handling witnesses. Never press a hostile witness unless he appears confused: obvious in theory but difficult in practice, and even professional counsel become heated and press witnesses imprudently from resentment. The art of cross-examination, Wedderburn explained, lay in discovering the witness's state of mind. If he was shaken he could be questioned directly. But if he was hostile and in a collected frame of mind, it was very difficult to make him bring out the conclusion which the examining counsel wanted if the preceding questions had alerted him to the trend of the examination. The art in this case was to follow the leading question with some neutral ones to put him off his guard before falling on him with the clinching question.

Never ask an adverse witness a question of opinion, Wedderburn continued, for 'a man's opinion can settle matters so easily with his conscience'. In cross-examination beware of disclosing the nature of the defence, even if this means foregoing an advantageous question. If Sackville's defence were known, the prosecutor's evidence would be adapted to it; and with regard to the opinion of the world at large, it was better to lay the defence before it as a whole rather than disclose it piecemeal and half understood, which might allow the public to prejudge the case a second time. Finally Wedderburn advised Sackville to observe the greatest candour, and show a contempt for seizing little advantages.

The prosecution's case could only be guessed from Ferdinand's narrative, but Wedderburn ran through its probable stages and how to handle the witnesses. Winzingerode was likely to be a witness who would improve his evidence under cross-examination, and the fewer questions he was asked the better. Wedderburn guessed that he had not known the location of the infantry behind which he ordered the cavalry to form; but it was unsafe to ask him this, as he would probably have sorted the matter out since the battle. Ligonier and Fitzroy should be made to state their orders distinctly, and Fitzroy asked whether the orders he delivered were correct; but they too should not be asked too many questions – and here Wedderburn's experience as an advocate introduced a further rule. One should never ask a prosecution witness questions of fact which would later be proved by defence witnesses. If he gave the same answer the prosecution witness would not state it so strongly: if different, it would raise a contradiction of one's proof. One might indeed examine a prosecution witness to trap him into making assertions which would later be disproved, and thereby lessen his credibility as a witness; but for this purpose one should examine only on collateral facts, and avoid the risk of inviting contradiction of facts essential to the defence.

Wedderburn foresaw that the final stage of the prosecution's case would be the cavalry's halts on the heath. This was not a charge in itself unless it was argued that the halts had been ordered simply to cause delay; and Granby being a man of honour should show under cross-examination their true reason and short duration. The danger Wedderburn feared was Granby's pliability. Since the battle he might have been influenced to change his views; for 'no means will be neglected to make out the charge'.

Other points of evidence for which Sackville must be ready included matters of opinion. Witnesses might be asked to state on oath what could have been achieved by marching sooner. Such evidence ought not to be admitted, but was unlikely to be rejected by the court. Sackville ought not to press his objection hard; but by just hinting at an objection he might use it later as a circumstance of hardship, taking merit from his own candour and entitling himself to introduce in his own defence as much evidence of opinion as he pleased.

Hearsay evidence was a more serious problem. Court martials had been known to admit evidence of what another party not on oath had said. If the Judge-Advocate allowed such hearsay Sackville must persist in his objections, for there was no safety in such a trial. Even if the court did not believe the evidence, the audience would go away repeating the story without weighing its credibility, and his reputation would suffer.

There were dangerous shoals ahead for a defendant with no legal training, and February was spent in methodical preparation of the case. Sackville had supplied a list of twenty-one witnesses to be brought over from Germany, adding that he had omitted the names of generals since it might not be easy to spare them. Fourteen of his list were called as witnesses at the trial, a much more generous treatment than Byng had received; and Sackville made no complaint that others had been prevented from attending. As the witnesses arrived in England they were questioned by Sackville or his lawyers, and the conduct of the case was prepared from their answers. The notes of these questions and answers seem to have been looked over and annotated during the trial in the light of the prosecution's evidence. Sackville's performance in court was based on expert advice and thorough preparation.

The day of the trial could not be fixed till the witnesses arrived; but at last, on 24 February, the Judge-Advocate was able to convene the court for the following Friday, the 29th of February. On the day before the trial Sackville was arrested for disobedience of orders, a formal procedure which did not confine him. Here again he had the advantage of Byng, who had been arrested long before the charges were made or the trial prepared, and kept in close confinement under guard in a garret.

And now came Sackville's last opportunity to evade his trial. When the Secretary at War informed the House of Commons of his arrest, the Speaker and many members objected to the court martial of a Member who was no longer a soldier as a breach of privilege. Sackville, however, refused this escape. On his instructions his brother-in-law Lord Milton stood up and assured the House that the trial was what Lord George earnestly desired. The House respected his wish, and the trial went forward.*

*The Parliamentary History omits the debate and the authority is Walpole; but he would scarcely have invented the proceedings of the House of Commons.

EIGHT

LORD GEORGE ON TRIAL

THE COURT ASSEMBLES

The cheerless late winter months of 1760 provided a rich harvest of aristocratic trials for the gossip-writers. Lord Ferrers had shot his steward in a fit of paranoid rage, and was languishing in Nottingham gaol awaiting his indictment and trial before his peers. Unless he were found to be insane he would provide entertainment for the mob at Tyburn. And on 12 February a court martial opened at the Horse Guards on Major-General Lord Charles Hay, a hero of Fontenoy like Sackville. In the legendary exchange of invitations between the French and British to fire first, Lord Charles had stepped forward in front of the 1st Guards at fifty yards range from the enemy, doffed his hat and drank to them, and introduced them to his company. His courage may have owed more than Sackville's did that day to the contents of his flask. Now he was charged with opprobrious and disrespectful speeches against Lord Loudon in Nova Scotia, tending to excite mutiny and sedition: he had said that Loudon was planting cabbages when he ought to have been fighting.

Before Lord Charles's judges completed their work on this grave sedition, Lord George's began theirs in a neighbouring room. At ten o'clock on Friday, 29 February, fifteen generals assembled in the offices of the Judge-Advocate-General at the Horse Guards, and the Deputy Judge-Advocate Charles Gould opened the proceedings. Gould was in his early thirties, a product of Westminster School and Christ Church, making a successful career in the military by-ways of the law, with a shrewd marriage to the plain elder daughter of his boss. Thomas Morgan, M.P., the Judge-Advocate, was an absentee from his duties which Gould performed for him, and the owner of vast estates in South Wales which Gould eventually inherited through his wife.

Gould took his place on the right of the president at the centre of the judges' table, with the other members of the court ranged in seniority to the right and left. Eight of them had sat on the court which had acquitted Sir John Mordaunt a couple of years earlier on a charge of disobedience in command of the Rochefort expedition, and among these were the two most active of Sackville's judges, Lord Albemarle and General Cholmondeley.

The Judge-Advocate (for so Gould is described in the records of the court) called the roll, and had now to administer the oath for capital cases: 'You shall well and truly try and determine according to your evidence in the matter now before you between our Sovereign Lord the King's Majesty and the prisoner to be tried. So help you God.' And in turn each member would swear to administer justice impartially; and because military law was uncertain, he promised that, in case of a doubt arising which was not explained in the articles of war, he would act according to his conscience and understanding and the custom of war in like cases. Each swore that he would not divulge the sentence till it had been approved by the king, or ever disclose the vote of any member.

But before Gould proceeded to the swearing-in, the prisoner was brought in and asked whether he objected to any member of the court. The only judges in the case who are still remembered as soldiers were James Abercromby, who had commanded the force repulsed on the Canadian frontier at Ticonderoga in 1758, and Lord Albemarle, who would command the force which captured Havana in 1762. But two had notable connections to which Sackville might have objected: Albemarle, the head of the Keppel family and chamberlain of the Duke of Cumberland's household; and Lord Granby's uncle Lord Robert Manners, who joined the court a week later. To neither of these did Sackville object; but he had already sent a letter to the court objecting to General Belford, and was asked to explain it, which he proceeded to do. Belford was a colonel-commandant of the Royal Artillery, and was described by

Sir Joseph Yorke as 'an excellent officer to whom we owe the figure our artillery makes': in particular the army owed its new light six-pounder guns to him. When Sackville became Lieutenant-General of the Ordnance he had (on the instructions, he said, of the Duke of Marlborough) taken over the management of the Royal Artillery from Belford. This had caused ill feeling, and when Sackville returned to England after Minden he noticed that General Belford was the only field officer of artillery who did not call on him. Nor did Belford recommend Sackville's ordnance aide-de-camp to his successor Granby.

The feud, if such it was, is the kind of thing which some men generate and others do not. The court was surprised that Sackville should have challenged this rough but honest member of the court, who was on oath to do justice impartially, and ruled that his grounds were insufficient. But Belford, who had asked to be excused as soon as the letter of objection was received, persisted when he heard Sackville's reasons and was allowed to stand down.

A more serious obstruction now arose. Asked whether he held any military commission, Lord George replied that he did not. He was ordered to withdraw, and two questions were raised by Lord Albemarle. Could a civilian be tried by court martial? And if so, could the court inflict any other punishment than death? The first question had already been answered by the law officers; but the court agreed to lay both questions before the king for submission to the judges, and adjourned for a week.

The king was furious. 'Angrily and indecently' he was pushing the trial on, and this unexpected delay was too much. Blue eyes popping out of his purple countenance, he ordered Lord Albemarle's mother to be dropped from his private evening parties, and cut her at the morning drawing-room. The Cabinet was obliged to behave more rationally, and consulted Lord Chief Justice Mansfield. The great Scots lawyer replied that the judges were all out on circuit or about to depart, and it was impossible to obtain their opinion – 'be assured you will have no answer'. 'I consider it as the court martial refusing to try him,' he scrawled to Newcastle.

The Cabinet met that evening at Lord Holdernesse's house to decide what to do, and was treated to a vehement harangue from the

Lord President of the Council, Lord Granville, to the effect that Sackville was not amenable to a court martial and should not have been granted one, and that the judges had nothing to do with the question. From this attack Newcastle was rescued by Lord Hardwicke, who threw his formidable legal reputation into the battle and asserted that it was perfectly proper to refer the jurisdiction of an inferior court to the judges. Mansfield concurred, but asked that as a judge his signature should not appear on the Cabinet minute.

What was Mansfield up to? Some time previously he had prevented the question from being referred to the judges, and now he was pretending that there was no time to get it. At court it was being said that he was running with the hare and hunting with the hounds: advising the Cabinet that the court martial had jurisdiction in order to please the king, but obstructing the attempt to obtain the judge's advice to save his friend Sackville. Newcastle reminded him that he was incurring the royal anger and implored him to obtain the judges' opinion over the weekend. Somehow he managed to assemble some of the judges in his chambers on the Saturday, and on Monday, 3 March, the opinion was written out and signed by Mansfield and ten other judges. It was a fine piece of legal equivocation. They saw no grounds at present to doubt the jurisdiction of the court martial; but should the question be brought before any of them judicially, 'we shall be ready without difficulty to change our opinion'.

A lawyer's reply, but enough; and the ruling has been adhered to ever since. On Friday 7 March the court reassembled and began its work before a crowded audience.

'ALARMED TO A VERY GREAT DEGREE'

During the intervening week the President, General Onslow, had been taken ill and retired from the case, and Sir Charles Howard took his place at the centre of the table. The others ranged themselves on either side of him, with Belford replaced by General Caesar and Lord Robert Manners taking the place of the ailing

Onslow. The charge was read; Sackville admitted his instructions to obey our good cousin Prince Ferdinand of Brunswick: and the first witness was called. During the next five days the Judge-Advocate took his witnesses through the evidence for the Crown, and the lines of the prosecution's case were revealed. They were much as Wedderburn had predicted: neglect of the earlier orders to be ready to move; late arrival of Sackville at his post at the head of the cavalry; disobeying the successive orders of Winzingerode, Ligonier and Fitzroy; and the halts on the heath.

The first witness was Colonel Hotham, followed by Major Stubbs and Colonel Johnston of the Blues. Then came the first of the staff officers who had brought orders for the cavalry to advance, Captain Winzingerode, speaking in French through an interpreter. A question from Lord George: did the witness understand the nature of the oath? Winzingerode bridled, and replied that oaths were as well understood in Germany as anywhere else. Apparently supposing that he resented being questioned by a prisoner, the Judge-Advocate explained politely that 'it is usual in this country for the gentleman upon his trial to have an opportunity of cross-examining the witnesses'.

Ferdinand's German witnesses were indeed shocked by the latitude which the court allowed to Sackville and the six lawyers who surrounded him. Derenthal complained that the judges lacked the firmness needed to contain Sackville's artifices and subtle loquacity, and described the Judge-Advocate as a pedant who asked a lot of silly questions. 'It's a world of intrigues and cabals,' he grumbled to Ferdinand, 'and the better one gets to know it the more disagreeable it becomes.' He regarded Albemarle as the most soldierly and intelligent member of the court, but feared that his connection with Cumberland, who was jealous of Ferdinand as his successor in the German command, made his good will doubtful. The rest of the court asked ridiculous questions, allowed the prisoner to say what he pleased, and digressed into matters which had no bearing on the charge. The Germans were received in the friendliest manner by the king when they appeared at court, and were dined by Newcastle and other political magnates; but as the weeks of hanging about London were protracted by the extraordinary English way of conducting a trial they became increasingly bored and impatient.

The second day of the trial saw all three bearers of the disputed orders in court. Winzingerode completed his evidence and was followed by Ligonier, now a lieutenant-colonel. Sackville made the point that he had not been a field officer when he delivered his orders: 'I call him captain, because that was his rank at the time.' None of the three bearers of the orders could wish to see an acquittal. If Sackville were not guilty it would become a question whether they had conveyed their orders correctly; and Fitzroy would further have to answer for his imprudent talking since the battle.

Steadily, question by question, the Judge-Advocate built up the story of Sackville's delinquency. A new point was added by Fitzroy, who revealed how Ferdinand had sent him with an order to hasten the cavalry, and how Fitzroy had elicited the additional 'to Lord Granby, for I know he will obey me'. In cross-examining, Sackville followed Wedderburn's advice, and confined himself in the main to pressing the witnesses for exact statements of times and orders. His most striking intervention was provoked by a question to Colonel Johnston about what Ligonier had told him, and his opinion of it. Sackville had been prepared for this by Wedderburn, and rose to protest: 'Sir, if we are to go into hearsay and opinion, you may sit here some six months. Colonel Ligonier does attend here on the part of the Crown; what passed between him and me, I dare say, he will declare upon his oath.'

That was temperately said, and on the third day came another opportunity to make the point and prepare to take advantage of it. Fitzroy, continuing his evidence, remarked that there had been no cavalry in the rear of the British infantry to support it, whereon the chatterbox General Cholmondeley interrupted: 'Then you are of opinion, if they had been broke, that the whole must have been sacrificed?'

Sackville rose to handle this as he had been advised: 'Sir, I do not think that a fair question, to ask only matter of opinion.'

The president offered to clear the court and discuss it; but Wedderburn's advice had been to make the protest without pressing it, in order to suggest hard treatment and open the way for the defence to use the same sort of evidence.

Sir [Sackville replied], I did not mention it as an objection to clear the court or prevent the truth coming out. I would not have desired the trial if that had been the case. . . . The reason I mentioned it was for the dignity of the court, and for the sake of the method of proceeding in courts martial, that the generals who sit here to judge should ask the opinion of so young a gentleman as Colonel Fitzroy. . . . Upon this question every officer is able to determine: if infantry is broke upon a plain, and cavalry near at hand to sustain them, there is no doubt but it would be of great service. Such questions of opinion cannot be for the information of the court, but for the audience.

I am tried for disobedience of orders. The question is, did I obey or disobey the orders of Prince Ferdinand? But whether the cavalry did or did not attack is not a charge upon me, but upon those who gave me the orders. . . . I hope I shall be equally indulged in being allowed the liberty of putting questions to the witnesses, as to matters of opinion.

The case was developing as promisingly as the prosecution had hoped, though Sackville had obtained a few useful admissions from the witnesses. Lord Barrington attended the trial and sent a brief report to Newcastle every afternoon when the proceedings had closed. It had been proved, he wrote, that Sackville had arrived late at his post; Winzingerode had given his evidence fully and well – 'very cautious yet very strong'; Ligonier's evidence was exactly what had been hoped; and Fitzroy's was what he had always said, with the extra plum of Ferdinand's remark that Granby would obey him. How Sackville would defend himself was still a mystery, but all was going well. 'Your Grace may rest assured that no cause ever was in a better way,' Barrington reported.

A critical moment for the defence would come when Colonel Sloper of Bland's Dragoon Guards was called. He had been putting round London his version of the delivery of Winzingerode's order, and had related it to General Elliot in Germany. His story was that the order had been delivered in front of his squadron where he could hear it; that it had been repeated in English and German; that Sackville had asked what the order meant and Sloper had told him it meant a move to the left; and that twenty-five minutes had been wasted by not obeying it. Sloper was regarded as violently hostile to Sackville. Personal dislike could account for this, but there are two leads which might explain it further. Horace Walpole says that Sloper was believed to be influenced by General Mordaunt, who resented Sackville's role in the inquiry into the Rochefort expedition: Sackville had been the most active member of the board of inquiry whose adverse report had led to Mordaunt's court martial. It is fair to mention however that Mordaunt, while making no secret of his resentment, had expressed sympathy to Newcastle for Sackville's plight, and declared himself to be 'too much of a gentleman to show his enmity at this time'. A second possible reason for Sloper's hostility was that in the preceding May Sackville had objected to General Bland's nephew Lieutenant Bland being given a vacant troop in the regiment, an appointment of which Sloper apparently approved, on the grounds that he was too young and junior.

Wedderburn had advised that if Sloper's evidence in court proved to be milder than what he had been saying in public, Sackville should not press him hard in cross-examination, for fear of forcing him to strengthen his evidence in order to justify what he had said in public. But if he were very hostile, he should be examined closely. Why had he told his story to Elliot and to no one else in Germany; and why had he then put it around in England? He should be pressed on the alleged repetition of the order in German, which Captain Hugo would deny; and on who else was present and heard the conversation.

Sloper had been saying in public that Lord George had shown confusion when he received his orders, and Wedderburn had given Sackville his advice about what to do if a witness were asked whether he had shown fear. In view of what was to happen in court it is worth quoting Wedderburn's advice in full:

No man of honour would answer the question, because a little reflection upon those delicate emotions of his own mind which lead to courage or timidity would easily convince him how impossible it is to decide justly from any appearances of the situation of another's mind in time of action. . . . A fair judge would not allow such questions to be put, but if the court suffers them to be asked and the witness does not decline to give an answer, one should not be surprised if he gives an unfair one. The only conduct for Lord George to observe in that case is to stifle his just indignation, to treat the questions and answers with the most perfect contempt, and when the opportunity presents itself to expose the weakness, ridicule and malice of such evidence.

Sloper was called after Fitzroy on the third day. Would he temper his evidence, or repeat the virulently hostile version of events which he had been spreading round London? It was soon clear that his story would not be softened. He related his tale of Winzingerode's order to move to the left, his own advice to the puzzled Sackville, and the long delay doing nothing till Ligonier arrived. He stated that he had heard Ligonier deliver an order to advance and that the movement was to be by the left, and had then spoken to Ligonier himself.

Here Sloper broke off, and asked the court whether he should relate what he had said. He was told to proceed, and went on:

I said, 'For God's sake, sir, repeat your orders to that man, that he may not pretend not to have understood them, for it is near half an hour ago that he received orders to advance, and yet we are still here'. – My oath obliges me to say all I said. – 'But you see the condition he is in.'

At those words there must have been a hush of expectation in the court, but for a few minutes the Judge-Advocate proceeded with questions on other matters. Then he turned back sharply. What, he asked, did Sloper mean by the phrase 'the condition he is in'?

My opinion [Sloper replied], is that my Lord George Sackville was alarmed to a very great degree. When his Lordship ordered me to advance, he seemed in the utmost confusion. The original orders were to the left; Captain Ligonier's orders were to the left. The cavalry afterwards made a move to the left, and the order his Lordship had given me, was to move with the regiment straight forwards.

'HE WILL HAVE LITTLE TO SAY IN HIS DEFENCE'

The 'impossible' had happened. Sloper had done what Wedder-burn had said no man of honour would do: he had impugned

Sackville's courage. A new dimension had been written into the court's proceedings: and whatever the verdict on Sackville's obedience, he would always carry the stigma of a man who had been publicly accused of cowardice.

Wedderburn's advice had been to treat such evidence with contempt and destroy it later; but it was too much for Lord George, and for the first time he lost his composure. Visibly agitated, he asked a member of the court in a whisper whether he would be allowed to answer Sloper when his evidence was completed. 'My Lord, why do you apply to me?' the member replied. 'You should address the President.' Sackville replied that he had asked him as a friend, and subsided into silence. The Judge-Advocate proceeded to the end of his examination, Sloper's evidence was read over, and Lord George rose to cross-examination.

SACKVILLE: Sir Charles Howard, if I may be allowed to say a few words touching this gentleman's evidence before I go any further.

GENERAL CHOLMONDELEY: I am never against any indulgence to the prisoner.

SACKVILLE: It is a little hard for me to be sitting here, and have a witness come against me with an opinion of this nature, and I forced to remain entirely silent. I shall only say a few words. This sort of attack I never heard before, from any one gentleman whatever, excepting from the private insinuations of this gentleman now before the court. I have heard of it since he has been in London, I am glad he has mentioned it in court, I –

LORD ALBEMARLE: Your Lordship will have an opportunity of observing upon that in your defence; but I am afraid we are going into an irregularity.

SACKVILLE: I will only say now that I shall prove my conduct that day with regard to every branch of it, and I shall shew that gentleman to the court in such colours for truth and veracity –

LORD ALBEMARLE: My Lord, this is being irregular.

SACKVILLE: Your Lordship may imagine what I must feel upon such an occasion; and it is difficult not to express it instantly.

LORD ALBEMARLE: I am very sensible of what your Lordship must feel, and sorry to interrupt; but the course of proceeding –

SACKVILLE: I submit to the opinion of the court, and must beg leave to suppose, for the present, that no evidence has been given. I shall now go on as if nothing of this sort had happened, and shall treat that gentleman in that part of his evidence with the contempt it deserves.

With that shot Lord George proceeded to the cross-examination. Sloper had answered the Judge-Advocate's questions in a fulsome manner which contrasted with the succinctness of the preceding witnesses. He now added a tone of contempt which annoyed the court. Asked by Sackville who had been present when Ligonier delivered his orders, he replied that if he known it was necessary to remember, 'as I had but little employment I should have particularly noticed it'. Sackville asked him to describe the cavalry's situation (a question asked of other witnesses) and received the reply: 'I did not range the cavalry nor the infantry; I cannot speak to the general position of the army.' This was too much for Lord Albemarle, who interposed sharply: 'If you do not know it that is an answer and say so.'

'Has your Lordship any more questions to ask?' the president asked Lord George.

SACKVILLE: I shall ask no more questions of this witness, since they only tend to declamation.

With that the court adjourned for the day, and Barrington's afternoon report to Newcastle purred with satisfaction. Sloper's evidence, he wrote, had been 'very long, and strong to the greatest degree, both as to the disobedience and the appearance of fear and distraction in Lord George Sackville, who seemed much moved by it'. Though Sloper's acrimony weakened the force of his evidence, Sackville's crime was appearing in ever more lurid colours. For one naïve observer, young Thomas Cowper, Sloper had quite simply 'proved' that Sackville had appeared agitated – 'whether with eagerness to engage or fear of being attacked every person is at liberty to judge'. The passage of time soon resolved even this doubt, and a few days later Cowper was asserting that Sloper had shown Sackville to be 'in great confusion, much frighted and terrified'.

Sloper completed his evidence on the following day, treating the court with the same insolent confidence as before, and at the close attempted to answer Sackville's aspersions.

SLOPER: I would just say a word upon what was mentioned yesterday by Lord George, he reflected upon me.

PRESIDENT: You have nothing to do but give your evidence. The court stopped Lord George from saying anything about it.

SLOPER: I would just go as far as Lord George did.

PRESIDENT: You are not to say anything but your evidence.

Sloper retired, to be followed briefly by Derenthal, with an apology from the Judge-Advocate for calling him to prove that Ferdinand had been impatient. 'If you go into this sort of evidence there will never be an end of the trial,' Sackville protested. Then came Colonel Pitt of Mordaunt's Dragoons, with evidence of the slowness of the march across the heath, leaving the Judge-Advocate with only one more witness of importance to call. Lord Granby's examination had probably been postponed till the end of the prosecution's case because of the sudden death of his wife as he was leaving Germany. It was about the advance across the heath that Granby could provide first-hand evidence, and it was clear that he thought the cavalry had moved too slowly and halted too much. He said that if they had moved at a trot as soon as Winzingerode delivered his orders, he thought they would have been in time to engage the enemy; and though he was not certain that, after the delay in obeying the orders, they would have been in time to do much execution if they had pushed on across the heath without halting, he believed that if they had gone on as fast as possible without blowing their horses they could have been up with the infantry fifteen or twenty minutes sooner. Granby's 'tenderness and decency' and evident wish to say all that he could in the prisoner's favour did more harm to Sackville than Sloper's acrimony.

After reading over Granby's evidence, Lord George wrote a note for his lawyers which shows the difficulty of remembering what had happened during those crowded hours at Minden. Granby's evidence had described the halting of the second line before they reached the fir-wood to allow the first line to come up and form a single line; then an order to march to the left near the fir-wood to make room for the two right-hand regiments; a halt by Elliot three or four hundred yards further on while Granby was ahead of his brigade; and finally, a brief halt afterwards to dress the line. Sackville remembered the first halt, and sending word to halt or march slower to allow the two displaced regiments on the right to come up. But as he remembered the sequence of events, on learning that Granby was advancing by Ferdinand's orders he had not stopped him again but pressed on with the right of the line and come up level with him, so that if Elliot had halted it could only have been momentarily. This note was written to aid the planning of the defence, and not for the court. It reveals Sackville genuinely puzzled to recall exactly what had happened and when. The certainties which some of the witnesses expressed in court might have given place to more tentative recollections if they had been questioned in private.

Granby finished his evidence on the sixth day of the trial, Wednesday, 12 March; and the Crown's case ended with the calling of two cavalry subalterns. Lieutenant John Wogan's evidence is memorable only for a reply whose modesty would have become some of the preceding witnesses. 'Do you remember anything more of that transaction?' he was asked, concerning Granby's orders for the second line to march. 'Nothing at all,' he replied. 'They cannot expect much from me, as I was only a subaltern.'

With the two lieutenants the Judge-Advocate closed the evidence for the prosecution, well satisfied with his witnesses and still unable to imagine what defence the prisoner could offer. Sir Joseph Yorke at The Hague, after hearing of the progress of the trial, was equally puzzled to know how Sackville could put up a serious defence against the Judge-Advocate's formidable evidence. 'The more I hear of the court martial', he wrote, 'the more I am astonished how Lord George Sackville could push matters so far. He will have little to say in his defence unless he has composed a libel against Prince Ferdinand, which I can't yet think him void of sense enough to have done.' This of course was what the government feared, and Charles Gould promised the Secretary at War that he would keep Sackville as much to the point as possible and hinder him from making irrelevant accusations. The only part of the prosecution's case which looked shaky was the charge that the cavalry had not been saddled as ordered at one o'clock, and for the sake of appearances it was decided not to print this passage in Ferdinand's narrative. On this point, Derenthal warned Ferdinand, 'your Highness may have received false reports'.

To give Sackville time to study the Crown's evidence the court adjourned for three days, and through Thursday and Friday the world waited to see how he would face his accusers. On Saturday morning a crowd stormed into the courtroom to see the spectacle. Young Thomas Cowper arrived too late, and even at the risk of his hat and coat was unable to fight his way through the door.

The members of the court took their places, and the prisoner was ordered into court. 'My Lord George,' said the president, 'you will please to proceed.'

LORD GEORGE'S REPLY

For six months Sackville had kept his silence, reserving his defence for the grand inquest he had sought. Now, he told the court, the time had come to unfold the whole of his conduct at Minden: it had never yet been done, nor could have been done by witnesses who saw only part of the scene and even that imperfectly. Without apparent irony he thanked the king for granting him a trial: 'I am very sensible of this last instance of his Majesty's goodness towards me.' Only by being tried could he discover the grounds on which he had been censured in public orders and dismissed from the army: 'I stand here a willing prisoner, nor should I have come to this bar but by my own desire.'

Lord George's defence consisted of an opening address, the examining of his witnesses, and a closing speech which summed up his evidence. The whole took up about nine days of the court's proceedings. No summary can do justice to his two addresses to the court. They bear the marks of Wedderburn's command of law and language; but Sackville's own unrehearsed interventions at critical stages of the trial, and his parliamentary reputation as a master of lucid exposition, leave no doubt that the defence is ultimately his own.*

*Sackville's addresses may be read in either version of the published proceedings of the trial, for which see page 267.

Lord George's Reply

Sackville opened his argument with the contention that to determine whether he was guilty of disobedience the court had only to establish what orders he had received, whether they had been obeyed, and if not, whether they could have been obeyed. What the cavalry might have achieved if it had engaged the enemy was irrelevant; and he must be judged by what he knew at the time, and not with hindsight.

I must here [he said] beg the court would look into my situation and not judge upon my supposed knowledge or upon facts since disclosed; but look upon me at the head of a right wing of cavalry, without any general disposition communicated to me, or any previous instructions given for my conduct, unacquainted with the ground, with woods or inclosures upon my right and left, and the country open only to the front, towards which front the original position of the cavalry was to have been.

This plea lies at the heart of the defence. The infantry battle had been masked from Sackville by the woodland on his left, and he knew nothing of his commander's intentions except that the cavalry had been ordered to wait for Hahlen to be cleared to enable it to advance to its line of deployment. In these circumstances he received unexpected and conflicting orders from junior officers, whose notions of what was happening elsewhere were hazy. Thus placed, he had to take a decision which, if wrong, might throw the army's order of battle into disarray and bring on disaster.

From this general argument Lord George proceeded to a detailed analysis of the Judge-Advocate's accusations. He began with the orders which preceded the action, and their execution up to the time when the cavalry's advance was halted by Malortie near Hartum. The order to reconnoitre the approaches to the Minden plain had been complied with as far as his duties as general of the day had allowed. The order to be saddled at one had been distributed to the regiments and obeyed. And though the order from Ferdinand's headquarters to march had miscarried, Sackville was the first general of his division to join the troops, and marched immediately.

This part of the charge, he said, had been included not so much to prove disobedience as to show his general negligence and give a plausible appearance to the charges which followed. The Judge-Advocate had implied that the battle was expected. Had that been so, no commander-in-chief would have failed to issue a general plan for conducting the battle, least of all Ferdinand with his talent for planning and exposition. The orders for saddling had been repeated so often in the previous fortnight that they no longer indicated an immediate battle; and Ferdinand's silence on the subject when Sackville reported the state of the pickets was a further reason to suppose that no enemy attack was expected. The army's situation in the early hours of 1 August was not one of expectation and readiness, with Sackville alone confused and unready, but of general surprise and confusion which he overcame. His approach march, far from being slow as one witness claimed, was fast enough to cause hurry in the rear of the column: an instance of the errors of officers who guessed what was happening elsewhere.

Listening to this argument, the Judge-Advocate knew that his own witnesses had already disproved this part of his case, and at the end of Sackville's address he rose to deny that the orders issued before the battle had been thrown in to swell the charge. He now pretended that they had been mentioned merely to show that Sackville was familiar with the ground. Sackville challenged this, and appealed to the court whether Gould had not constantly examined his witnesses about the execution of those orders, poking into the minutest details even down to the forming of quarter ranks. 'If they had been examining a major of cavalry they could not have done it more closely.'

The first part of the charge was thus demolished, and Gould eventually withdrew it. The next item concerned the orders brought by Captain Winzingerode. Sackville pointed out that in the half hour of waiting near Hartum before Winzingerode's arrival, he had sent on the British artillery, which had found itself with no orders, without sending for instructions to Ferdinand. He had disliked the situation of his own troops, hemmed in and likely to come under fire from enemy batteries in their cramped position; and everything he knew indicated that the cavalry could only intervene in the approaching battle by advancing past Hahlen when the pickets cleared the village. Thus when Winzingerode galloped up with an order to form one line and advance to sustain the infantry it was exactly what Sackville wished and expected. He took immediate steps to obey it.

But had he been given the orders he claimed to have heard? On this point he would produce five witnesses; and the prosecution had only Winzingerode himself. For Colonel Sloper was not to be believed. 'In what manner his evidence was given I need not remind the court . . . he comes into court prepared and obliged to support by his oath the credit of the tales he has so often told.' And if Sloper's behaviour had not already destroyed his credibility, Sackville's witnesses would prove that what he had sworn could not be true. It should already have been possible to prove by cross-examining Sloper that Sackville could not have spoken to him to receive his advice, but Sloper would not give a direct answer to any question;

and accurate as his memory was in other particulars, he could not remember the name of any one officer he at any time saw with me except Captain Hugo, and him only because Captain Winzingerode's speaking to him in German was a circumstance he had introduced in the relation he had given out of doors, and durst not venture entirely to forget it in court.

With that suggestion of perjury Sackville set Colonel Sloper's evidence aside, and turned to Winzingerode's claim that he had told Sackville the cavalry was to move to the left. He conceded that Winzingerode had given his evidence with candour. He did not challenge his truthfulness, nor doubt that he believed he had explained his orders in the manner he now stated. Winzingerode was cautious at this distance of time about the exact words he had used (unlike Sloper, who had sworn to the very words which Winzingerode was too honest to recall). It was natural for him to suppose he had expressed himself clearly and indicated a move to the left; but five witnesses had understood the order as meaning an advance to the front.

Winzingerode had also given evidence of Ferdinand's impatience for the cavalry to appear, inferring that it showed the prince's sense of Sackville's delay. It did not. It showed only that Ferdinand had a great need of cavalry where he had not posted it. Winzingerode learned of the prince's impatience when he met Ligonier as he was galloping back after delivering his orders. If Ferdinand knew where the cavalry was posted, his impatience could not arise from a well-founded belief that Sackville had delayed its arrival – 'unless it were possible to imagine that twenty-four squadrons could move faster than Captain Winzingerode, who went full gallop and was not then come in sight of the prince'.

The next item of the charge Sackville said he was at a loss how to state. Was it that he had disobeyed the order delivered by Captain Ligonier, which was immediately complied with, or the order delivered by Fitzroy, which differed materially from Ligonier's? Or was it that he had hesitated between two different orders delivered almost simultaneously, which seemed to everyone present to have been intended by Ferdinand to be the same order, and had gone a few hundred yards to the prince to clear up the muddle?

The facts of the case were that he was clearing the Saxe-Gotha regiment from his line of advance, and collecting information which would justify him in departing from the literal words of Winzingerode's order to advance in a single line, when Ligonier galloped up. The interval between the two orders was seven or eight minutes; not as Sloper claimed on one occasion a quarter of an hour, and on another occasion half an hour. The order which Ligonier delivered, and which only Sloper disputed, was to advance and exploit the enemy cavalry's confusion. This order, clear and explicit, removed every doubt; and as Ligonier testified, Sackville drew his sword and gave the order to march. Ligonier claimed that he had then said as the line moved forward that Sackville was to march to the left; but no officer near Sackville heard him, and with the drums beating it was possible that he had said something of the kind which no one heard.

Scarcely had the advance begun when Fitzroy arrived with an order to move with only the British cavalry and to the left. Sackville was amazed. To move to the left was contrary to all he expected or had understood from the earlier orders; he could see no reason to divide his force in face of the enemy's great superiority in cavalry; and if cavalry were needed urgently on the left, why send for the British squadrons which were half a mile further away than the

Hanoverians? Fitzroy asserted that he and Ligonier had left the prince at the same time with the same order; Ligonier was sent for and asserted that his own order was correct. Since neither would give way, and the prince was near by, he went to him for an explanation. For the difference between the two orders, said Sackville, no tolerable reason had yet been given. But five officers would corroborate his version of his conversation with Fitzroy and Ligonier, neither of whom could corroborate the other, since both claimed that they had heard nothing which passed between Sackville and the other. It was much more probable that a man should be right about the words he had heard, than the man who related the words he imagined he had spoken. This was no reflection on the truthfulness of Ligonier and Fitzroy: their hurry and eagerness accounted for their lapse of memory.

What should Sackville have done? Verbal orders delivered by young staff officers were liable to error.

The distinctness or indistinctness of two young aides-de-camp might have decided the fate of an army . . . Entrusted with such a command as I bore . . . I determined to act upon more certain grounds, having already experienced too much of the confusion of orders sent by aides-de-camp.

Sackville therefore rode off in search of Ferdinand; but as he rode along Fitzroy continued to insist that his order was correct; and finding that the wood opened on to the heath sooner than he expected, Sackville realized that it was at least feasible for cavalry to move to the left. That being so, Fitzroy's order might be the one to follow (for Sackville had heard nothing about moving to the left from Ligonier) and in that case the British cavalry only were wanted. He sent Captain Smith back to fetch them, and rode on to find the prince.

And with that Sackville came to the final article of the charge, that he had advanced across the heath too slowly, and had halted unnecessarily and in disobedience of Ferdinand's orders. Those orders were to form eighteen squadrons in a single line and advance to sustain the infantry. Acting under such orders, every halt he made was in his judgement necessary. Here again he asked the court to enter into his situation. No one realized that the battle was won. If Ferdinand had meant to throw the cavalry into a pursuit he would have ordered the first cavalry which arrived to advance immediately, without waiting for the rest of the force. But Ferdinand said nothing about pursuit or even attack. His stated intention was to support the infantry with a formed body of horse. Sackville was to advance into a battle which was still supposed to be raging in full fury, ready to charge or be charged. The marching of cavalry in line was a matter of judgement; and those qualified to judge would know whether an extended line of squadrons could advance fast yet in good order.

I have ever found the greatest difficulty [he told the listening row of generals] in preserving intervals, or even the appearance of a line, without a constant attention to their motions, and stopping the first appearance of irregularity. To attack with velocity and vigour, you must advance without hurry and confusion. . . . Whoever attempts to bring squadrons after being blown or hurried to an attack will soon find that the vigour and weight so peculiar to the British cavalry will be lost. . . . These are the principles upon which I thought it proper to conduct a wing of cavalry.

This was an argument which the court was disposed to hear with sympathy, and on which it had already pressed two of the cavalry commanding officers called by the prosecution. Cholmondeley had questioned Sloper about it.

GENERAL CHOLMONDELEY: I have seen cavalry move so quick that they could not move at all afterwards. Some we had in training; and they are all gone now [*sic*]. Now I desire to know whether you mean by quickness, whether they must have gone a little trot, a full trot or a very hard gallop to have come in time to charge the enemy or support the infantry.

COLONEL SLOPER: I think a trot would have done it, and not a very fast trot; but had the front gone fast enough to have obliged the regiment I commanded to have galloped, I think it would have come up fit for business, and would have beat any three French squadrons it would have met with.

For that boast retribution lay in wait. Sloper's regiment was indeed to meet three French squadrons later that year at Warburg, and they overthrew it.

Lord George's Reply

Later on the day of Sloper's examination Colonel Pitt of Mordaunt's Dragoons was questioned on the same subject by Lord Albemarle.

LORD ALBEMARLE: You say Lord George marched slowly. I dare say as much as possible to avoid confusion. I therefore desire to know whether, at any time, whenever Lord George marched at the head of a line of cavalry, he did not march them more slowly in order to avoid confusion, I do not mean particularly that day.

COLONEL PITT: His Lordship always marched very slowly in all marches.

On the premise that he was required to bring up the cavalry in regular order, Sackville could defend the pace of his advance. Every halt had been necessary. It was alleged that he halted Granby's brigade after he knew that Ferdinand had sent Granby a direct order to hasten; but that charge was answered by Granby himself, who understood the order as being addressed to the whole line. Had the order detachèd Granby's brigade from his command, he would have been wrong to halt it. But it did not detach Granby, or relieve Sackville of his responsibility to execute the order.

Thus did the cavalry advance across the heath, eighteen squadrons being met at a full trot by Captain Smith as he returned from locating the infantry. Whether those were the infantry which Ferdinand intended Sackville to sustain, it was impossible to say, for the prince's orders had not been precise. But no other line of infantry could be seen, and in halting behind those eight battalions Sackville fulfilled his orders as exactly as it was possible to do.

Sackville closed his address with a general point about the evidence which was called by both sides: the uncertainty of conjectures about time and distance in a battle. His own witnesses would contradict many of the intervals of time hazarded by the witnesses for the prosecution; but already the Crown's evidence abounded in contradictions of time. He gave some instances, and could have extended them. At every phase of the battle the discrepancies between the witnesses' guesses at the passage of time are astonishing. No witness claimed to have looked at his watch; and Fitzroy neither carried a watch nor asked anyone the time during the battle.

NINE

THE JUDGEMENT

THE EVIDENCE FOR THE DEFENCE

This defence [said Sackville at the conclusion of his address] is intended not for the world, but for the information of the court. . . . All I desire at present is that mankind would suspend their judgments of my conduct till the evidence is closed. Then I trust in the goodness of my cause, which has supported me under a load of calumny, and emboldened me to ask for this trial, that under your favourable judgment the candid will with pleasure acquit me, the prejudiced be obliged to retract their rash censures, and that I shall once more be restored to the good opinion of my country, and of my sovereign.

With that Sackville handed the text of his address to the Judge-Advocate for the records of the court, and called his first witness. He proposed to deal with the prosecution's case phase by phase, recalling his witnesses as necessary, and to begin with the eve of the battle and the approach march in the early morning. His first witness was Colonel Hotham, already called by the prosecution and still playing his cards close to his chest. He was followed by the assistance quartermaster-general, Lieutenant Bisset of Brudenell's regiment. Then came three officers who did not conceal their warm support for Sackville. Of these perhaps the most effective was Captain Richard Lloyd, one of his aides-de-camp, who was cool-headed and explicit. Another aide-de-camp, Captain John Smith of the 3rd Guards, was the officer who had persuaded Sackville to let him fetch the British cavalry while he went in search of Ferdinand: he was to play a dramatic part in a later stage of the trial, and his career would suffer for it. The third of this trio, the camp

The Evidence for the Defence

quartermaster Lieutenant James Sutherland, is described in the
memoirs of Percival Stockdale as 'a blunt, honest man and a gallant
Caledonian'. Stockdale, who had served with Sutherland in the
Welch Fusiliers, used to breakfast with him at his lodgings during
the trial, and found Sutherland indignant at what he called the
malignant prejudices and false testimonies of the Crown's witnesses. It will be remembered that he had already provoked a
quarrel with Captain Ligonier on the day of the battle.

The last witness of the day was Colonel George Preston of the
Greys, who confirmed that his regiment had been saddled at one in
the morning. When the court rose no doubt remained that the
charges against Sackville in the hours preceding the battle were
unfounded. All the witnesses had also been asked what Sackville
called 'the general question', which he said he would have the
mortification of asking all who had seen him in order to answer
Sloper's aspersions. 'Did you observe anything in my looks,
manner or behaviour during that whole day, different from what it
was at any other time?' All replied with different degrees of
emphasis that they had not. 'I cannot say I did,' replied Hotham;
and 'No, really, I did not observe any alteration,' from Colonel
Preston. The junior officers spoke with warmth. 'Not in the least,'
replied Lloyd with characteristic succinctness and conviction.
'Indeed I did not,' said Sutherland. 'No indeed,' Jack Smith replied
with a touch of drama, 'I believe Lord George would have gone to
death that day had it been necessary.' Bisset was full and clear: 'The
orders Lord George gave me, and the conversation I had with him,
were the same as at any other time; the orders were distinctly given
as at other times.'

From this day a change began to take place in the public's
attitude. Sackville's address had been lucidly argued, and expressed
with force and elegance; and what had seemed indefensible was
being defended. 'In general the speech was much admired', James
Hamilton recorded; and Ferdinand's Germans sourly acknowl-
edged its effect. 'He opened with a great harangue,' Derenthal
reported to Ferdinand, 'one knows he is a better parliamentary
orator than a general.' So far Sackville had forgone to criticize the
prince, except obliquely by suggesting that he had not expected the

battle; but Derenthal heard that he had said afterwards that
Ferdinand had not been ready and that there had been confusion.
The king reassured him, however. He sympathized with
Derenthal's anxiety, but Sackville would not be allowed to attack
the prince – '*ich habe es ihm stopfen lassen*'. The Germans urged
Lord Barrington to put an end to what they regarded as abuses in
the conduct of the trial; in particular Sackville's division of his
defence into a succession of topics which allowed him to recall his
witnesses as often as he pleased.

The court resumed on the Monday; and before proceeding to the
next item of the charge Sackville explained that he wished to
establish the facts about the march of the artillery, and called two
battery commanders from the Celtic fringes, Captain Griffith
Williams and Captain Forbes Macbean. They were Woolwich-
trained professionals, clear-headed and expert judges of distance.
To bring up their gun-teams they had to know the ground, and
Williams was the only witness called by either side who had
thoroughly reconnoitred the long wood on the flank of the cavalry
before the battle, using a plan supplied by the army's artillery
commander, the Count of Schaumburg-Lippe. He thought that the
map before the court rather underestimated the size of the wood.

To uninformed spectators the two gunners did not seem to aid
the defence, for they showed that the artillery had marched
successfully through the wood. In fact, however, they proved that
the trees and undergrowth on the flank and front of the cavalry were
too thick for troops to pass except in a column of not more than four
abreast on a track; and that when Ferdinand's messenger the Duke
of Richmond came to bring on the artillery he knew nothing about
the interior of the wood and they ignored his directions. They
confirmed the confusion of the morning, and how Sackville had
ordered the guns forward like a man who knew his mind. Macbean
had not spoken to Sackville during the day, but Williams was able to
answer the 'general question' whether he had seen anything
unusual in Sackville's appearance. 'I neither did, nor suspect it,' he
replied, 'especially as I received my orders very distinct from Lord
George.'

Pursuing his plan to examine each stage of the charge in turn,

Sackville spent the next two days examining his witnesses about the orders brought by Winzingerode. The first was Colonel Hotham, called into court for the third time. He was exact and guarded as always, firmly refusing to assert anything of which he could not be sure. Sackville's purpose was to prove that Winzingerode had not ordered him to move to the left but to the front; that he took immediate measures to clear his line of advance; and that the interval between the coming of Winzingerode and Ligonier was only a few minutes. Hotham made a good beginning. Winzingerode, he said, had delivered an order that the cavalry should form a single line as a third line to sustain the infantry, and advance.

SACKVILLE: What did you understand by advancing?

HOTHAM: As I could not then know the position of the infantry, I could give no other interpretation to the word than the obvious meaning of it, to move forwards.

SACKVILLE: Did I make him repeat his order?

HOTHAM: You did.

SACKVILLE: Did he explain it in any other manner than by repeating his order?

HOTHAM: I did not hear him explain it.

The questioning then turned to Colonel Sloper's evidence.

SACKVILLE: Did you hear him [Winzingerode] speak to Captain Hugo in German?

HOTHAM: I did not.

SACKVILLE: Did you hear or see me speak to Colonel Sloper, or Colonel Sloper speak to me?

HOTHAM: Not that I remember.

The disinterested air of strict truth with which Hotham safeguarded his position was making him after all an excellent witness for the defence. The Judge-Advocate tried to probe his assertion that he had heard nothing pass between Sackville and Winzingerode except the bare orders.

JUDGE-ADVOCATE: Do you remember having heard any mention made either by Captain Winzingerode or Lord George Sackville of trees or a wood on the left?

The Judgement

HOTHAM: I have just said that I remember no conversation between them, but only what I have recited.

JUDGE-ADVOCATE: I did not mean to ask you the same question, only to see if I could bring anything to your memory.

HOTHAM: No.

JUDGE-ADVOCATE: Do you remember pointing to trees on the left by Captain Winzingerode or Lord George Sackville?

HOTHAM: I remember Captain Winzingerode had his sword in his hand; but I do not remember his pointing with it particularly one way or another.

The next witness, and the last of the day, was the Hanoverian aide-de-camp Captain Hugo, for whom Sackville's friend Colonel Irwin interpreted. Like Hotham, Hugo said that he had understood Winzingerode's order to mean an advance to the front, and denied that Winzingerode had spoken to him in German. He thought the interval between Winzingerode's departure and Ligonier's arrival was seven or eight minutes (Hotham had guessed between five and ten). To the general question about Sackville's appearance he replied: 'I did not in any manner perceive it.'

Wednesday, 19 March, the tenth day's sitting, saw Hugo's evidence completed, and he was followed by Bisset, Lloyd and Sackville's ordnance aide-de-camp Captain Joseph Broome, to confirm Winzingerode's orders and the measures taken to obey them. Broome, called for the first time, was asked the general question and replied: 'No, but on the contrary: the orders I heard given were very distinct, and to all appearance without the least sign of fear.'

Bisset's evidence produced a clash between Sackville and General Cholmondeley which gives us a glimpse of the atmosphere in which the proceedings were conducted. Court-martial procedure was loose, misunderstandings were easy, and tempers flared quickly; but both the prisoner and his judges were concerned to restore decency to the courtroom. Bisset had admitted that after seeing the enemy during a reconnaissance beyond the wood to the left, he had not reported the fact to Lord George. Why had he not discharged this indispensable duty, asked Cholmondeley. Bisset explained that he had gone away without Sackville's leave, to satisfy his own curiosity, and had thought that the French on the left were not of interest to Sackville, whose concern was the enemy in front. At this Lord George rose to protect his witness.

SACKVILLE: . . . Here is a gentleman, a subaltern in the army, doing his duty as assistant quartermaster-general. A question is put to him which is prefaced as a matter of blame . . . that may tend to accuse himself. What I say may be wrong . . . but I have felt too much what it is to suffer in character myself, not to be tender of other people's.

At this there was a very loud clapping from some of the audience, which the court reproved; and nettled by the applause, General Cholmondeley broke in again, spluttering angrily.

CHOLMONDELEY: Unable as I am to answer the noble lord in speaking, I cannot pretend to flowers of rhetoric or ornaments of speech; the homespun overflowings of an honest heart I will always express. But since the noble lord has been pleased to animadvert upon me, I have a right in my turn to animadvert likewise upon him. I do say that I have observed things upon this proceeding that I never observed in any proceeding before. The noble lord has begun by syllables, syllables have begot words; and at last I suppose they will grow up into sentences, that have been added to the witnesses' depositions, as in the case of Captain Hugo just now.

Captain Hugo said *hors de vue*; my lord did not like the expression; and when it was put down, it was *hors de front*. I did not take notice of that at the time. As to Mr. Bisset, I really think he lies under great obligations to me. His answers as to the distance that he saw that he went from the cavalry to the enemy's infantry with Captain Roy were very extraordinary. I thought that it would look very strange if this gentleman had gone abroad to his duty the next day, and Captain Roy had been called and had contradicted him. I tried to set him right. I put a question to him that was very clear – my questions always are very clear. He still did not comprehend me. I explained to him further: I illustrated it by shewing him this snuff-box and that standish, and then asked him what was the distance. He then understood me, and all was set right. Now I do say that Mr. Bisset is therefore obliged to me. And now, sir, I suppose I may go on.

SACKVILLE: Sir Charles Howard, though I am a prisoner these are things that I ought not to hear in silence. I have never done anything unbecoming the character of a man of honour; my standing here proves how highly I value that character; here and in every other place I shall always be ready to assert and maintain it. It had not only been unbecoming in me, but I should have been highly criminal, had I attempted to put words into the mouths of witnesses. I appeal to you, sir, to the Judge-Advocate, and to all present, that Captain Hugo used the words that are put down. He said at first that he did not know whether the Saxe-Gotha regiment was *hors de vue*; at the end of his sentence he himself explained this expression by *hors de front*. The first expression would have been ridiculous, for no man can suppose that a regiment could have gone away out of sight in two or three minutes; the second was plainly his thought, and I did not imagine there could be any harm in repeating it to the Judge-Advocate as the proper expression to be taken down.

Sir, I shall only say that my whole conduct during the trial has very little deserved such reflections: no man can accuse me of the least uncandid proceeding. I should be sorry to have the least difference with the court; I was very far from meaning to animadvert upon the General; I expressed myself, I am certain, with all possible moderation – I meant to do so, I should have been absurd to have done otherwise: I stand here a prisoner unfortunately, and that gentleman sits there as my judge.

SIR CHARLES HOWARD: My lord George, I am very sorry your lordship should have thrown any reflection on any member of the court.

SACKVILLE: Sir, I protest I don't know what I have said that could give the least cause for that. What is it that I have said so improper?

SIR CHARLES HOWARD: You said unfortunately that gentleman sat there as your judge.

SACKVILLE: I said, sir, that it was unfortunate for me to be a prisoner. I did not say that it was unfortunate for me that any gentleman here should be my judge.

LORD ROBERT BERTIE: I only understood my lord that it was unfortunate to be judged.

CHOLMONDELEY: I protest that I understood my lord in the same sense before he explained himself; and I am very sorry if any expression of mine should have given his lordship any umbrage. And as for Mr. Bisset I hope he is satisfied that I did not mean him any harm by my question; I have too much tenderness for witnesses to do such a thing. I protest upon my honour I would not ask a question that could hurt him in the least. I hope, sir, you are satisfied; and I hope, although the noble lord and I have both been a little warm, that he thinks no more of it. I am persuaded he must think I have too much honour, if I was not upon my oath, to do him any injury.

When one contemplates this exchange one cannot wonder that the king and his political servants were infuriated. Instead of hurrying the prisoner towards the required verdict, Sackville's judges were behaving like gentlemen conducting a dialogue with an equal, giving him elbow-room and striving patiently towards the truth. The court did however at this point ask Sackville to alter his method of conducting the case. Now that he had finished with the Winzingerode episode he was asked to depart from his plan of proceeding from item to item of the charge, and to examine each witness at large on the rest of the affair. He had asked the court's approval for his procedure at the outset, and now assented to their change of opinion. 'I shall obey the direction of the court,' he agreed; and from Tuesday, 20 March, the fifth day of the defence, he examined each witness on all that had happened from the arrival of Ligonier to the end of the battle. This was the point at which he intended the destruction of Colonel Sloper.

THE ATTACK ON SLOPER

During Sackville's examination of the Winzingerode episode his witnesses had thrown doubt on parts of Sloper's evidence, in particular on his version of Winzingerode's orders and whether he had heard them delivered. But the strongest witness against Sloper had still to be heard. Captain John Smith had not been present when Winzingerode delivered his orders, having ridden off beyond the right of the line to load his pistols. He returned when Sackville was ordering Captain Hugo to move the Saxe-Gotha regiment from his front. According to Sloper's story, Ligonier soon afterwards delivered another order to Sackville at the head of the right-hand squadron of Bland's, where Sloper heard him and spoke to him about Sackville's condition. Smith, however, told the court that he was standing at the right squadron of Bland's when he saw Ligonier approaching, having as Smith supposed delivered an order to Lord

The Judgement

George, who was at the head of the right squadron of the next regiment, the Inniskillings. He saw Sackville turn about, draw his sword, and order the line to march. The line moved forward, and Colonel Sloper asked Smith whether they were going to charge. It seemed so, Smith replied. 'I have not thrown away my picket poles,' said Sloper; 'do for God's sake tell Lord George the line is not ready, and beg him to stop one minute.' Smith rode over to Sackville and delivered the message, to which Lord George replied: 'Tell Colonel Sloper to throw them away as we move up, for I will not halt the line now it is in motion.' Smith returned to Sloper who, instead of obeying the order, halted the squadron and said, 'I shall do it quicker, never fear. I shall not stop a moment.'

If Smith was telling the truth, his story not only made Sloper look ridiculous for fussing about his unreadiness at a time when he claimed he was complaining of Sackville's delay, but showed that Sloper had not been near Sackville when Ligonier delivered his orders. It had already been affirmed by Sutherland, Lloyd, Bisset and Hotham that Sackville had not been near Sloper's post at the right-hand squadron of Bland's when Winzingerode delivered his orders; and later Lieutenant Whiteford, who had carried the standard in the centre of the right squadron of the Inniskillings, testified that he had seen Sackville near him as Ligonier rode up. If Smith was believed, Sloper's credibility was finally destroyed.

Here was a head-on collision of evidence. Someone appeared to be lying; and much of the subsequent heat in the proceedings was caused by the Judge-Advocate's efforts to re-establish Sloper's credibility.

Smith's evidence, which took the story through to the end of the battle, lasted the better part of three days, and at times the strain of the ordeal made him a nervous witness. Nevertheless he stood up to the questioning with spirit.

JUDGE-ADVOCATE: Can a regiment of dragoons attack with their picket poles on, without any material disadvantage?
SMITH: Yes, they can do it.
JUDGE-ADVOCATE: Without any material disadvantage?
SMITH: I think a piece of wood stuck in a man's bucket is an inconvenience. . . .

JUDGE-ADVOCATE: Did any of the enemy's shot come near the British cavalry?

SMITH: Yes.

JUDGE-ADVOCATE: Did you ever say since the battle that Lord George Sackville was apprehensive of the shot, and wished to be moved?

SMITH: I have no sort of objection to answering that question, but it may bring on many more of the same kind; I shall tell all the conversation I've had about it.

JUDGE-ADVOCATE: It is necessary to ask it, as it affects his evidence. It is a question I'm unwilling to ask: if I thought there was anything improper in it, I would retract it.

LORD GEORGE SACKVILLE (*to the Judge-Advocate*): Do you mean by apprehensive that I was afraid of the shot?

JUDGE-ADVOCATE: He will explain that.

SMITH: If I answer the question at all, I must say what passed between my Lord George and me, which was the foundation of it.

(*Question repeated.*)

SMITH: Yes, I have very often, and my Lord George conveyed to me at the time that he did not like being halted there at all. I think I remember him making use of the words, being put in a hole there; I mean the first ground where we halted.

JUDGE-ADVOCATE: Nobody is more desirous of having this explained than I am. In what sense did you use the words the Lord George was apprehensive of the shot?

SMITH: The line was brought forward upon my explaining the ground to be better, and as soon as my Lord saw the shot take place he remarked to me, the line was within shot. I think at the time he pointed forwards and said I hope they will not keep us here long.

SACKVILLE: I should be sorry this should go away in this manner, therefore beg leave to ask a question. What do you mean by the word apprehensive, a personal apprehension in regard to myself, or apprehension that that was a bad position for the cavalry?

SMITH: The latter undoubtedly.

SACKVILLE: You say I pointed forwards. Now I ask you whether, if our position had been forwarder, we must not still have been more within shot?

SMITH: We should not only have been nearer, but we should have been within sight of the enemy's batteries, which we were not then. They were all chance shot.

SACKVILLE: Had we gone forward about as far as the windmill towards

The Judgement

the battery where you mean, should we not then have been out of what I
called the hole, and have had ground to have acted upon?
SMITH: Yes.
SACKVILLE: I thank the court for this indulgence, in letting me ask these
questions at this time.

Smith's nervousness made him a telling witness on the delivery
of Fitzroy's orders, as he related how the two aides-de-camp
disputed their orders. He came close enough to hear Sackville say:
'Why, sir, Mr. Ligonier says the whole. Don't be in a hurry,
Fitzroy.'

'My lord,' Smith said he heard Fitzroy reply, 'we bring the same
order.'

It is extremely difficult [Smith continued] to say what followed. There
were several speaking together, I could not hear them; I felt distressed
myself, and therefore if what I say should appear to be unconnected, it is
not my fault: I recollect seeing Captain Ligonier speak at that instant, but I
cannot upon my oath say what the words were. My Lord George appeared
to me to be angry with Mr. Fitzroy. I heard him say to them, I wish you
would agree what your orders are, I am ready to obey either. Captain
Fitzroy appeared to me to be the most pressing in his manner; and I saw
that he prevailed so much upon Lord George by his eagernesss that he
asked Captain Fitzroy which way he would have him go, and Captain
Fitzroy pointed to the rear, towards our left. I cannot say what the words
were; something about the way runs in my memory. . . .

Three witnesses subsequently supported Smith's account of the
dispute between Fitzroy and Ligonier: Lloyd, Bisset and the
laconic Sutherland, Hotham having gone off to the second line
when Sackville ordered the advance. Lloyd was a particularly
impressive witness, cool, brief and firm under cross-examination.
Asked by the court, he gave his opinion that the route Sackville
would have followed by the windmill was much the shortest way to
join the infantry, and that the cavalry could have intervened in the
battle if they had not been halted by Fitzroy. In the audience young
Thomas Cowper, who had hitherto been prepossessed against the
prisoner, reported that Lloyd 'gave a very clear and distinct
evidence much in Lord George Sackville's favour'.

'Our court martial goes on very slowly,' wrote Newcastle at the end of Smith's evidence, 'but the evidence against Lord George is strong, beyond measure.' Newcastle was whistling in the dark to keep his spirits up, for the case had shifted profoundly in Sackville's favour, as Horace Walpole reported to his friend Horace Mann in Florence.

The colour of it is more favourable for him that it looked at first. Prince Ferdinand's narrative has proved to set out with a heap of lies. There is an old gentleman of the same family who has spared no indecency to give weight to them. . . . Lord Charles Hay's court martial is dissolved by the death of one of its members – and as no German interest is concerned to ruin *him*, it probably will not be resumed.

The Judge-Advocate, however, did not intend to let the defence discredit one of his major witnesses without a fight. Sloper himself had delivered a letter to the court demanding that some of the prosecution's witnesses should be re-examined to confirm his evidence; and Gould not only intended to do this but also to call fresh witnesses. The opportunity to raise the matter came on 25 March with the expiry of the annual Mutiny Act. The trial had outrun its expected time, because of the week's delay caused by the referral to the judges and the unexpected depth of Sackville's defence, and with the Mutiny Act the authority of the court expired. A new court would have to be constituted under a fresh warrant.

This meant that the whole proceedings of the trial were invalidated and a new trial would begin. The prosecution would be entitled to re-examine its witnesses and to produce new witnesses in support of the charge, this time with full knowledge of the nature of the defence. This would have been a monstrous affront to natural justice; but Gould was willing to bargain. If the prisoner agreed, instead of examining all the witnesses again the previous evidence would be read out in court and confirmed by the witnesses on oath, which would save many days of hearings. In return for this agreement, the prosecutor would call no new witnesses to support the charge.

But from this offer the Judge-Advocate excepted Colonel Sloper's evidence. His veracity had been impeached, and to reestablish it Gould informed the court that he intended to reexamine witnesses and call new ones. Sloper's evidence had been challenged on three counts: that Sackville's manner and appearance had not been as he described it; that he had cooked up his story after Sackville had been censured in general orders; and that Sackville had not been at the right of Bland's and could not have been addressed by Sloper. On these counts the Judge-Advocate intended to call new evidence.

This was the first Lord George had heard of the proposals. He had not received copies of the law officers' opinions on the legality of the procedure, which the Judge-Advocate had only received that morning, and he was at a loss how to reply.

I am very unfit to speak on opinions of this sort which are matters of law without the least warning [he protested]. What occurs to me at present is this, that it is so contradictory to what I hear is law, so contradictory to common sense, that it surprises me. . . . This is fishing out evidence to throw a slur upon my character. . . . I am talking perhaps very unlearnedly. If I had had time, I might have had opinions also.

Such is the record of the court; but according to a member of the audience Sackville went further, telling the Judge-Advocate that if he had been a soldier he should have expected honour from him; if a lawyer justice; but that as he was neither, he expected nothing. The official record shows Gould replying mildly that he had not expected to be attacked for want of candour. Sackville agreed to the reading of the evidence, and was promised a copy of the law officers' opinion. How far the Judge-Advocate would be allowed to call fresh evidence was not made clear; nor was it firmly established whether Lord George would be allowed to reply to it.

The rest of the day and part of the next was spent in reading over the evidence, and then the defence resumed its examination of witnesses, ranging from the order of Ligonier and Fitzroy to the halt behind the infantry and the close of the battle. Sackville wound up his case with a final appearance by Hugo and Hotham; and on

Saturday, 29 March, the eighteenth day of the trial and the tenth of the defence, the cross-examination of Hotham completed Sackville's evidence.

'People', wrote the poet Thomas Gray, 'wonder at (and some there are that celebrate) his dexterity, his easy elocution, and unembarrassed manner.' One who did not celebrate Sackville's skill was Captain Derenthal, whose prolonged attendance at the court had been futile and who was at last released and allowed to return to duty in Germany. He complained bitterly at the delays: the judges who had allowed Smith to talk for twenty hours, and the Mutiny Act which had caused the court's authority to expire. 'Perhaps a country can have too many laws –' he grumbled, 'they are certainly very inconvenient here. It is a country with many peculiarities, and one has to be born here not to tire of them.' The Duke of Newcastle looked forward to a satisfactory conclusion, but not quite so confidently as he had at the outset. 'The famous court martial will finish next week, and I hope as honest men and men of honour should do.'

THE CLOSING SPEECHES

But the final battle of the courtroom was still to be fought. As soon as Sackville concluded his case, he inquired what new evidence the prosecutor wished to call, and asked that it should be heard immediately so that he could take it into account in his final address. An altercation then broke out about whether the fresh evidence should be heard before or after his concluding address. 'I am frightened every time I talk of law,' said Sackville; and the Judge-Advocate replied: 'I should be glad his lordship would not talk of law, I am not a military person, I do not really see why that should be thrown out, I have not the honour of wearing a military garb; but I hope I have endeavoured to conduct the prosecution with tenderness and candour.'

Lord George proceeded to argue that he had not impeached Sloper's veracity but only challenged his facts, and that therefore the Judge-Advocate had no right to call fresh evidence at this stage of the trial. He slashed angrily at Gould.

The Judgement

As to the Judge-Advocate I wish, as he observed, he either wore a military garb, or were a person of such eminence and reputation in the profession of the law, as might entitle him to lay down the rules and practice of the courts of justice in such a manner as the prisoner might have no doubt of the truth of what was asserted to be law. I wish one of the judges of England was to sit here, the prisoner then would be certain of being tried by the real laws of this land, and not by laws made occasionally for him. . . . If there is a point of law, you refer to the Judge-Advocate, why? because you don't know the law, not because he does. . . . Other courts never determine in any matter without the advantage of being informed of what can be offered on both sides. This court, ignorant themselves of a matter of law, can only receive their information from the prosecutor.

This attack may have been pertinent to the state of the military courts, but its personal acrimony was not deserved by Gould, though the aspersion on Lord George's courage was enough to excuse his anger. He softened his attack by adding, 'I have a great respect for Mr. Gould's character as Judge-Advocate, and think he sits there and executes his office as ably as any man I ever saw in his place.'

But the dispute continued, on the question whether Sloper's veracity had been impeached. At some point in the debate a remark of Sackville's was greeted with a loud clap in the audience which the court resented. 'In this court', Sackville let fly, 'a prisoner has an additional security. He is sure their honour will bind them, if the oath did not. Standing under that security I defy the Prosecution. Let Colonel Sloper stand forth from a witness become the agent of a prosecution.'

'I hope', the Judge-Advocate replied, 'the witnesses brought in support of the prosecution will also have the protection of the court. To hear of a witness turning into an agent for the prosecution is not right.'

Sackville did not object to the hearing of additional evidence on what the Judge-Advocate called the *alibi*: the contention that Sloper could not have talked to Sackville because he was elsewhere. On the other issues the president cleared the court for an hour and a half of discussion. It was resolved not to admit any new witnesses to Sackville's appearance and manner, because it might operate in support of the charge; but to admit evidence to prove that Sloper had told his story immediately after the battle. The additional evidence on the alibi would be called after Sackville had addressed the court; the evidence that Sloper had told his story before he read the order of censure would be called at once.

Three witnesses were called on that point. Lord Granby's evidence was brief. Sloper had told him a day or two after the battle that three officers had come with orders to march and form a third line to support the infantry, 'something to that purpose'; that Sackville did not obey them, 'something to that purpose'; 'to the best of my knowledge he said Lord George was in a hurry, and confused, something to that purpose, I don't remember the exact words'. But Granby did not know whether the conversation had taken place before or after Ferdinand's order of censure.

Granby obviously hated his role as a witness, and his answers did not help the prosecution. Colonel Harvey was more definite, that Sloper had told him his story an hour or more before the Inniskillings received Ferdinand's order of the day. Ligonier asserted positively that he had delivered his orders in front of the right squadron of Bland's; and that he spoke to Sloper, who leaned on his arm, urged him to repeat his order, and said 'you see the condition he is in'. 'I answered, yes,' Ligonier added.

SACKVILLE: In what sense do you mean the word condition: you see the condition he is in?

JUDGE-ADVOCATE: My lord, it is my duty to inform you that the answer to that question may make against you.

LIGONIER: That Lord George was perplexed, I cannot say why, confused. Colonel Fitzroy had delivered his order for the British cavalry to advance before this conversation passed between Colonel Sloper and me.

SACKVILLE: Three orders were subsisting.

JUDGE-ADVOCATE: My lord, you must not observe upon the evidence.

SACKVILLE: Do you apprehend that confusion meant a perplexity in orders, what did Colonel Sloper mean by confusion?

LIGONIER: He really did not explain what he meant. He observed he was confused, I do not know from what motive he judged.

The day's hearing was now at an end, and the court adjourned till the following Wednesday, four days off, to allow Sackville time to marshal his evidence and prepare his closing address.

'Lord George Sackville, is your lordship ready with your defence?'

Sackville rose to read the statement which would bring together a fortnight's evidence for the defence. He thanked the court for its patient attention through the long and tedious examination of witnesses, and proceeded to a narrative of his conduct in the battle, placing each decision in its context. His defence, thought the ingenuous Thomas Cowper, 'was artfully and very judiciously put together'.

I have shown [Lord George concluded at the end of this narrative] that in the first part of the day I was not deficient in diligence or activity, that I made every preparation for executing Captain Winzingerode's order that a few minutes would permit; that I instantly obeyed Captain Ligonier; that upon Colonel Fitzroy's order, and the dispute between Captain Ligonier and him, I was justified in going to the prince. The order I there received from his Serene Highness did not determine either of them to be right; the Prince's order I immediately put into execution.

He knew of no circumstances in which, with the information he had at the time, he could have acted differently. But with the information he had since received, he thought he could have done much more service if he had disregarded Fitzroy's order and marched the cavalry forward by the windmill. And now he borrowed a phrase of censure from Ferdinand's general order and turned it to his own advantage. 'I should then have fallen upon the flank of the enemy, and I make no doubt but the British cavalry would have shared with the infantry the glory of the day. And as mistakes were then fortunate, *the victory might then have been rendered more brilliant and complete.*'

Thus Sackville laid his conduct before his judges.

What opinion you may form of my abilities as an officer I do not presume to say. That is now an object of little importance to me, and his Majesty is the best judge of the merits of his officers. But I am persuaded that you will with pleasure on this occasion exercise the amiable part of your jurisdiction, and acquit me of the present charge of disobedience.

The speech, it was reported to Newcastle, made a visible impression on the court in Sackville's favour. 'It was sensible, not void of elegance, and though not eloquent, was moving.' But the judges had still to hear the Judge-Advocate's reply; and before he addressed the court he called five witnesses to prove that Sloper had been present when Ligonier delivered his orders. First came the two squadron leaders of the Inniskillings, but neither was conclusive. Major Marriot had seen Ligonier pass the front of his squadron and ride on towards Bland's. He had then ridden over to the right-hand squadron of the Inniskillings to ask permission to throw away his picket poles, and did not see Lord George there at that instant: when he did see him there, he did not see Ligonier with him. Major Hepburn had not seen Ligonier delivering his orders in front of the right squadron of the Inniskillings, but could not have been sure of doing so as he was frequently in the rear of his squadron; he had seen Ligonier returning from Bland's, but not going to Bland's. When the line advanced he thought he had given the order to advance to his own squadron, but could not be sure whether he was in the front or the rear at the time.

Such vague and negative evidence was little help; and Ligonier, who followed them, was hardly more positive. He did not remember Captain Smith delivering Colonel Sloper's message about picket poles to Sackville, or seeing Captain Smith while he was with Lord George. Again the evidence was negative. The final witness of the day was Cornet Erle of Bland's Dragoon Guards. He had been posted in the right-hand squadron of his regiment, and had seen Sackville in front of his squadron and Ligonier galloping up to him, with Sloper near by. The regiment had not stopped to throw away its picket poles, but was in motion in front; he did not remember seeing Captain Smith. Erle confessed, however, that he was not near enough to hear or even see Sackville and Ligonier talking, or to hear any orders Sloper might have received.* Nor did he remember whether Sackville was at the head of Bland's when the line advanced.

---

*This is made clear in the Sackville version of the *Trial*: the official *Proceedings* are obscure.

The Judgement

The final day of the trial came at last on Thursday, 3 April, the twentieth day of the sittings. One last witness made a momentary appearance. Colonel Johnston of the Blues was asked whether he had seen Ligonier when he brought his orders; confirmed that he had seen him pass and had called out to him; affirmed that he saw him go on to Bland's. This was at least positive, but the right of Bland's was five squadrons away from the Blues, and it would have carried more weight if a witness who was nearer could have been found to affirm how far Ligonier had gone.

Now came the final speech of the Judge-Advocate. Almost at once he launched into a defence of Colonel Sloper's credibility. This witnesses's character and reputation, he said, had been treated in a manner which decency would hardly have admitted; and if he became heated under cross-examination it was because he had been threatened with equal warmth by Sackville. The main attack on Sloper's truthfulness, the question whether Ligonier had delivered his order in front of Bland's where Sloper could hear them, had now been fully answered, Gould asserted. As for the other points with which Sackville had tried to discredit him, no evidence had been brought forward that he had asserted outside the court that Winzingerode had spoken to Hugo in German. If Sloper could not remember which other officers were present, nor could Sackville's witnesses. And if the defence witnesses had not heard Sloper speak to Sackville after Winzingerode's departure, that might be because they had been sent off on various missions to prepare for an advance. The argument that Sloper was displaying malice by repeating in court what he had said elsewhere could be used against any witness who had expressed his views before the trial. Nor could Sloper have been influenced by Ferdinand's order of censure, for he had expressed his views before it reached him. One witness or another had lied in the course of the proceedings, and which it had been was submitted to the judgement of the court.

Turning to the particulars of the charge, the Judge-Advocate withdrew the allegation that Sackville had been late at his post. The period within which Lord George was answerable for loss of time therefore began with the delivery of Captain Winzingerode's orders; and if these had been obeyed immediately the perplexity over the difference between the orders brought by Fitzroy and Ligonier need never have arisen. That Winzingerode had indicated that the cavalry were to pass through the trees to the left was corroborated by Sloper and by Granby (Gould did not remind the court that Granby had spoken to Winzingerode separately and had not heard the order delivered to Sackville). Against these positive declarations the defence could produce only the statements of Hotham, Hugo and Bisset that they did *not* hear the trees or the left mentioned. This negative evidence, said the Judge-Advocate, was not enough to set aside two witnesses who swore expressly to the point.

To execute the order in the manner intended there was only one obstacle, the artillery which some witnesses said was still passing on the left; but if indeed it was there it could have been halted immediately and the cavalry could have passed through it in five minutes. Towards the front, the defence maintained that it took more than five minutes to move the Saxe-Gotha regiment; but he was assured by soldiers that it could have been done in two. The estimated time between the delivery of Winzingerode's order and the march of the cavalry on Ligonier's arrival varied from the two minutes of Captain Smith to the fifteen of Sloper; but the balance of evidence suggested that Sackville took longer to move than was necessary to clear the Saxe-Gotha regiment. The Judge-Advocate did not mention the enemy in Hahlen as a possible hindrance to an advance.

When Ligonier arrived (the Judge-Advocate went on) both he and Colonel Sloper declared that his order as delivered was to move to the left; but even if Lord George misunderstood and the misunderstanding persisted after Fitzroy's arrival, the urgency of the orders was not in doubt, and it was proper to obey one or the other, rather than hesitate obeying neither. The time lost by this hesitation could reasonably be put at a quarter of an hour. If Sackville had immediately ordered the cavalry (or the British cavalry) to move while he sent to Ferdinand or even went himself, there would have been no cause for blame.

Finally the Judge-Advocate came to the advance across the heath. Sackville had said that the pace at which he led the line was a matter for judgement. The court would also exercise its judgement, and decide how far the discretion vested in the cavalry commander had been properly exercised. If there had been any unjustifiable delay, they would consider it a breach of the orders under which Sackville was acting. In particular, when Sackville halted the second line after Lord Granby had received orders to press on, he took that decision upon himself at his peril.

The Judge-Advocate concluded by giving his final directions to the court. He set aside all question of the effect of disobedience on the battle; and laid Sackville open to the verdict of guilty if he were found not to have obeyed his orders with all practicable speed at every moment of this complicated sequence of events and clashing personalities.

If any of the orders brought by Captain Winzingerode, Captain Ligonier or Colonel Fitzroy appear not to have been obeyed, with all the expedition which under the several circumstances now before you in evidence shall appear to have been practicable; or if any blameable delay was afterwards made in the march . . . I submit you will be under the disagreeable necessity of finding his lordship guilty.

The net was wide and the mesh was small. Unless a clear distinction was maintained by the court between obedience and judgement, it would be difficult not to find Sackville guilty on these terms. But the Judge-Advocate added a significant rider. 'In your judgement you will have regard to the degree of the offence, with respect to the proportion and the motive of the delay.' Here was a clear direction to the court that the offence was not an absolute one; that the court was entitled to consider its degree; and that on their views of the seriousness of the offence their sentence should depend.

The Judge-Advocate's reply should have closed the proceedings. But additional evidence had been introduced after Sackville's final address, and Sackville understood that the court had agreed to allow him to make some final remarks. In fact the matter had been left unsettled, and the president demurred. It was to General Cholmondeley, with whom Sackville had had an angry collision, that he owed yet one more indulgence from the court. 'I really did understand that there had been such a promise,' Cholmondeley interjected; 'if my lord enters too particularly into it, the court may stop him.'

Sackville was allowed to proceed with his remarks, which he confined to the additional evidence called by the prosecution on his position when Ligonier delivered his order. It was difficult, he said, to fix with precision the part of a line where a general might have stood while he received an order; but it was easy to establish whether he was at the extremity or not. His witnesses had not attempted to be positive where he was, but only that he was not at the right of Bland's, the extremity of the line. Four witnesses who were with him and heard the order delivered all believed that he was somewhere about the right of the Inniskillings or, as Colonel Hotham said, the left of Bland's. Against this evidence the only contradiction came from Ligonier, who could well have been mistaken in the hurry of his coming, and Sloper, whose evidence Sackville rejected. None of the prosecution's additional witnesses carried weight against his own witnesses. The two majors of the Inniskillings spoke from imperfect memory, and neither saw Ligonier deliver his order. Colonel Johnston proved nothing except that he had seen Ligonier pass along the front of the Blues. And Cornet Erle remembered indistinctly and was unable to answer the crucial question where Sackville had been when the line advanced.

With a final appeal to the court to look on the Judge-Advocate's summing up as that of a prosecutor and not a judge, and an assertion of the truthfulness of his witnesses, who had stood up in an unfashionable cause and had nothing to gain by falsehood, Sackville brought the proceedings to a close. He thanked the court for its patience, and relied on its honour. 'If I am guilty, let me be declared so: if I am not guilty, let the court shew by their sentence that they will with pleasure protect the innocent.'

UNFIT TO SERVE

The final reports from the courtroom were such as to warm the hearts of the king's servants. The Judge-Advocate's reply had been 'masterly and much to the purpose . . . had made a great impression on the audience'. 'I have heard great encomiums on the Judge-Advocate,' Lord Barrington reported to Newcastle. 'It affected Mr. Wedderburn greatly while he delivered it, and he left the court with the most visible signs of uneasiness in his countenance.'

Among the affected, needless to say, was young Thomas Cowper, whose opinion veered between each speaker in turn. The Judge-Advocate's reply, he wrote, 'very concisely and very fully, in thirty-five minutes . . . confuted every article in Lord George's argument'. But Sackville's final remarks to the court struck him as 'pathetic and moving'. 'It would be vain for me to attempt to convey to you an idea of this Lord's eloquence, all I can say is that it surpasses anything that ever I heard.'

Gould's reply was certainly concise and to the point; but it may have made a less profound impression on the members of the court than on the politicians and the audience. He 'confuted' Lord George because he had the last word – or almost the last, for Lord George's final remarks on the additional evidence showed that he still had plenty of ammunition. The Judge-Advocate's perspective was that of a civilian and a lawyer. No breath of the battlefield entered his address. From his lucid arguments he had banished the fog of uncertainty, the milling staff officers, the clouded memories of men with many things to attend to. He moved twenty-four squadrons of cavalry through woodland with the ease of a piece on a chessboard. He obscured the distinction between obedience and judgement, laying down confidently what a commander ought to do in case of doubt. But the generals on the court would not do this. They had handled troops, and would remember that a battlefield was not like a committee room: that was why a court martial was a court of honour and equity.

When they were ready to give their verdict, it would be collected by the Judge-Advocate beginning with the most junior member; and those who found the prisoner guilty would pass sentence, subject to the mitigation of those who found him not guilty. No sentence of death would be passed unless two-thirds of the court concurred. And before the sentence was published the proceedings

had to be reported to the king and his pleasure taken. To fair-copy
the record for the king would take a week.

In this interval rumour and speculation throve. The king vowed
that he did not know the verdict but was happy about it, and
Newcastle suspected that he *did* know it. Lord Ligonier, the
commander-in-chief, assured the king that he too was in the dark,
but suspected that the sentence was death. Newcastle found that
death was the common guess in London, and hoped it was wrong
for the typical reason that 'it will embarrass extremely'. In the
meantime the king was considering how to retaliate against
Sackville's witnesses, and as an intermediate measure Lord Granby
was directed to remove the offending officers from the staff and
return them to their regiments to keep them out of Ferdinand's
way.

One thing must have been clear to the judges: that no
recommendation to mercy would avail. Byng's judges, with no
alternative to the death sentence, had unanimously recommended
mercy, and their 'hardened brute' of a sovereign had refused it. His
German feelings and his whole conduct since the battle made it
clear that he was determined to secure a conviction and to execute
the harshest sentence. Yet an acquittal would be embarrassing,
both for relations with the German generalissimo and for the royal
prerogative which had dismissed Sackville without reasons given.
The verdict was guilty.

On the day when Lord Barrington reported the sentence to the
king, one of his majesty's judges reported on a forger who was due
to be hanged in Sussex on 19 April. His petition for the royal mercy
was supported by many local people, but the trial judge reported
that he had seen nothing to make the prisoner an object of
clemency. On 16 April, the day when the king confirmed the
sentence on Sackville, Lord Ferrers was brought from the Tower in
his own carriage to be tried by his peers for murder. He too would
go to the gallows, his plea of insanity talked down by Charles Yorke.
The common law was a harsh and merciless world, for the great as
well as the humble.

But common law did not bind the court which tried Lord George
Sackville, nor had the common-law judges pronounced on the

The Judgement

court's powers of sentence. With a free hand it proceeded to its decision, of which Sackville learned in a letter from the Judge-Advocate informing him that the king had confirmed the sentence. The court's verdict found him guilty of having disobeyed Prince Ferdinand of Brunswick. Its sentence was recorded in these remarkable words:

It is the further opinion of this Court, that the said Lord George Sackville is, and he is hereby adjudged, unfit to serve his Majesty in any military capacity whatever.

With that Charles Gould informed Sackville that he was his lordship's most humble and most obedient servant.

TEN

THE ELUSIVE TRUTH

THE KING'S REVENGE

The sonorous words echoed down the centuries and reverberated off Sackville's later eminence, ringing with the irony that a man so judged should have gone on to conduct a world war. Yet though the sentence sounds damning, it was really so lenient that the ministry was furious. 'The most abominable and most surprising sentence,' Newcastle bubbled; 'I can't call it an acquittal though very near it.' The court had done the minimum that was necessary to save the king's face, and did no more than affirm that his dismissal of Sackville had been justified. A rumour was reported by Thomas Gray that nine of the judges had voted for death; but he added, 'I do not affirm this.' Nor is it credible. The atmosphere of the court makes it inconceivable that the trial could have led to Sackville's execution, and if a nominal death sentence had been passed the king could not have been trusted to commute it. And Sackville was guilty of nothing which warranted even the gesture of a capital sentence. 'You will have regard to the degree of the offence,' the Judge-Advocate had charged the court; and the court did just that.

Nor was the sentence such as would have been passed as a lesser alternative to death. Sackville himself did not believe that a death sentence had been discussed; but since the judges had complaisantly found him guilty, he was surprised that the sentence was phrased so mildly. He was told that the more stringent members of the court had wished to declare him 'incapable' of serving, but had been overruled by the majority in favour of the milder and unusual word 'unfit'.

Still, it seemed safe at last for Newcastle to kick the fallen general. He had professed to pity him after Minden; but now he paraded his loyalty to Ferdinand and the German cause by huffing to Granby about the inadequacy of the 'very extraordinary sentence . . . so short of what we had reason to expect, and I may say of the merits of the question'. 'However,' he wrote to the like-thinking Sir Joseph Yorke, 'the King and Prince Ferdinand are fully justified, and consequently everything they had done approved.' Without delay a copy of the sentence was forwarded to Ferdinand.

The next step, inevitable and perhaps proper, was to remove the disgraced soldier from the Privy Council, and at the next meeting the king called for the council book and ordered his name to be struck from the list of Privy Councillors. He was also struck off the Irish Privy Council in Dublin, and these abasements were duly reported in the *London Gazette*. For the angry king, however, that was still not enough, and the next blow made even some of the ministers wince. He still had some further power to damage Sackville, and if he could not have his blood he could at least add ignominy to the sentence. He gave way, said Horace Walpole, to 'the ungenerous impulse of loading it with every insult in his power'. The king ordered the sentence to be published in army orders, written into the order book of every regiment in the army, and read out on parade, the last an unprecedented gesture except at a flogging or an execution. The Secretary at War Lord Barrington disliked the suggestion; but Lord Ligonier approved, old rogue that he was, and was glad to gratify his royal master. His nephew and heir had been involved in the case, and he paused in his quest for nymphets to compose what Walpole rightly called 'some barbarous additions to the sentence'. And so the sentence on Lord George Sackville was read out to every British regiment, with the following embellishment which was published in the *Gazette* and passed on to Ferdinand for his further gratification:

It is his Majesty's pleasure that the above sentence be given out in public orders; that officers being convinced that neither high birth nor great employment can shelter offences of such a nature; and that, seeing they are subject to censures much worse than death to a man who had any sense of honour, they may avoid the fatal consequences arising from disobedience of orders.

'Humming words indeed,' exclaimed Newcastle. 'Undoubtedly Ligonier composed this magnificent sentence,' the field-marshal's biographer declares. Magnificent it was; and the Augustan insults with which the executive loaded the disgraced Sackville are quoted by historians with tireless admiration, as though blows from officialdom confirmed his guilt. Imperialist historians like Sir John Fortescue, the historian of the British army, and the naval historian Sir Julian Corbett, recoiled from Sackville as a military failure and were glad to use him as a scapegoat for the loss of America; and liberals, disapproving of his share in the attempt to coerce the Americans, were happy to blacken his character.

Yet, as Sackville said many years later when his enemies wheeled out the words of censure on his admission to the House of Lords, the comment annexed by the executive formed no part of his sentence and he was not bound to submit to it. And from the Woolsack the keeper of the king's conscience stepped down to declare that the Crown had acted unjustly and that nothing in the charge or sentence justified the stigma. So spoke a Lord Chancellor under another sovereign. He pronounced as a lawyer; but how shall we, who do not judge as lawyers, pronounce on Sackville's crime?

No motive for disobedience was established at the trial. Of physical fear there was no evidence except Sloper's. All the witnesses show that, till Ligonier arrived, Sackville behaved as usual and gave his orders clearly, though there was as much long-range cannon-fire then as later. When he prepared to execute Winzingerode's orders he intended to advance straight into the fire of the enemy's batteries rather than move off to a flank behind the allied infantry. Unless he and his staff were lying about how they understood the orders, his decision to advance was rational; and even if he had heard Winzingerode and Ligonier ordering him to move to the left, he had grounds to question them. The allied army had been surprised by the enemy; and he knew nothing of the army commander's planned response except that he had been placed in command of the cavalry force which conventionally held the right flank of the line of battle, and that he was to be guided to the windmill at Hahlen where he could expect to find the French

cavalry opposite him in superior numbers. Unexpectedly he was
halted short of his forming-up position by the enemy in Hahlen;
and while he waited for the pickets to clear the village he was
considering the message he had received from Ferdinand that the
infantry might be extended across his front. A movement to his left
through a disruptive belt of woodland made little sense, since the
shortest and quickest route to support the infantry was straight
forward by the windmill and round the head of the woods into the
plain. Winzingerode, who had come from the left, was probably not
even aware of this, and certainly knew little about the enemy's
dispositions, as he admitted in court. But such considerations
probably weighed little with Sackville. When Winzingerode and
Ligonier brought orders to advance and support the infantry, these
orders fell naturally into the pattern he expected, and his mind
concentrated on executing them. If Winzingerode or Ligonier
explained distinctly and audibly that he was to move to the left, he
either did not hear or was functionally deaf to their explanations.
But it is not certain that either of them did so.

Then came Fitzroy, with his conflicting order that only the
British cavalry was to move; and Sackville understood for the first
time that he was to move to the left. It was now that Sloper referred
to his 'condition', by which he explained to the court that he had
meant 'alarmed to a very great degree' and 'in the utmost
confusion'. This was taken by some of the audience to mean that
Sackville was afraid. Sackville sought to interpret Sloper as
meaning that he showed, not physical fear, but anxiety because he
was perplexed; and he succeeded in drawing this interpretation of
Sloper's meaning from Ligonier. One might argue that Ligonier
said this from a decent reluctance to impute cowardice; but
Derenthal, retailing Sloper's evidence to Ferdinand with no motive
for sparing the prisoner, wrote merely that Sloper, 'very strong and
personal', had said that Sackville had been confused and had not
known what he was doing.

That Sackville was confused is possible. For the first time in his
life he was commanding a major force in battle, with a critical
decision suddenly thrust on him. In a short space of time he had
received three conflicting orders, and could not even discover

which of them was the latest. One order directed him to advance; another to divide his force in face of the superior French cavalry; and a third order apparently required him to break the army's order of battle, uncover the flank, and march most of his force through woodland towards the centre and rear of the army. This was the moment which would throw him into perplexity; and other witnesses could have been called to testify to his confusion. It is likely indeed that he was confused. His doubts may have been increased by lack of confidence in Ferdinand, for which he had some reason; and his temperament may have predisposed him to receive Ferdinand's orders with contempt or misunderstanding. That is not to say that he deliberately disobeyed his orders, but only that he felt it necessary to be sure of them. His sending back Captain Smith to bring on the British cavalry while he was on his way to Ferdinand strongly suggests a sudden belated realization that he might have misunderstood his orders: evidence that his doubts were genuine, and not a cover for fear or disobedience.

All Sackville's staff supported this interpretation; and if it is correct he can be acquitted of deliberate disobedience. Yet the cumulative impression of his successive delays raises other criticisms, of inadequacy and misjudgement. His ignorance of the woodland on his left can be explained by the duties which had prevented him from reconnoitring it on the day before the battle, and by his assumption that he would come into action further forward in the plain which he had reconnoitred. But when he was halted unexpectedly for half an hour between the woodland and the marsh he ought to have sent look-outs to watch the far side of the woods, a precaution which any master of foxhounds would have taken. He might then have kept in touch with the infantry's progress on his left, and discovered the depth and density of the woodland.

After the cavalry passed through the wood his advance was slow and deliberate. He defended this in the light of what Ferdinand had said to him and the state of the battle as he knew it. He moved his force with the deliberation required by the manuals and army instructions; and Granby's exasperation shows that one cavalryman with tactical flair had grasped the need for speed at the cost of field-day order. Again there is no proof that Sackville executed his orders with contumacious slowness; but he executed them without judgement.

That in itself was enough to justify his removal from his command. Ferdinand had to be able to rely on his British general, and Sackville seems to have fallen short of the tactical reliability his commander-in-chief had a right to expect. Coupled with their bad relations, this would have justified Ferdinand in asking for his removal. But Ferdinand was also convinced that Sackville had disobeyed him. This belief was unjustified. It rested on misinformation about the early morning movements of the cavalry, ignorance of what Sackville could see in his situation beyond the woods, and the prejudice instilled by the angry Fitzroy. The method Ferdinand chose for removing Sackville was malicious, humiliating and public. His admirers justified it as an example of the prince's skilful diplomacy; but it owed much to personal dislike. Sackville was unable to live with the censure, which was what Ferdinand intended; and his attempt to justify himself in the army enabled Ferdinand to stigmatize his conduct as disloyal. He was recalled, dismissed from the army and disgraced.

Given Sackville's character and influence, there was perhaps no other way to silence him, and it was necessary to protect Ferdinand at his expense. But historians are no longer under that obligation; and if one asks how far Ferdinand himself contributed to the confusion for which Sackville was broken, his secretiveness leaps to mind. He had commanded the allied army for twenty months, and knew its problems and its limitations. The elaborate trap which he laid for Contades at Minden depended on careful planning and a swift response. Yet when he saw the signs of enemy movement he confided in none of the generals who would have to spring the trap. In consequence Wangenheim was surprised on the left; and on the right Anhalt missed the significance of the French deserters' story, delayed its transmission, and allowed the enemy to occupy the key village of Hahlen.

Next to the briefing of the generals, Ferdinand's plan depended on smooth staff-work and communications. For want of these there was confusion when the alarm was raised. The orders to turn out and march were not properly delivered; and for want of previous briefing the British columns were uncertain what to do, the British generals received no warning, and the British artillery were at a loss for orders. When the battle began, Ferdinand's orders to his British troops miscarried. This was partly due to language difficulties, but that was not all. The order delivered by von Taube to the British infantry was not in the words which Ferdinand remembered, and it launched them into a premature advance. They were stopped by Richmond and Taube, only to be launched again, an error never explained but surely due to misunderstanding. The leftward incline of the advance was probably due to the fact that neither Spörcken nor Waldegrave had received any general orders for the battle, and continued in the direction of their approach march. About the string of orders which Ferdinand sent to Sackville his memory differed from that of his messengers; but it seems certain that he allowed Fitzroy to introduce additional confusion when he agreed that he should bring up the *British* cavalry. Whether Ferdinand or even Fitzroy understood the implications of the phrase 'British cavalry' one will never be sure – Ferdinand's own narrative is unreliable on this as on other details. But his assertion that he sent for only the British cavalry to save time is a later gloss; and he allowed Fitzroy to fetch the more distant British regiments, leaving the nearer German regiments where they were. Nothing in his string of orders gave Sackville guidance or explanation: that was left to the judgement of young aides-de-camp.

The commanders had not been briefed, and the staff machine did not work smoothly. Did Ferdinand compensate for these defects by his mastery of the battle? He knew his business, but he was no heaven-born *Feldherr*. He responded actively to the confusion caused by the British infantry's advance, calling forward the artillery and switching battalions across the rear of the British brigades to fill the gap opened by their leftward incline. But whether he made the best decision on how to use Sackville's cavalry is doubtful. The first summons carried by Winzingerode was intended to move the whole of the right wing of cavalry laterally behind the front to deal with the unexpected – the exposure of Waldegrave's infantry to the French cavalry. At that moment

Ferdinand feared disaster and a breakthrough, though he did not explain this to Sackville. The second summons carried by Ligonier and Fitzroy a few minutes later had a different purpose: to exploit the defeat of the French cavalry. This could have been done most quickly by Sackville advancing to the front and wheeling into the left of the French; and it was only later, with the final French and Saxon attacks, that Ferdinand again needed the cavalry in a support role. Even then they could have acted most effectively by advancing and charging the Saxon flank. But Ferdinand was chained by his first clumsy attempt to adjust his order of battle. The cavalry of the right wing was moved through the woodland on a devious course which brought them out far to the rear of the infantry.

And now the battle had changed, and the enemy were in full retreat. But Ferdinand lacked the swift intuition to sense it. For a brief period there was a chance to break into the disintegrated French centre and destroy the whole left wing of the enemy army before it could escape across the Bastau. But when Sackville rode up to Ferdinand the prince told him nothing about the changing situation, said nothing of exploitation or pursuit, but gave him orders to form a line and move up to sustain the infantry. With that he turned his back on his only uncommitted reserve and rode away. The opportunity vanished as swiftly as it came, and the French were soon safe behind the Bastau. Ferdinand had allowed the enemy to retreat almost unscathed across the bridges, just as he allowed them to retire up the Weser in the following days.

A CHARGE OF PERJURY

Lord Ligonier did not do Sackville the courtesy of telling him that the sentence with its vicious addendum was to be published in army orders, and only by chance did he learn what was happening. He had already had a taste of the difficulties ahead when he asked Bute immediately after the trial for leave to pay his respects to the Prince of Wales, and was refused. The king had forbidden Sackville to come to court, and the Lord Chamberlain notified Leicester House of the royal ban. Though the prince grumbled angrily at his grandfather he gave way, and Bute assured the Vice-Chamberlain that the prince would not think of seeing Lord George while it was disagreeable to the king. To Sackville, Bute explained that the prince could not receive him so soon after the sentence. He advised him to tell his friends that he would not attempt to impose himself on the prince, and to wait for better times.

Sackville was disappointed, but he faced and cleared another hurdle, the House of Commons. He had been warned that the ministry was thinking of a motion to expel him; but they were deterred by the fact that the court martial had not imposed the expected marks of ignominy, and in any case Lord George sat for a family borough and would be returned to the House immediately. But how would the House receive him? Some private member might be instigated to insult him, and he was advised to choose a quiet day and a thin House for the ordeal. His début took place six days after the sentence was published, and all was well. 'None of the great men chose to look towards me,' he reported; 'others in general very civil and attentive.'

Great was Sir Joseph Yorke's disgust at the news that Sackville was not to be expelled. He had looked forward to his expulsion, and was embarrassed to explain to foreigners how Lord George could still be giving laws to his country when a peer of ancient family was treated like a common criminal – Lord Ferrers was hanged on 5 May, and Walpole reported that the mob almost pitied him. 'So they would Lord George, whose execution they are so angry at missing.'

As long as the old king lived the ministers continued to ignore Lord George, with the exception of the great judges Lord Hardwicke and Lord Mansfield – lawyers' careers were less dependent on the revolving wheel of politics than the common herd of statesmen. By others Sackville was treated with at least the respect due to a ducal family, and it was beyond the power of the king to do him further harm. Not so for the officers who had testified for him in court: 'Every officer who was bold enough to speak truth upon his oath in my favour is now labouring under the weight of his Majesty's displeasure.' Captain Hugo was stripped of his commission in the Hanoverian army. Sackville wrote to him about the possibility of entering the service of another state, expressing his strong regard and friendship and telling him to call on him for money if he needed it to buy a commission in Denmark. He could pull no strings at present, since no British minister at a foreign court would risk the king's displeasure by a private recommendation. 'I must have resource to patience till time shall alter circumstances.'

Another witness on whom the royal anger fell heavily was Jack Smith, whose evidence had challenged Colonel Sloper's. No sooner was the trial over than he was forbidden to mount guard and ordered to sell out of the army. And a worse fate hung over him. When Charles Gould brought the proceedings of the court martial to the Secretary at War he pointed out the contradictions in the evidence, and was asked for a report. No one questioned that it was Smith rather than Sloper who had perjured himself. Gould sent Lord Barrington his observations on 12 May, and the papers were immediately forwarded to the Attorney-General and Solicitor-General for their opinion on whether to launch a criminal prosecution for perjury. The penalty was seven or fourteen years' transportation. The Attorney-General Charles Pratt puzzled over the evidence and sent his colleague Charles Yorke some thoughts on 'this ugly business'. For three months they sat on the papers, and in the meantime Sloper, back in Germany with his regiment, collected statements from his officers to support his own evidence. These were sworn before the Deputy Judge-Advocate in Germany, forwarded to the Secretary at War, and published as a pamphlet.

There were two points on which the law officer saw a suspicion of perjury: whether Lord George had been near Sloper at the head of Bland's Dragoon Guards when Ligonier delivered his orders, or out of earshot near the Inniskillings; and whether Smith had fabricated his story of Sloper's picket poles. On both questions the weight of evidence was finely balanced. On Sackville's position Smith himself could not plausibly be indicted, since he had only said that he *thought* Sackville could not have been at the head of Bland's regiment because he had carried an order from him to Sloper. Smith would be supported by the positive statements of Lloyd and Sutherland that Sackville had been with the Inniskillings, by what Lieutenant Bisset said he believed and by the doubts of Colonel Hotham; and Sackville would also be called to support him. If Lloyd and Sutherland were indicted for asserting as fact that Sackville had been at the head of the Inniskillings, they were as likely as Smith to be acquitted on the balance of probabilities. As for the alleged order to Sloper to throw away his picket poles, Sloper and Smith would receive equal credit from the jury; and though Sloper would be supported by the strong negative evidence of what witnesses had *not* seen, Smith would be supported by the positive evidence of Sackville that he had delivered Sloper's message and taken back Sackville's reply.

On where Sackville was posted the defence would argue the possibility of error in the rapidly changing circumstances. About this even the Judge-Advocate admitted doubt, and pointed out how fine a point of time was involved. If Sackville had really given Smith the picket-pole order, he must have done so in the short interval between Ligonier's arrival and Fitzroy's; and in those moments Gould now thought that Sackville might have moved a little to the left towards the Inniskillings, and doubted how far Fitzroy could be certain of his facts.

What would a jury think? In a trial for perjury the characters and motives of the witnesses were crucial, and a jury would never convict when the accused was supported by witnesses of fair character and there was a reasonable possibility of a mistake. Pratt thought that the balance of the evidence was against Smith; but the only people who could give positive evidence on the picket-pole order were Smith, Sackville and Sloper, and a jury was unlikely to find against Smith on the evidence of one witness against two. 'Captain Smith is a gentleman: his character will be supported by witnesses of the first rank. The crime is odious and the punishment infamous.'

Yorke agreed, and on 15 August the law officers reported against a prosecution. The threat which had been hanging over Smith was removed, and if Sackville recovered his influence his future was secure. But again one must ask what was the truth as distinct from the legal expediency of the matter. The success of Lord George's defence rested in large measure on whether he could discredit

Sloper's evidence that he had heard Winzingerode and Ligonier ordering him to move to the left. There is reason to believe that Sloper was biased by malice and prejudice, as Sackville declared in court, and that his memory was liable to error. Sloper asserted, for example, that Winzingerode had arrived just after the line was formed, though all other witnesses estimated the interval as half an hour. If, as the Judge-Advocate suggested in his summing up, the discrepancy can be explained by Sloper having timed the forming of the line from the short later movement forward to gain space beyond Hartum, this acquits Sloper of bias on the point only to demonstrate how inexact was his memory of times and sequences. Again, when Sloper urged Ligonier to repeat his orders, he told him that half an hour had passed since the delivery of Winzingerode's orders, though in court he reduced this to a quarter of an hour: an indication that he had addressed Ligonier under the influence of strong feelings, whether of impatience or anger. Later, Sloper timed the short advance which the cavalry made after Ligonier's arrival as having taken place just before Ligonier arrived, with circumstantial details of Sackville riding up and ordering him to put his regiment in motion. Yet it is clear from all the other witnesses, including Ligonier himself, that it was after receiving Ligonier's order that Sackville drew his sword, turned about and gave a general order for the line to march.

Sloper's performance as a witness is therefore far from flawless. But that is not to say that he perjured himself, and one must look at the specific parts of his evidence which were challenged in court. His account of how Winzingerode delivered his orders is entirely unsupported. Alone of the witnesses he claimed to have heard Winzingerode ordering a move to the left; nor did anyone hear Sloper explain the order in this sense to Sackville. He said that Winzingerode had repeated his order a third time in English, which Winzingerode himself denied; and out of court he had said that Winzingerode had spoken to Hugo in German, which no one else had heard and which Hugo denied. Four officers of Sackville's staff said that they had heard only the order to advance, even when it was repeated, and denied that they had seen Sloper near them at that moment. Support for the prosecution came from Granby's statement that Winzingerode had told him when he passed the second line that the movement was to be to the left; but Winzingerode had said this several hundred yards away from Sackville, nor is there any evidence that this was even the order which Ferdinand had sent. After the trial Sloper obtained an affidavit from the chaplain of Bland's that he had heard Ligonier deliver his orders twice in French and once in English, and that Sloper had then offered his explanation of the orders. This is disturbing; but the chaplain had had ample time to read the record of the trial and to be primed by his commanding officer, and his evidence should carry no more weight than that of Colonel Hotham and three other witnesses who had heard the orders delivered and gave their evidence in court.

Then there was the question of Ligonier's orders. Sloper claimed to have heard him order an advance to the left. But Ligonier himself did not claim to have delivered his orders in this plain and audible fashion. He said that he had added the explanation 'to the left' while riding beside Sackville as the line advanced; and unless Sloper was also riding alongside the general and the aide-de-camp instead of leading his regiment it was impossible for him to hear this above the beat of the drums. When Fitzroy arrived and the line halted, Sloper took Ligonier aside and urged him to repeat his orders, saying that Winzingerode had delivered the same orders already. This appears to show that he had heard both Winzingerode's orders and Ligonier's; but the Judge-Advocate conceded that Sloper could have learned the nature of Ligonier's orders from Ligonier himself, a point on which no evidence had been produced. In that case Sloper's words did not prove that he had heard Ligonier delivering them.

Had Sloper been in earshot at all when Ligonier delivered his orders? His post was at the head of the right squadron of Bland's Dragoon Guards, on the extreme flank of the line. It was there that he claimed to have heard the orders; and Ligonier himself said that he had delivered them there. But Hotham, Lloyd, Sutherland and Bisset all testified that Sackville had received the orders at or near the right squadron of the next regiment, the Inniskillings; the lieutenant carrying the standard of the Inniskillings said that he had seen Ligonier riding up to Sackville near by; Smith claimed to have seen Ligonier riding towards Bland's *after* delivering his orders, and Sutherland that when Ligonier was called back to Sackville to argue his orders with Fitzroy he came from the direction of Bland's. Here again is a massive conflict of evidence. Five officers were subsequently called by the prosecution to confirm that Ligonier had delivered his orders at the head of Bland's. None of them was conclusive; but Sloper managed to collect three affidavits after the trial from officers of his regiment that they had seen Ligonier with Sackville at the head of the right squadron of Bland's, and another to say that Sackville had been at the head of the squadron when the line advanced.

But the trump concealed in Sackville's hand at the beginning of the trial was Captain Smith's story of Sloper and the picket poles. If it was true that he had carried messages between Sackville and Sloper, it proved that Sloper was not with Sackville when Ligonier delivered his orders and the line advanced. Smith's evidence that Sloper had halted to discard his picket poles in spite of Sackville's order was later contradicted by five officers of the regiment, who swore that Bland's had never been behind the rest of the line. But that, if true, was not significant. The cavalry's advance, interrupted immediately by the arrival of Fitzroy, was so short (ten or twenty paces according to one witness) that by the time of Smith's return to Sloper with the order to keep moving the whole line must have been on the point of halting.

How can this succession of contradictions in the evidence be explained? Was Sloper lying or in error? There was error in his evidence, certainly; malice in court, and anger provoked by Sackville's cross-examination; and later, a desire to demolish Smith's ludicrous portrayal of him fussing about his picket poles.

Alternatively, were Sackville's witnesses lying? Perhaps one can never decide the truth of such a question without seeing the witnesses in court and knowing what the spectators knew about them. But that Hotham, Bisset, Lloyd and Sutherland should all have perjured themselves is incredible. In the case of Smith a faint doubt creeps in. In any ordinary circumstances one could dismiss the suggestion. As the law officers remarked, he was a gentleman, with too much to lose by such a crime. Aged twenty-nine at the time of the court martial, Captain Smith came of a respectable though not distinguished Kentish family. They bore the coat of arms of Thomas Smith, the Elizabethan Customer of the port of London, from whom also were descended three more eminent families, the Viscounts Strangford, the Smythes of Sutton Place of whom the last descendant Sir Sidney Stafford Smythe, Chief Baron of the Exchequer, died in 1788, and the Smiths of Leeds Castle. The links through which Jack Smith's branch of the family had descended were obscure. It was known that his great grandfather had been a colonel in Ireland, and his grandfather Captain Cornelius Smith had commanded the Custom House yacht at Dover. His father, Captain Edward Smith, had died of wounds as a frigate captain in the West Indies in 1743. This seems to have been a family of solid public service, and so it continued. Jack's younger brother Edward was present at the death of Wolfe at Quebec six weeks after the battle of Minden and later became a general. Of Jack's three sons the eldest became a colonel, the youngest a diplomat and minister to the Porte; while the most famous of the three, Admiral Sir William Sidney Smith, was the defender of Acre against Napoleon. Of Jack Smith's own character Perceval Stockdale, whose favourable views of Lord George Sackville and Lieutenant Sutherland have already been quoted, wrote that he was 'a man of sense and spirit; a man of warm, generous and sincere heart; with whom no consideration upon earth could ever prevail to suppress the truth when he thought it was his duty to declare it'. Could this man's evidence, vivid and circumstantial, have been a fabrication?

In one circumstance the answer could certainly be yes: if there were a homosexual conspiracy between Sackville and Smith. The threads leading towards such a guess are fragile, and there is a more solid explanation for Sackville's choice of his aide-de-camp. Jack's home territory seems to have been in the Tonbridge region of Kent, in the heart of Sackville territory. Was it not natural for a general to choose as his aide-de-camp an officer whom he knew, and to use his patronage on behalf of a neighbour? And would not the aide-de-camp do what he could to defend his general? Captain Smith had been Sackville's aide-de-camp for at least two years before the battle of Minden; Joshua Reynolds had painted his portrait 'to be sent to Lord George'; and one can imagine this highly strung and partisan officer going to great lengths to protect a friend and patron. But if one speculates about his secret motives, it would be equally proper to ask what passion or jealousy may have lain behind Colonel Sloper's bearing as a witness.

In neither case can the question be answered. There was, however, a streak of opportunism in Jack Smith which still leaves one uneasy. His father's death when he was thirteen had left his mother with four children to bring up; and the fact that Captain Edward Smith was still only commanding a frigate when he died at the age of sixty suggests that he had not been able to call on any great influence to further his career. How Jack obtained his commission in the 3rd Guards and his brother made his military career we do not know, but perhaps the Sackville family had had a hand in it.

Very soon after the court martial Jack launched a venture which calls in question Stockdale's eulogy on his sincerity. Deprived of his career, he tried his luck in the marriage market. Two years earlier, shortly before he went to Germany with Sackville, he had met a family called Wilkinson who were staying in Bath for the health of their invalidish elder daughter Mary. Mr Pinckney Wilkinson was a rich elderly London merchant with a house in Hanover Square, a place in Norfolk and only two daughters to inherit his fortune. Jack Smith cultivated the elder girl; but as far as the family knew, he did not keep in touch with her when he went to Germany. In June 1760, however, with his career gone and the shadow of a charge of perjury hanging over him, Smith heard that the Wilkinsons had brought Mary to try the waters at Tunbridge Wells. He contrived to meet her in the street, forced himself on the family for dinner and later for breakfast, and without delay made a secret proposal of marriage to the girl.

When Mr Wilkinson learned what had happened he objected strongly to his daughter marrying a man with no money and no profession, who had behaved like an adventurer. Under his remonstrances Smith agreed to stay out of Tunbridge Wells as long as the Wilkinsons were there, and retired to Lord George's country house, Stoneland Lodge (now Buckhurst Park) at near-by Withy-

A Charge of Perjury

ham. The Wilkinsons returned to London in September; but they had not long been back when the wife of the rector of Withyham called on Mary, introduced herself as a friend of Jack Smith, and said that he was dangerously ill at Stoneland Lodge and was asking for her. Threatened with a revival of his daughter's affair, Pinckney Wilkinson warned her that if she married without his consent he would never see her again. But in vain. A day or two later she eloped, and was married to Jack in Withyham church by the 'worthy parish priest and ever faithful friend' of Lord George Sackville (as Richard Cumberland described him), with the rector's wife as one of the witnesses.* One begins to remember Lord Shelburne's assertion that Lord George Sackville surrounded himself with low adventurers.

This story proves nothing about Smith's evidence at the court martial, but it is clear from the records of the trial that both he and Sloper were biased witnesses. Whenever time was lost, Sloper's estimate is the highest, Smith's the lowest. On Sloper's estimate of the interval between Winzingerode's arrival and Ligonier's we do not have Smith's opinion; but his estimate of two minutes between the arrival of Ligonier and Fitzroy is hard to reconcile with his story of carrying messages about picket poles. The extreme clash between Smith's evidence and Sloper's concerns the interval between Sackville's departure to find Ferdinand and the delivery of Smith's order to bring on the British cavalry, which Sloper gave as twenty minutes and Smith as two or three.

Bias was at work on both sides; but when two groups of respectable witnesses disagree about the details of a battle, confusion of memory is a likelier explanation than conspiracy, and whatever one may think of Jack Smith, some of Sackville's witnesses were respectable men. Sackville himself was uncertain about the number of halts on the heath, and no witness was wholly accurate about what happened and when, or about the words that were spoken. Errors have been shown in Sloper's evidence, and many lapses of memory on the part of Prince Ferdinand or his

*The Rev Sackville Spencer Bale had gone to Westminster School in 1733, a couple of years after Sackville had left it.

messengers. These instances of error could be multiplied. To take a trivial one, when Ligonier galloped across from the woodland in company with Captain Lloyd to deliver his orders to Sackville, he believed afterwards that he had ridden diagonally across to the Blues, whereas Lloyd, with no strong motive for contradicting him, remembered riding across to the Inniskillings. The discrepancy is easily explained by the diagonal course which made the place where they joined the line a matter of opinion, and by the blurred lateral vision of men galloping with the wind in their eyes and searching ahead, as anyone who has ridden across country will recognize.

Some of the contradictions are not so easily dismissed; but in every instance one must take account of breathless messengers, preconceived ideas and the fading memories of a few crowded minutes after a lapse of seven months. 'The history of a battle', wrote the Duke of Wellington a few weeks after Waterloo, 'is not unlike the history of a ball. Some individuals may recollect all the little events . . . but no individual can recollect the order in which, or the exact moment at which, they occurred, which makes all the difference to their value or importance.' This was true of Minden, as of Waterloo.

ELEVEN

UPHILL ALL THE WAY

RESURRECTION

One need hardly say that Sir Joseph Yorke crowed lustily over the king's vindictive pursuit of his 'superb and inactive General' when the trial was over. That was not the ordinary attitude, however. At the other end of the spectrum General James Murray, commanding at Quebec since the death of Sackville's protégé Wolfe, wrote to him that his whole garrison had read the proceedings, and 'there is not an officer in it who does not blush that such a sentence should have been pronounced by a British court'.

On most people the impression created by the trial was more equivocal. It had cleared Lord George in some degree but not entirely, and there seemed to be enough substance in the charge to justify the king's earlier action in dismissing him. 'Upon the whole,' an observer in the court wrote to Newcastle between trial and sentences, 'though I cannot think his Lordship so blameable as his enemies represent him; yet when your Grace sees the tryal, I am convinced you will think that his Majesty could do no otherwise than he has done with regard to his Lordship.' Horace Walpole concluded that the question had turned on a very few minutes: 'Enough was evident to prove that Lord George, at best, was too critically and minutely cool at such a moment of importance.'

Many people thought that it had been a mistake for Lord George to insist on a trial. He should have dropped his demand when the government admitted that there were no specific charges, and his friends could then have put it about that he had been sacrificed to a German general. Thus, when passions had time to die down and

243

Frederick the Great and Ferdinand went out of fashion, the tide would have turned in his favour.

That was a doubtful argument. It was true that Lord Cobham had been reinstated after the fall of the ministry which dismissed him in 1735, but his dismissal had been a disreputable political reprisal; nor had he been dismissed from the army, but only from the colonelcy of his regiment. For Sackville to submit quietly to implicit accusations of disobedience and cowardice in battle was another matter, and he could scarcely have been reinstated with that accusation hanging over him unanswered. The trial, unfortunately, did not clear him, and only time would show whether he had a future. Walpole was convinced that he had. 'He is a peculiar man, and I repeat it, we have not heard the last of him.' With that Walpole turned to other topical matters. A parcel of books which he sent out to Horace Mann in Florence included the trials of Sackville and Lord Ferrers, and 'a fashionable thing they call Tristram Shandy'.

Having failed in his bid to be received by the Prince of Wales, Lord George had simply to follow Lord Bute's advice and bide his time. In the meantime life was not intolerable. He attended Parliament, circulated in society, and took a hand in the borough politics of Kent. As for his enemies, he must have had some fun with the news from Germany. Colonel Sloper had said in his evidence that Bland's Dragoon Guards could have crossed the Minden heath at a gallop and still have beaten any three French squadrons. On 31 July at the battle of Warburg three French squadrons caught his regiment in the flank and scattered it. Sloper must have acquired a taste for collecting written statements, for he issued one of his own: 'I do hereby declare that the first Regiment of Dragoon Guards on the affair of the 31st of July in my opinion behaved with resolution and bravery, and I also declare that I never said any thing to the contrary.'

Sackville may also have been amused by a small publishing triumph. During the trial he had shared the cost of a shorthand writer with the court, and must have started printing the proceedings before the trial was over. His own version was thus the first to appear. It is also the more entertaining one. The official

Proceedings reported the evidence in the third person, and omitted most of the dialogue between Sackville and his judges and between the members of the court. Sackville printed the lot, and in the first person – 'with all the foolish questions and absurdities of his judges', as the poet Thomas Gray remarked.

The event for which Lord George was waiting was the death of the king, which could not be long in coming. In the early morning of 25 October the old man drank his chocolate, had a heart attack on his closet-stool and 'with a noise louder than the royal wind' fell dead. He had lived for seventy-six years and reigned for thirty-three, and Sir Joseph Yorke intoned that he died 'in the height of his glory, loved, honoured and respected by all Europe'. Lord Chesterfield put it differently. 'He died unlamented, tho' not unpraised because he was dead.'

At the solemn funeral in Westminster Abbey many an eye was dry; but not the Duke of Newcastle's.

He fell into a fit of crying at the moment he came into the chapel, and flung himself back in a stall, the Archbishop hovering over him with a smelling-bottle; but in two minutes his curiosity got the better of his hypocrisy, and he ran about the chapel with his glass to spy who was or who was not there, spying with one hand and mopping his eyes with the other. Then returned the fear of catching cold; and the Duke of Cumberland, who was sinking fast with heat, felt himself weighed down, and turning round, found it was the Duke of Newcastle standing upon his train, to avoid the chill of the marble.

George II died just six months after embellishing Sackville's sentence. Lord George lost no time, and on the evening of the king's death wrote to ask Lord Bute for permission to pay his duty to the young king immediately. He came to Court and kissed hands, but it caused such an uproar that he was asked not to appear again. It would have been imprudent to affront the late king's ministers by resurrecting Sackville so promptly before the politics of the new reign had time to take shape. Pitt in particular was bitterly opposed to his reinstatement, as an insult to the late king's memory and to Prince Ferdinand – and a reflection on himself. Again Bute had to ask Sackville to wait in patience, promising this time to rehabilitate him at the end of the war.

Sackville therefore fell back on his base at Knole and local politics. But at least he was in a better position to help his friends. Captain Hugo was reinstated in the Hanoverian army and promoted major, and James Sutherland received a captaincy. The Hothams as usual did best. Charles became a courtier, a Knight of the Bath and eventually a general, and George III wanted to appoint him tutor to the future George IV. His brother John, placed on the list of the Prince of Wales's chaplains immediately after Minden, in due course attained his bishopric.

Jack Smith never returned to the army, but some years later in 1774 became a Gentleman-Usher to Queen Charlotte. His speculation in marriage had not prospered, however. Though a local newspaper reporting the wedding had described Miss Wilkinson as 'an agreeable young lady with a very large fortune', her father had kept his word and did not forgive her. Refusing to see her, he cut her off in his will with a £40 annuity, leaving his fortune to his younger daughter who married Lord Camelford. Four years later Mr Wilkinson relented a little. Mary received an allowance of £400 a year, and a codicil in his will provided that it should continue after his death, the capital of £10,000 being held in trust for the children so that Jack Smith could never lay his hands on it.

Mary Wilkinson thus turned out to be no heiress; nor did the couple find each other agreeable. Soon Mary was complaining of Jack's temper and violence, and in 1772 a separation was arranged by which she retired to Bath with the custody of her three sons, her husband receiving £200 a year for his consent. Jack, however, broke the agreement about the children as they grew up, alienated them from their mother, and sent his second boy Sidney to sea when he was thirteen in breach of his mother's wishes. Sidney sneaked his clothes out of the house while his brother kept their mother in conversation.

Captain Smith continued to cultivate people of influence, though Lord George ceased to appear in his life. His sons were baptized by the chaplains to Lord Vere and Lord Chancellor Bathurst and by an archdeacon, as the family bible recorded. The godparents included four earls, Lady Robert Manners and the Duchess of Dorset. But it was probably not through these connections that young Sidney was placed in Sir George Rodney's flagship, and promoted by him to the command of a ship at the age of eighteen, though Jack claimed that it was through his influence that Sidney had been made a post-captain and set on the ladder of promotion to flag rank. His brother-in-law Lord Camelford took an active interest in Jack's ungrateful children, found the purchase money for Charles's company in the army, and used his interest in the navy for Sidney, receiving no thanks for his efforts.

Captain Smith himself continued to serve at court, rising to Gentleman Usher Daily Waiter and in 1799 to Gentleman Usher of the Privy Chamber, a post which he held till his death in 1804. His home in later years was a curious cliff-top house at Dover, with a vast view across the straits to the coast of France. At the foot of the cliffs near the castle he excavated a dwelling known as The Caves, or alternatively as Smith's Folly. To this eccentric boathouse he sometimes retired in hot weather to write letters and do his private business.

So much for Lord George's supporters. Among his critics, Colonel Sloper continued in the army, to become commander-in-chief at Madras in 1784 and a full general in 1796. Of Lord Granby, who became commander-in-chief in 1766, Lord George always wrote with contempt, referring to promises extracted from him 'in the midst of riot and dissipation'; and he called Granby's death during the war scare of 1770 a boon to the army. Towards Prince Ferdinand he never ceased to express his bitterness. On the news that the prince had fallen out with the much liked and respected General Spörcken he commented: 'All these things will rise up in judgment against H.S.H. if ever he lives to see a day of adversity.' And in 1762 he wrote to his friend General Irwin that if Ferdinand should be successful in the field and the Hereditary Prince suffered a reverse, 'his Serene Highness will be at the summit of human happiness, that is, as far as so wicked a mind can taste anything that resembles happiness'.

Sackville implied that Ferdinand was possessed by jealousy; and even before the old king died this view had been supported by a fresh scandal which threatened the army in Hanover. Ferdinand removed General Imhoff from the command of the Brunswick troops for abandoning the line of the river Ohm. At least some of the blame seems to have lain with Ferdinand, who had dithered and consulted Westphalen instead of marching promptly to Imhoff's support, and another scandal was feared; but unlike Sackville Imhoff departed without a fuss to the Brunswick garrison.

Still, the affair did not pass unnoticed in England; and as General Murray had predicted to Sackville the tide of English opinion was turning against Ferdinand as it had already begun to turn against Frederick. Ferdinand's massive reinforcement of the Prussians after Minden at the expense of the army in Hanover had been a shock even to George II – 'the old gentleman does not know how to digest it,' gossiped Thomas Gray. By 1761 it was being said in Parliament that the German war had never served British interests, and that England had been paying Frederick to fight his own battles against England's natural allies the Austrians. By now the expense of British supplies in Germany was becoming a major scandal, and a committee concluded that Prussian officials were usurping the authority of the British commissariat staff and defrauding the British government. Sackville spoke in Parliament against these expenses in Germany, and was heard and answered civilly.

Peace was signed at last in 1763, but still it was not convenient to employ him. He was put off with a promise that he should have his rank in the army and a civil employment at the end of the session, though the king flinched at his request for a military post. But when the end of the session came he was put off again, for fear of undermining the newly formed Grenville ministry. This time Sackville was tougher and threatened to go into opposition, and was allowed to come to court and treated with marked attention by the king. The wheels of politics revolved for another two years, and in 1765 his moment came. The Rockingham ministry took office and appointed him to the lucrative office of Vice-Treasurer of Ireland, though Newcastle called his appointment 'hard of digestion', and he was readmitted to the Privy Council. Thus five years after his condemnation he achieved two vital steps towards rehabilitation: admission to political office, and recognition that he was fit to serve the king as a Privy Councillor.

Sackville's post lasted no longer than the short-lived ministry, and in 1766 he was out of office again, one of only three or four office-holders dismissed by Pitt. But he was back in the inner circle of politics, allied to Newcastle's political heirs of the Rockingham connection. Unlike Pitt they were not prepared, for the sake of past history, to forgo the support of an able parliamentary speaker and an influential borough-owning family, especially when Sackville settled at Stoneland Lodge in Newcastle's own county of Sussex. He dined with Rockingham and Burke, and it is ironic to find Newcastle inviting him to meet the assize judges in a party which included another Sussex magnate of the Rockingham group, Ferdinand's erstwhile aide-de-camp the Duke of Richmond. In these years the anonymous *Letters of Junius* began to appear, and some people attributed their venomous invective to Sackville. But he won the respect of Burke. 'I esteem Lord George in some things, and admire him in many others,' he wrote a few years later.

But life was not all smooth for the 'Minden coward'. He felt let down by Bute, who had acquiesced in his expulsion from office by Pitt, now Earl of Chatham, and retaliated by campaigning against Bute's son-in-law Sir James Lowther. Speaking with great bitterness against Lowther in the House, Sackville let fall the phrase 'avoiding the combat', and faltered in confusion, unable to remember how he had meant to go on. He asked the members near him where he had got to, and received the reply from the benches in front, 'about avoiding the combat, my Lord'.

Two years later Lowther instigated the combative Captain George Johnstone to insult Lord George during a debate. Sackville had let fall the phrase 'the honour of the country', and Johnstone remarked that 'he wondered that the noble lord should interest himself so deeply in the honour of his country, when he had been hitherto so regardless of his own'. How would the man of Minden rise to the occasion? Critical watchers thought that his reaction was slow, but in due course he challenged Johnstone and exchanged two pistol shots with him in Hyde Park. Sackville received a hit on the barrel of his pistol, and Johnstone declared that he had never known a man behave better in a duel.

By now Sackville had changed his name. For many years the widowed Lady Betty Germain had lived at Knole, and her childless husband had expressed the wish that his estate at Drayton in Northamptonshire should pass to one of the Duke of Dorset's family. When Lady Betty died in 1769 she left the estate to Lord George, with the condition that he should take her name; and as Lord George Germain he is best known to history. He was now a rich man, and in the vast, romantic house at Drayton he left two memorials of his taste. The William and Mary dining-room was refurbished in the Adam style by William Rhodes, and an elegant Georgian drawing-room was created in the Elizabethan wing.

In politics Lord George was finding that his Rockingham allies were out on a limb. In 1770 Lord North succeeded the decayed and depressive Chatham as Prime Minister, and rapidly created the stable political system which George III had been seeking for the past ten years. Only the death of the king or a major war was likely to shake North's ministry, and the long careers of Robert Walpole and Newcastle showed that under a stable ministry there was only one road to office for an ambitious politician. He must prove his nuisance-value and make it worth the ministry's while to buy him in.

This Lord George proceeded to do, with effective speeches on the major issues of the day. One of these issues was the suppression of a Carib revolt in the West Indies, and the dispatch of troops to fight them in the hot season. 'Lord George', Walpole recorded, 'summed up the whole barbarity, rashness and folly in one of his most pointed speeches, full of pith, matter, irony and satire.' Gradually he loosened his connection with the Rockinghams. That tight group of political friends were digging themselves with Burke's assistance ever deeper into an ideological pit which blocked their road to power. With Wedderburn's help Lord George drew closer to the government. The American question troubled the scene; he allied himself with the hard-liners in the ministry; and a few months after open rebellion broke out in 1775 he was appointed Secretary of State for the American Colonies. The man who had been declared by a court martial to be unfit to serve in any military capacity became the director of the war beyond the Atlantic.

From the wilder shores of opposition came the joyous baying of hounds as the city radicals set on the new minister. 'The Ghost of Minden is for ever brought in to frighten him with.' John Wilkes and Alderman Sawbridge were at his throat 'attacking him with the British cavalry'. Germain might conquer America, said Wilkes, but it would not be in Germany – a joke which Lord George repeated with relish in the Cabinet. More crudely Colonel Luttrell said that the only safety for the royal army lay in flight, and Germain was fit to lead it. Embarrassed by these attacks, Germain at first seemed more subdued in the House of Commons as a minister than he had been as a private member.

There were many, however, who welcomed him with high expectations. One was Sir William Hamilton, not yet chained to his Emma, who wrote from Naples rejoicing in Lord George's appointment – 'if it is possible to bring us out of our present confusion I am confident he will do it'. 'I always had the greatest opinion of my friend Lord George,' he added in a later letter, 'if there is a sound head in England I am sure it is that of his Lordship.' His friend Charles Greville agreed; so did the American loyalist refugee, Governor Thomas Hutchinson. 'I don't know of any person more to the general satisfaction than Lord George,' he confided to his journal. 'He has the character of a great man.' A year later his opinion had not altered. 'His character in private life is amiable, his good sense qualifies him for his department, and his firmness of mind renders him equal to the subdual of the American rebellion.'

The first impressions of Lord George in office matched these hopes. James Cunningham found him well and busy, and in good spirits – 'he drives business on, obviating all difficulties as well as he can'. 'The force gone or going to America is greater than I ever expected,' Hutchinson wrote, 'owing much to Lord George Germain's zeal.' Richard Cumberland, then a minor official at the Board of Trade, which was subordinate to the American Department, compares him with his predecessor Lord Dartmouth in a striking passage in his memoirs.

A very short time sufficed to confirm the idea I had entertained of Lord George's character for decision and dispatch in business: there was at once an end of all our circumlocutory reports and inefficient forms, that had only impeded business and substituted ambiguity for precision: there . . . was no trash in his mind; he studied no choice phrases, no superfluous words, nor ever suffered the clearness of his conceptions to be clouded by the obscurity of his expressions . . . he was so momentarily punctual to his time, so religiously observant of his engagements, that we, who served under him in office, felt the sweets of the exchange we had so lately made in the person of our chief.

Cumberland may have been biased, for reasons which will appear. But another memoir-writer, Nathaniel Wraxall, gives a plausible twist to a similar picture of efficiency. 'In business he was rapid, yet clear and accurate; rather negligent in his style, which was that of a gentleman and a man of the world, unstudied and frequently careless, even in his official despatches. But there was no obscurity and ambiguity in his compositions.'

For seven years Lord George bore the main burden of the great world war for America. I have argued in another book that he bore it with courage and intelligence. It was the most complex war that England had ever waged, with the three chief maritime nations of Europe ranged against her in many theatres of war across the globe. The campaigns waged in America, 3,000 miles beyond the ocean, involved an effort without parallel in the history of the world. Dependent on ocean convoys for all their reinforcements and equipment and virtually all their food and forage, the armies in the Americas fought a war which challenged most of the accepted precepts. As Secretary of State Germain was responsible for putting plans before the Cabinet and translating Cabinet decisions into action. It was he who co-ordinated troops, shipping, naval escorts and supplies, and drove the responsible departments to deliver on schedule. As the political director of operations in America he showed imagination and intellect in searching for an effective counter-insurgent strategy. And in the Cabinet he fought consistently to maintain the strategic initiative in a war waged against France and Spain all over the world, struggling against the counsels of timidity which would have locked up the navy and army in defence of the home islands. For nearly two centuries he has been lampooned as a disastrous failure and blamed for nearly every British reverse in a war waged against great odds. That view can no longer be sustained. Compared with the war ministers who preceded and followed him – the younger Pitt and his colleagues, and the overrated elder Pitt – he emerged with credit.*

That the disgraced soldier should have made a successful war statesman is no paradox. As a general in the field he may have been working on the wrong level, and by temperament he was unsuited to coping with the personal strains and clashes of national interest in a situation which in our own century was to tax the relationship of Montgomery with Eisenhower – the command of a national contingent under a foreign supreme commander, especially one like Ferdinand who was neither self-confident nor confiding. No man is right for every situation, and though Sackville fell short of the best at Minden his clear, far-reaching mind was to bear the strain of conducting a great war with confidence and equanimity.

But this is the story of Minden, not of the American war; and it may be that the war statesman throws light on the military commander. The Secretary of State showed moral courage; conviction even to the point of inflexibility about the course he was pursuing; clarity of mind; determination to push down obstructions and overcome inertia. His comments on the war show a shrewd professional understanding of tactics.

But Sackville's conduct at Minden, so far as it was not dictated by the course of the battle, was rooted in his personality more than in his intellect or in his qualities as an administrator and planner. At Minden he was acting under stress of urgency and confusion, and reacting to the behaviour of other individuals – of Ferdinand and his messengers, and in some degree perhaps of the British staff. Lord George's later career shows some signs of the impatient, indiscreet and irritable temper which marred his relations with Ferdinand. There was also his homosexuality.

*For an account of Germain's role in the American War of Independence see my book *The War for America, 1775–83* (1964). I have expanded on the theme of insurgent warfare in the Bland-Lee Lecture for 1975, *Could the British Have Won the War of Independence?* (Clark University, 1976).

There had been scattered sniping at this in the seventeen-sixties – an allusion in a poem by Churchill, a sly backhander in an apocryphal letter of Junius. But scarcely had Sackville taken office when he was slashed in a scandalous poem *Sodom and Onan*, published in 1776 by 'Humphrey Nettle'. The author's real name was William Jackson, factotum to the bigamous Elizabeth Chudleigh, Duchess of Kingston, and its real target was the writer Samuel Foote, against whom the duchess was waging a vendetta. The passage in which Lord George was noticed attacked the king for his appointment as Secretary of State.

> As heaven's Vicegerents Kings on Earth are placed,
> But George the seal majestic hath disgraced;
> Inveigled by Scotch Insinuation
> To pardon Sodomites and damn the Nation.
> Sackville, both Coward and Catamite, commands
> Department honourable, and kisses hands
> With lips that oft in blandishment obscene
> Have been employed. . . .

This sort of abuse was echoed by his fashionable enemies in the clubs of St James's. He was a 'Minden buggering hero', an outcast for his 'cowardice and sodomy'. But though all this provided fuel for his enemies' prejudice and distaste, one might suppose that it could be dismissed as irrelevant to his public character. Unfortunately the matter went further; for during his tenure of the American Department he appointed to high positions – and they were very personal appointments – two men whose characters lay under question. One of them was Richard Cumberland, clerk of reports at the Board of Trade, whom Germain promoted to the secretaryship of the board; the other was the loyalist refugee Benjamin Thompson, who became under-secretary in the American Department. Both were men of talent in other fields, Cumberland as a dramatist and Thompson as a scientist and reformer.

About Cumberland there was no public scandal, and suspicion arises almost entirely from two passages, separated by almost twenty years, in the private diaries of Samuel Johnson's friend Mrs Thrale. 'I have a notion, *Dieu me pardonne*,' she confided to her journal in 1777, 'that Cumberland is a –. . . . N.B. he is a profess'd favourite of Lord George Sackville, who made his fortune for him. . . . Effeminacy is an odious quality in a He creature, and when joined with low jealousy actually detestable.' In 1796 she returned to the theme. 'Something always did whisper in my heart, that Cumberland did like the *Masculine* gender best, I have given a hint on't in this book somewhere a vast many years ago, and all his manner, and all his works confirm my old suspicion.'

In 1780 Cumberland was sent on a diplomatic mission to Spain, and from Madrid he wrote to Lord George thanking him for his continued protection, and sending his love to Mr Thompson. The phrase was an unusual one from a subordinate writing to a Secretary of State, and it referred to an unusual man. Benjamin Thompson, later created Count Rumford by the Elector of Bavaria, is best remembered for his achievements as a scientist, a reputation which he inflated with his gift for self-advertisement. Born in New England, he was endowed with good looks and charm which, before he was twenty, won him a rich and much older wife. His next conquest was Governor Wentworth of New Hampshire, whose eye he caught with his striking taste in dress, and who gave him a commission as major in a provincial regiment to the rage of the junior officers. 'Is not this a sweet gentleman?' Thompson wrote of the governor in camp accents to a friend, 'one exactly suited to our taste. . . .' Early in the Revolution he fell foul of the local committee of safety, converted his property into cash, and sailed to seek his fortune in the Old World. A letter of introduction from Governor Wentworth brought him to Lord George's notice, and soon he was living in his household, attending Lady George and her daughters to balls and dancing with the girls when they could get no other partners. He was regarded, Lord Glenbervie recalled in his journal many years later, as the favourite simultaneously of father, mother and daughter; 'a boy of beauty and a hundred arts', Glenbervie quoted in Latin. 'The ill-fame of the father then, and of the daughters since, have served to keep the scandal alive with regard to them. This anecdote reminds one of what was said of Caesar' (again Glenbervie dropped into Latin): 'a husband to all women, and a wife to all husbands.'

Lady George died in 1778, and in 1780 Thompson was appointed Under-Secretary in the American Department, and the loyalist Samuel Curwen recorded that he 'always breakfasts, dines and sups with Lord George, so great a favourite is he'. A year later his appointment came to an abrupt end. In after-life he let it be understood that it was because he was tired of being held responsible for Germain's ineptitude; but current rumour said that he had been in communication with a French spy. Germain sent him to command a new regiment of loyalist cavalry in America, where he saw some skirmishing in the final days of the war.

The fighting over, Thompson sought his fortune in Europe. Attending a parade in uniform he aroused the interest of a general, who introduced him to the Elector of Bavaria; soon he was an established favourite and was offered the post of adjutant-general and aide-de-camp.

Returning to England he obtained permission to enter the service of Bavaria, and was knighted by George III before his departure. From Munich he wrote to Lord George rejoicing in his new honours.

How near would this approach to happiness could I but enjoy with all these, the society of my best, my only friend! Look back for a moment, my dearest friend, upon the work of your hands. *Je suis votre ouvrage.* Does it not afford you a very sensible pleasure to find that your child has answered your expectations?

This may have been no more than a sentimental way of thanking an elderly man who enjoyed helping talented young men; but others viewed Thompson's success sardonically. In 1791 on a visit to Munich the future Marquess Wellesley was astonished by the power of 'Sir *Sodom* Thompson, Lord Sackville's *under* Secretary'. Seven years later the British government refused to accept Thompson as Bavarian Minister in London; ostensibly because he was a former British subject and under-secretary, but in fact on grounds of character.

Inevitably people will ask, does all this matter? Nothing is proved, and if it were, no harm is visible: what concerns us is Lord George's public character. But it does matter, because public and

private character are not wholly separable. Lord George was using
his ministerial patronage in an unacceptable way. Patronage in itself
was not objectionable: it was the force which powered the political
system, a shimmering waterfall of gold which cascaded from rock to
rock as it descended from the heights. Nor was patronage obliged to
promote talent: family, friendship and reciprocal advantage were
stronger claims. But in promoting Thompson Lord George stepped
outside the bounds of accepted convention. It was fair to help one's
godson or nephew, one's steward's son or a voter in one's borough;
but it was not proper to promote an unconnected young man of no
standing or proved ability and of doubtful reputation. One can
follow the impact of Thompson's connection with Germain in the
diary of Thomas Hutchinson, the loyalist who had so warmly
welcomed Germain's appointment to the American Department.
Rumour first reached him in February 1778 from Mr D'Oyly, a
resigning under-secretary in the American Department. Hutchinson recorded his visit: 'He speaks freely of Lord George's taking
Thompson into his family. Some points look strange.'

Eighteen months passed before Hutchinson made another entry
on the subject. In October 1779 Lord Polwarth called and referred
to Thompson as 'that scoundrel'. He 'wondered at Lord George,
that he would give such cause for the world to insinuate such things
of him'. 'I was astonished', wrote Hutchinson, 'at the freedom with
which he spoke of what it's shocking to think of.' A few months later
'Mr. Thompson (Lord George's) called', and in the course of
conversation repeated a remark which the king had made in private
to Lord George. Hutchinson was shocked by the indiscretion.

It shews also that Lord George is extremely incautious in trusting such an
account of his conversation with the King to a young man, especially as it is
not possible they should have lived so long together without Lord
George's having discovered that Thompson has not the faculty of
retention. This brings to mind the conversation I had with Lord Polwarth.

Hutchinson's comments were not the malicious gossip of
fashion, but the private dismay of a serious-minded American who
approved wholeheartedly of Lord George's determination to defeat
the rebellion.

I have dwelt on Sackville's homosexual reputation in the belief that it was his Achilles' heel. It may help to explain the strangely hostile reaction which he aroused in many people – a hostility which seems to go beyond what his reserve and arrogance could account for in themselves. It may explain his difficulty in forming happy working relationships with some of his colleagues, and the recurring hints of instability which flit through his life. It may shed some light on the web of passions in which the Minden affair is tangled. But it does not destroy his claim to have been a courageous and successful war minister in adversity.

All able men have their uses, and the most tragic sight in public life is a clever man trapped in a situation for which he is unfitted. Sackville in later life directed with shrewdness and courage the most difficult war of the century. But no worse appointment could have been made to the command of the British corps in Germany, which he inherited by accident. Strategic grasp and administrative system were subordinate to the need to cooperate with the German commander of this international force. Sackville's successor Lord Granby hated paperwork, and had limited intellectual horizons; but he was a quick and cooperative tactician, and easy to work with. These were the qualities most needed in the British commander.

Six years after Lord George took office as Secretary of State came the news of Cornwallis's capitulation at Yorktown; the House of Commons lost faith in the war and voted to end it. Lord George, who maintained to the last that Britain must fight on or cease to be a great power, and that even now the war could still be won, resigned to make way for a nonentity who would fall in with the prevailing mood of Parliament. But before he left office he performed one final service to the country by taking part in the decision to send a massive naval reinforcement to the West Indies. For years he had maintained in the teeth of the Admiralty that the only way to defend the British colonies and retain the strategic initiative was to seek a decisive naval superiority overseas at the expense of the home fleet, and accept the risk of invasion. The Yorktown catastrophe had been the result of allowing the French to achieve a local superiority in the western Atlantic; and in January 1782 Admiral Rodney was sent out to the Caribbean with a colossal reinforcement of seventeen sail of the line to redress the balance. There, when the ministry had fallen and Rodney's own recall was on the way, his victory in the battle of the Saints restored the naval position in the western Atlantic and demonstrated that the British navy had not lost the global command of the seas.

But by then Lord George was in retirement with a peerage. He had sought it to efface for ever the stain of Minden, and chose the title Viscount Sackville, recovering his family name and the name under which he had stood his trial. But instead of marking his final vindication and acceptance, his peerage was to bring down on him what Cumberland called 'one of the last and most painful trials of his life'. When it was announced, Lord Carmarthen rose unexpectedly in the House of Lords to read out the sentence of the court martial and the rider which George II had attached to it, and to move that Sackville's presence would be derogatory to the honour of the House. A succession of peers with Minden connections rose to support him. The Duke of Richmond, a close political collaborator of Sackville's ten years earlier, dwelt at length on Lord George's delay in obeying Prince Ferdinand's orders, asserting that he had had his watch in his hand the whole time and that an hour and a half had elapsed between the first order and the arrival of the cavalry. Fitzroy's brother the Duke of Grafton spoke for the motion. So did Granby's adjutant-general Lord Pembroke (he had not arrived in Germany till 1760, but like Carmarthen he had been a friend of the Ligoniers), and Granby's nephew the Duke of Rutland. Lord Shelburne, who had been present at Minden and had an old professional grudge against Sackville, said that his appointment as Secretary of State had begun the war with 'the grossest insult to the Americans that could possibly have been devised'. Pitt's son Lord Chatham joined in the attack; so did the half-mad Lord Abingdon, later to be imprisoned for a libel.

General Burgoyne's nephew Lord Derby denounced Sackville's peerage as 'a great and serious insult to their Lordships, to see a person created a peer whose disgrace was entered in the orderly book of every British regiment'.

Sackville's attackers were members of the Opposition – Carmarthen and Pembroke had both been deprived of their lord-lieutenancies two years earlier for supporting a motion against the government – but this cruel and personal attack on a retired politician did not fall within the conventions of political decency. The House rejected Carmarthen's motion by 75 votes to 28; and it is said that Sackville considered challenging Carmarthen but was dissuaded by his boyhood friend and Cabinet colleague Lord Amherst. 'It is not a *cas combattable*,' thought the fashionable wit and sinecurist George Selwyn, 'it is more offensive than if it was.'

But even now Carmarthen and his friends had not finished with 'the pederastical American Secretary'. Eleven days later Sackville took his seat in the House of Lords, and Carmarthen renewed the attack in his presence. Again he read the sentence and its rider, and denounced Sackville's peerage as an abuse of the royal prerogative. Lord Abingdon added that it connected the House with 'one whom every soldier, and every soldier as a man of honour, is forbid to associate with'. This time Sackville was there to reply. He did so with temperance and generosity. Carmarthen, he said, had acted in a fair and manly way. But his sentence was no disqualification from sitting in the House. It had been pronounced twenty-two years ago, amidst faction and clamour. He had been punished without a hearing; and had insisted on being tried, though those who wished to deflect him had warned him that a capital sentence would be executed. He had always regarded his recall to the Privy Council as a virtual repeal of the sentence, and as Privy Councillor and Secretary of State he had held posts of more importance than a peerage. As for the executive's comment which Carmarthen had included in his motion, it was neither part of the sentence nor consonant with justice.

'Able, dignified and manly' was how one Member of Parliament described this speech; but it offended two of his hearers, and Lord Southampton now intervened. We met him last as Charles Fitzroy, and hitherto he had decently kept out of the debate. But he had understood Sackville to say that the court martial was factious, and rose to protest that he had not been motivated as a witness by factious views. To this Sackville agreed, and explained that he had meant no such thing: he had been punished before he was tried, in an atmosphere of faction. Lord Derby rose again to say that Sackville's remarks on the rider to the sentence aspersed the character of George II, that 'wise and magnanimous prince'.

It suited opponents of the ministry to reflect on the present king by praising the peppery George II. But not all the Opposition joined in the baiting of Sackville. The great Rockingham party, soon to take office, had given very cool encouragement to Carmarthen, for they had not felt that their hands were being stained by their long political association with Sackville after 1765. Nor did Sackville defend himself alone, for this time his friends were ready. Lord Mansfield's heir Lord Stormont, Secretary of State for the Southern Department, delivered a warm eulogy on his old colleague; and Sackville's former under-secretary Lord Walsingham quoted Blackstone's attack on martial law, 'which is built upon no settled principle, but is entirely arbitrary in its decisions': it was 'in truth and reality no law'. As for the sentence and its rider, Walsingham asked: 'Was the loose censure of a Judge-Advocate to be considered "a censure worse than death" to a man of honour?'

Lord Chancellor Thurlow took this argument further, in a speech described as one of the most powerful ever heard in the House. Whoever had advised the Crown to issue the orders which accompanied the sentence had advised the Crown to act unjustly, he said. A stigma had been published which was infinitely worse than the charge or the sentence could justify. Sackville had been found guilty only of disobeying orders, which might in some cases be actually laudable, in other cases due to inadvertency, incompetence of judgement or professional ignorance. None of these justified the stain which the Crown had cast upon Sackville.

This time ninety-three peers voted the motion down, and the common reaction to it was disgust. 'Cruel and ill-mannered,' Selwyn called it, 'not becoming one man of quality to another; at the same time an unpardonable insult to the Crown.' 'In every light odious', thought Walpole, and it 'tended to destroy the best prerogative of the Crown, that of pardon'. Shelburne's performance had been especially distasteful. To express George II's contempt for Sackville he had quoted the old king's words and mimicked his all-too-imitable manner, 'a pantomime fitter for the *tréteaux des boulevards* than for a chamber of Parliament'. This vulgar exhibition took place in the presence of two of the royal princes, George II's grandchildren.

It is difficult to grasp today the cruelty of Carmarthen's motion, and how shocking it was to all who respected the Crown's prerogative. Sackville must have suffered deeply. 'If we are not misinformed,' said his obituary in the *European Magazine*, 'the circumstances of this opposition dwelt in the mind of his Lordship even to the last moments of his life.' He did not forgive Carmarthen, and two years later he rebuffed an overture from the younger Pitt's newly formed and precarious ministry and refused to allow his son-in-law to serve in it, because its Foreign Secretary was Carmarthen. In vain the king, Pitt, Thurlow and Lord Sydney appealed for his support. It would be foolish, he admitted to Thurlow, to bear resentment for things said while he was in office. But he had retired before he entered the House of Lords, and 'the attack made upon me by my Lord Carmarthen was so unprovoked and of so personal a nature that I can never act with or have the least connections with him'. He thanked Thurlow for his goodness and support when they had sat together in the Cabinet; 'and I shall ever feel with particular gratitude the manly and able part which you took in defending me against the illiberal attack of my Lord Carmarthen'.

Lord Sackville lived three years after his admission to the Lords. He often visited his house in Pall Mall and spoke regularly in Parliament; but in the country he lived the life of an old-fashioned squire, entertaining his friends, helping the unfortunate, and reproving the singing of the village choir on Sunday. He had friends who remained loyal, and not merely for the sake of his hospitality. William Knox, who had served him in the American Department, never forgave the statesman Henry Dundas for precipitating his resignation, and wrote when Sackville was dead of 'the superiority of his understanding, and the pure disinterestedness of his heart'. William Eden, climbing ambitiously towards the peerage, was another who praised Sackville when he was no longer alive to help or hinder; and a recent acquaintance, Gibbon's friend Lord Sheffield, agreed. 'He had many good points,' he replied to Eden; 'he was fair and downright, he had a right understanding. I began to take much to him.' Richard Cumberland asserted that misfortune had not spoiled his nature in these last years. 'The same Providence that gave him strength to endure laid afflictions upon him that put that strength to the trial: I am warranted in saying that they neither hardened his heart, depressed his spirit, nor soured his temper.'

Sackville was a strange man, as Horace Walpole had written long ago, and had provoked strong enmities as well as friendships. The shadow of Minden hung over him to the end. As death approached he asked that a friend who was to visit Drayton should be let known – 'he hesitated a little and then added – to let him know that I am dead'. He wanted his composure in the face of death to be marked, Lord Sheffield explained. Cumberland was with him two days before he died, when he struggled to extinguish one last resentment before he took the Sacrament.

You see me now [he said] in those moments when no disguise will serve, and when the spirit of a man must be proved; I have a mind perfectly resigned and at peace within itself. . . . Tell me not of all that passes in health and pride of heart, these are the moments when a man must be searched; and remember that I die, as you see me, happy and content.

EPILOGUE 1854

Ninety-five years had passed since the battle of Minden, and at Balaclava another British cavalry force was drawn up for battle. There were no Minden regiments in the Light Brigade; but in the Heavy Brigade, which had attacked gallantly in the morning, were the Greys and Inniskillings, firm friends who had charged side by side at Waterloo.

An arrogant aide-de-camp galloped up to the general commanding the cavalry with a written order from the commander-in-chief to advance. The order was obscure and the general was posted where he could not view the battlefield as his commander-in-chief could do. Puzzled and irritated, he questioned the aide-de-camp, who impatiently cut him short with the words that the cavalry were to attack immediately. 'Attack, sir?' the general replied. 'Attack what? What guns, sir?'

The aide-de-camp flung out his arm in an insolent gesture: 'There, my Lord, is your enemy, there are your guns.'

Captain Nolan was wrong, and General Lord Lucan was appalled by his interpretation. 'Surely', Sackville had said at his trial, 'a General Officer may be allowed to question even an aide-de-camp's explanation of the orders he brings.' But to Lucan Queen's Regulations were clear. All orders brought by aides-de-camp were to be obeyed as if delivered personally by the general who sent them. With a shrug of his shoulders he rode over to Lord Cardigan at the head of the Light Brigade and quietly gave him orders to attack. Cardigan remonstrated, but Lord Lucan shrugged his shoulders again and replied, 'We have no choice but to obey.'

Under the eyes of the hushed ranks of the Greys and Inniskillings the Light Brigade moved forward to its destruction.

NOTES ON THE BRITISH
REGIMENTS

Below are given the official titles in 1759 of the Minden regiments and their subsequent evolution.

The Blues: The Royal Regiment of Horse Guards. Later: The Royal Horse Guards (The Blues). 1969: The Blues and Royals (Royal Horse Guards and 1st Dragoons).

Bland's: 1st or King's Regiment of Dragoon Guards. Later: 1st King's Dragoon Guards. 1959: 1st The Queen's Dragoon Guards.

Howard's: 3rd Regiment of Dragoon Guards. 1928: 3rd Carabiniers (Prince of Wales's Dragoon Guards). 1971: The Royal Scots Dragoon Guards (Carabiniers and Greys).

Scots Greys: 2nd (or Royal North British) Regiment of Dragoons. Later: The Royal Scots Greys (2nd Dragoons). 1971: The Royal Scots Dragoon Guards (Carabiniers and Greys).

Inniskillings: 6th or Inniskilling Regiment of Dragoons. Since 1935: 5th Royal Inniskilling Dragoon Guards.

Mordaunt's: 10th Regiment of Dragoons. Later: 10th Royal Hussars (Prince of Wales's Own). 1969: The Royal Hussars (Prince of Wales's Own).

Napier's: 12th Regiment of Foot. 1881: The Suffolk Regiment. 1964: 1st battalion The Royal Anglian Regiment.

Kingsley's: 20th Regiment of Foot. 1881: The Lancashire Fusiliers. 1968: 4th battalion The Royal Regiment of Fusiliers.

Welch Fusiliers: 23rd Regiment of Foot (or Royal Welch Fuziliers). 1881: Royal Welch Fusiliers.

Home's: 25th Regiment of Foot. 1887: The King's Own Scottish Borderers.

Stewart's: 37th Regiment of Foot. 1881: 1st battalion The Hampshire Regiment. 1946: The Royal Hampshire Regiment.

Brudenell's: 51st Regiment of Foot. 1887: 1st battalion The King's Own Yorkshire Light Infantry. 1968: 3rd battalion The Light Infantry.

NOTES ON SOURCES

To save space, no references to sources are given in the text. For the same reason the list of printed works is confined to some suggestions for further reading; but a full list of the manuscript sources is given.

MANUSCRIPTS

The most fruitful collections used were:

Public Record Office, London. Correspondence with commanders in Germany (SP 87/28–30, 32, 34–5), correspondence and legal opinions on the court martial (SP 41/23, SP 44/135), records of Judge-Advocate-General (WO 71/24, 134; WO 72/4), Chatham Papers (PRO 30/8, LXXVI and XC).

British Museum. Additional manuscripts: Newcastle (32894–904), Hardwicke (34357–8, 35365, 35893–4, 35639, 36223), Bute (36796), Calcraft (17494). Map collections: Captain Roy's map of the battle laid before the court (30520 (1)).

Royal Archives, Windsor Castle. Cumberland Papers.

Drayton House, Northamptonshire. Papers of Lord George Germain.

William L. Clements Library, Ann Arbor, Michigan. Germain papers.

Kent Record Office, Maidstone. Sackville papers; Amherst papers.

Nottingham University Library. Newcastle papers.

Cardiff Central Library. Bute papers.

Hull University Library. Hotham papers.

Material was also found in the following collections:

National Army Museum, London. Plan of battle of Minden (6906/4), MS copy of letter from T. Thompson (6807/142–13), Misc. single letters (6807/453), order book of the Greys (M/F16/3).

Notes on Sources

Hanover, Niedersächsiches Staatsarchiv. Papers relating to Prince Ferdinand, series 9E, 38A.

Rice University, Houston, Texas. Papers of Sir William Sidney Smith in the Fondren Library.

Mount Stuart, Bute (Bute papers); *Bury St Edmunds and West Suffolk Record Office* (Grafton papers); *Hove Central Library* (order book of Frederick Mackenzie); *Glenharvie, Dumfriesshire* (two letters in Stewart of Shamballie papers); *Garrowby, Yorkshire* (Hickleton papers in the possession of Lord Halifax); *Lincolnshire Record Office, Lincoln* (Chauncy papers); *Halifax Central Public Library* (Lister papers); *Comrie, Perthshire* (Dundas of Beechwood papers); *Mitchell Library, Glasgow* (journal of John Burrell); *Cheshire Record Office, Chester* (letters of William Cowper, junior); *Durham University Library* (order book of 3rd Dragoon Guards); *Knole, Kent* (a few papers retained when the remainder were deposited in the county record office); *Sheffield City Libraries* (Fitzwilliam/Rockingham papers); *Huntington Library, San Marino, California* (miscellaneous letters; Hamilton-Greville correspondence).

PRINTED MATERIAL: A GUIDE TO FURTHER READING

Two superb printed sources are the indispensable foundation. The correspondence of Prince Ferdinand (*Geschichte der Feldzüge des Ferdinands von Braunschweig-Lüneburg*, vol. V, ed. C. H. P. Westphalen) is largely in French. The proceedings of the court martial are best read in the version published by Sackville, *The trial of the Rt. Hon. Lord George Sackville at a Court Martial. . . .* The official version (*Proceedings of a General Court Martial Held at the Horse Guards . . . upon the Trial of Lord George Sackville*) differs in minor details which can be explained by divergent transcriptions from the shorthand (and contains some obscurities which can be cleared up by reference to the Sackville version). The official version, however, omits much of the legal arguments about procedure, the names of the questioners, and the interjections of the judges and arguments between them, as well as between Lord George and the Judge-Advocate. Their publication by Sackville provoked the president of the court to insert an advertisement in the *London Gazette* protesting that the *Trial* was published without authority and that the particular observations of members and by the Judge-Advocate ought not to have been published. The official proceedings have a fuller version of the Judge-Advocate's final speech.

Notes on Sources

Biographical

There is no satisfactory biography of Lord George. Louis Marlow's *Sackville of Drayton* is lively but scrappy and undocumented. Alan Valentine's very hostile *Lord George Germain* has all the apparatus of scholarship, but is inaccurate and misleading. Gerald S. Brown, *The American Secretary: the Colonial Policy of Lord George Germain, 1775–1778* is a work of sound scholarship confined in the main to a period of Lord George's later life. There is an up-to-date and perceptive account of his political career in Sir Lewis Namier and John Brooke, *The House of Commons, 1754–1790*, vol. iii. Lord George's conduct of the War of American Independence is examined in my *War for America, 1775–1783*. Contemporary personal accounts of Lord George's character can be found in Richard Cumberland's *Memoirs* and in his *Character of the Late Lord Sackville*; in E. G. Fitzmaurice's *Life of Shelburne* (very hostile, indeed malevolent); the *Memoirs* of Perceval Stockdale; and N. W. Wraxall's *Historical Memoirs of My Own Times*, vol. I.

Among the innumerable printed collections in which political and biographical source material is scattered, the most useful are: the Historical Manuscripts Commission's volumes of the Stopford-Sackville, Rutland, Hastings, Matcham, Bathurst and Laing papers; *The Correspondence of William Pitt* (ed. W. S. Taylor and J. H. Pringle); *The Letters from George III to Lord Bute* (ed. Romney Sedgwick); *Horace Walpole's Correspondence* (the Yale edition, ed. W. S. Lewis and others), and Walpole's *Memoirs of the Last Ten Years of the Reign of George II* (ed. Lord Holland); A. M. W. Stirling, *The Hothams*; *The Grenville Papers*, vol. I (ed. W. J. Smith); *The Correspondence of Thomas Gray*, vol. II (ed. Paget Toynbee and Leonard Whibley); *Letters and Journals of Lady Mary Coke* (ed. J. A. Horne); *Thraliana: the Diary of Mrs. Hester Lynch Thrale (Later Mrs. Piozzi), 1776–1809* (ed. Katherine Balderston); *The Diaries of Sylvester Douglas (Lord Glenbervie)* (ed. Francis Bickley); the *Parliamentary History*; and *Henry, Elizabeth and George* and *The Pembroke Papers* (both edited by Lord Herbert). An account of Captain John Smith's marital speculation is in Thomas Pitt, Lord Camelford, *Narrative and Proofs*; and there is further information about this and the Smith family in Professor H. H. Finlay's *Edward Beaumont Smith and the Exchequer Bill Affair of 1841* (Tasmanian Historical Research Association, 1962).

The German Campaigns and the Battle of Minden

Of the many general histories of the Seven Years War in Germany,

Notes on Sources

English readers will probably find Sir Reginald Savory's *His Britannic Majesty's Army in Germany*, written by a distinguished soldier, the most helpful, and Sir Lees Knowles's *Minden and the Seven Years War* the least. In a smaller compass than Savory, Sir John Fortescue's *History of the British Army*, vol. II, is prejudiced but highly readable. Two articles by graduates of the Staff College, F. E. Whitton's *Service Trials and Tragedies*, and David Fraser's 'The Trial of Lord George Sackville' in *History Today* (1974), enter into the difficulties of Lord George's situation under a barrage of conflicting orders delivered by young staff officers.

Among original sources are the court-martial records and the correspondence of Prince Ferdinand, mentioned above. Jacob von Mauvillon's *Geschichte Ferdinands Herzog von Braunschweig-Lüneburg* is an interesting though adulatory account of Ferdinand's character and campaigns by one of his staff officers. The correspondence of Frederick the Great (*Politische Correspondenz Friedrichs des Grossen*, vol. XVIII) places the operation of Ferdinand's army in their wider strategic context. A regimental view of military life in Germany is that of Major Richard Davenport of the 10th Dragoons (Mordaunt's) (*To Mr. Davenport*, ed. C. W. Frearson, Society for Army Historical Research, Special Publication No. 9, 1968). A letter about the battle written by H. Montgomery is printed in the *Gallipoli Gazette*, vol. XXV, no. 97, p. 39.

Contemporary pamphlets

An early attack on Sackville's conduct at Minden was *A Letter to a Late Noble Commander of the British Forces in Germany*, which was followed by *A Second Letter* . . . and by *Further Animadversions on the Conduct of a Late Noble Commander at the Battle of Thonhausen*. Other hostile pamphlets include *The Conduct of a Noble Lord Scrutinised*, *A Reply to his Vindication*, the satirical *A Consolatory Letter to a Noble Lord* and *Proceedings of a Court Martial . . . Together with Their Remarkable Sentence* (a spoof based on the published exchange of letters between Sackville and Fitzroy). For libellous abuse nothing rivals *A Parallel between the Cases of Admiral J. Byng and That of Lord G. Sackville, by the Captain of a Man of War*.

In defence of Sackville there appeared *Remarks on a Pamphlet Entitled The Conduct of a Noble Lord Scrutinised*, John Douglas's serious *The Conduct of a Noble Lord Candidly Considered*, *A Seasonable Antidote against the Poison of Popular Censure* (a protest against the habit of making scapegoats of commanders), Sackville's own *Short Address to the Public* and *His Lordship's Apology*, the incompetent *A Vindication of the Rt. Hon. Lord George Sackville* (described by Lord Hardwicke as 'most absurd'), *Yet One Vindication More of the Conduct of L— G— S—* (which is little better), *An Answer to a Letter to a Late Noble Commander, Truth Developed and Innocence Protected*, and *An Apologetical Oration on an Extraordinary Occasion* (a well-written apologia published after the trial).

Some documents in the case are printed in *Lord George Sackville's Vindication of Himself, in a Letter to Colonel Fitzroy*. . . . After the trial Colonel Sloper issued *Colonel S—r's Letter to the S—y at War, with Genuine Affidavits Relative to the Evidence Given on the Tryal of L—d G—e S—e.*

INDEX

Index

Index

Index

Index

Index

Index

Index

Walpole, Sir Robert, 250
Walsingham, Lord, 261
Wangenheim, Gen., 56, 62, 80, 82–3,
  87, 93, 97–100, 112, 131–2, 142–4,
  230
Warburg, 57; battle of, 196, 244
Washington, George, 20
Waterloo, battle of, 242, 264
Watson, Col., 94
Wedderburn, Alexander, 175–7,
  183–4, 186, 188, 192, 222, 250
Wellesley, Marquess, 256
Wellington, Duke of, 30, 73, 242
Wentworth, Governor Sir John, 255
Werle, 56
Werra, river, 157
Werre, river, 77, 140–41
Wesel, 48, 50, 76
Weser, river, 20, 24, 50, 56, 59f, 62ff,
  67, 69ff, 74–7, 79–80, 82, 88, 90,
  99f, 141, 151, 156, 232
Wesergebirge, 62
West Indies, 18, 250, 258
Westminster School, 29, 179
Westphalen, C.H.P., 19, 22, 52, 59, 60,
  62ff, 67–9, 71, 75–8, 80, 84, 142–3,
  149, 152–3, 158, 248
Westphalia, 21, 25, 36ff, 48, 50, 52,
  56, 60, 62, 67–9f, 74–5, 146, 156
Whitefoord, Gen., 37

Whiteford, Lieut., 208
Wiehengebirge, 62, 74, 82, 90
Wilkes, 251
Wilkinson, Mary, 240–41, 246
Wilkinson, Pinckney, 240–41, 246
Williams, Capt. Griffith, 108–9, 112,
  202
Winzingerode, Capt.: at Minden,
  115–18, 120, 125, 129–30, 176, 190,
  203f, 207f, 216, 218–20, 227–8, 231,
  236–7, 241; at court martial, 183–5,
  187
Withyham, 240–41
Wogan, Lieut. John, 191
Wolfe, Maj.-Gen. James, 29, 239, 243
Wraxall, Nathaniel, 34, 252
Wutginau, General, 56, 100, 121, 124

Yarmouth, Lady, 167
York, Duke of, 19
Yorke, Charles, 172, 223, 234–5
Yorke, Maj.-Gen. Sir Joseph, 39,
  53n, 54, 58, 61, 70, 147, 149, 152f,
  156, 158, 162, 169, 174, 191, 226,
  233, 243, 245
Yorktown, 258

Zastrow, Gen., 19, 64, 85
Zorndorf, battle of, 49
Züllichau, battle of, 75